SHELDON LETTICH

SHELDON LETTICH:

FROM VIETNAM TO VAN DAMME

by Corey Danna

BearManor Media
2022

SHELDON LETTICH:
FROM VIETNAM TO VAN DAMME

© 2022 *Corey Danna*

All rights reserved.

Published in the United States of America by:

BearManor Media

4700 Millenia Blvd.
Suite 175 PMB 90497
Orlando, FL 32839

bearmanormedia.com

Printed in the United States.

Typesetting and layout by BearManor Media
Cover art by Alan Pirie Design / Samurai Guinea Pig

ISBN—978-1-62933-987-0

TABLE OF CONTENTS

Through Blood, Sweat, and Tears: FOREWORD by George Saunders

For nearly four decades, Sheldon Lettich has been at the forefront of the action film genre, penning such iconic movies as *Bloodsport*, *Lionheart*, and *Double Impact*, starring one of the legends of action-noir, Jean Claude Van Damme. He has arguably defined the male action star of the 1980s, 1990s, and the genesis of the new millennium.

I met Sheldon in 1996 when, on his suggestion to the producers, I was brought on board a project called *Perfect Target*, a script badly in need of a rewrite. Together, Sheldon and I toiled over this imperfect piece of clay, eventually developing a screenplay that morphed into a rather decent flick. Sheldon carefully and patiently worked with a budding screenwriter (myself) to craft a well-structured script that hit all the intrinsic beats of the requisite genre. Not only was Sheldon my guiding light and mentor in this enterprise, he was also the director of the film, which starred Daniel Bernhardt as the hero lead, lending Van Damme-esque muscular integrity to all things kickass.

I had the opportunity to watch Sheldon direct his actors, compose scenes, and otherwise invoke both excitement and pathos out of both character and story. Not every director can master the multiple tasks of handling actors (notorious for extremes in temperament and insecurity), deliver good storytelling and frame (no pun intended) a final product that is both fun and satisfying. Sheldon is one such artist who has fulfilled all these parameters and has done so not on just one picture but over a dozen in his varied career. On a film both he and I wrote in 2005, called *The Hard Corps*, I journeyed up to Canada to watch Sheldon in action, directing Jean Claude and

Vivica Fox. Now you must understand that in person, Sheldon is a man of medium stature who comes off more as an erudite college professor versus that of a guy who directs muscular sweaty men hell-bent on the cinematic kill. One would expect a fellow with multiple and legendary action-film credits to be six foot four on the hoof and possessed of a body any longshoreman would envy. Sheldon is not such a dude – he is a regular gent, yet gifted with, and paraphrasing Rudyard Kipling, "the virtue of he who can walk with kings yet blessed with the common touch." This modest legend [Lettich] directed Van Damme strategically and compassionately, evoking one of the star's most sensitive performances.

Sheldon's sense of humor is also one of unsuspecting grace and surprise. One could easily be engaged in a serious sociological or political debate with him, when, quite out of the blue, Mr. Lettich will disarm you with irreverent commentary, thus disabling whatever point or treatise you were trying to make as a devil's advocate. You would be forced back into your primeval hole of iniquity and lick your wounds inflicted by Sheldon's soft yet scathing commentary on how little you pretended to know on a given subject.

I believe many of Sheldon's filmmaking gifts stem from a fascinating first-hand life experience. He served as a radio-operator in the Vietnam debacle toward the end of that dreadful conflict, hiking and sludging through muck and blood with the toughest of hombres and watching friends and peers die at his side. Sheldon is himself an action hero, borne from hard trials in the merciless jungles of Southeast Asia. He was not afforded the luxury of pretending to be a tough guy for the camera; he had to live the role of a true-blue hero.

I remember once discussing with Sheldon on our way to get Chinese food for one of his legendary parties – wherein I rather arrogantly stated that I had dreamed of greatness in the film or television industry. I asked him if he ever had such aspirations. He merely shrugged and in typical subdued fashion responded:

"George, I never aspired to greatness. I'm just happy that I made it this far doing what I really liked to do."

I have known Mr. Lettich for over twenty-five years and have seen him in action, both personally and professionally. A devoted family man, married for forty years with three lovely daughters, Sheldon is a two-legged hen's tooth in Hollywood. Such luck is rarely enjoyed by the majority of us who struggle in the antediluvian slime of Tinseltown, with all its moral infirmity and pretense. Sheldon has circumnavigated triumphantly the primal muck of ignominious temptation. His is a most enviable circumstance as through the years he has risen to great estate, inspiring others to excel and vanquish the absurd number of obstacles the film business proffers.

I have learned much from Sheldon and owe a great part of my career, such as it is, to his involvement, participation and priceless guidance. On a global field of play, he has almost single-handedly defined the male action star in his films – and represents an era which is in its twilight – a time when men were men and kicked the shit out of one another when needed. Today's male action star is invariably wearing a cape or dressed in tights, or a suit made from super-titanium, or other alien alloy utilized to ward off evil and other nefarious elements threatening Western Civilization or the galaxy at large.

The action star of Sheldon's age (and truth be told, mine as well) is all but gone. John Rambo is part of a heroic yesterday. When Sheldon assisted Sylvester Stallone in *Rambo III*, the net was cast again to bring back hard an action star of beloved yore. The blood-drenched heroes of Sly, Van Damme, and Schwarzenegger are all but gone in the modern epoch of action fealty. Yet the legends continue to be appreciated and most importantly remembered.

The stuff of legends is imbued inexorably in the name of Sheldon Lettich. He shall join the pantheon of other greats, Howard Hawks, James Cameron, John McTiernan, Tony Scott and John Woo.

For me, Sheldon will remain more than a legend and master craftsman.

Sheldon triumphed over time and incomprehensible challenges. He gored himself into the history books and his place therein has been earned through blood, sweat and tears.

He will forever be my big brother and dearest friend.

A guy like Lettich comes around once in a rare generation.

I fear we will not see his like again.

George P. Saunders
December 12, 2021

INTRODUCTION

In the era of parachute pants, leg warmers, and Cabbage Patch Kids, who would have thought we would still be discussing the films from the 80s the way we do. The fandom those properties have spawned just continues to grow year after year. Some of the films have been remade, they've had sequels, and even what is now being called a 'requel', a remake that doubles as a sequel. The book you are about to read isn't about any of those things. There is a major connection though.

Before modern special effects, most everything would be done in camera. When you would do a film like Sam Raimi's horror masterpiece *The Evil Dead* (1981), all those crazy, elaborate special effects were done in real time, live on the set. During this time, all the horror films would employ this method; it's all that was available.

During this same time period, action films were done the exact same way. The majority of explosions, car crashes, or crumbling buildings, were all done live on the set. What the action film had the horror ones didn't were the action stars. These men and women were given roles in these films because, in a sense, they were their own special effect. They were hired for how they looked or what they could do over their acting abilities. Guys like Steven Seagal, Jeff Speakman, or Sylvester Stallone all had their own unique set of skills which made them stars. There was an amazing amount of action stars had the look or martial arts skills which would earn them acclaim around the world.

As time would pass and movies evolved, so did modern technology and these performers were no longer needed by major studios. They could take any actor and make them look like they were performing these amazing feats with the use of computers. The 'real' action heroes were left to do the best they could in smaller budgeted films released direct to video. By the late 90s, you couldn't find a Jean-Claude Van Damme film playing at the local multi-plex and the age of Computer Generated Imagery (CGI) had taken over.

The stories you are about to read in this book take place in the era of film so many of us refuse to let die. Jean-Claude is also a major presence in many of these stories simply because of the relationship he had with our subject, they made history together. Sheldon Lettich had very little film experience when he was tasked with writing the script for *Bloodsport* (1988). The film became a worldwide phenomenon and launched both men into another realm career-wise. This book will take you into the stories behind the films Sheldon has worked on, how his work has helped to launch the careers of others, and give you a look into who this guy actually is.

Through the jungles of Vietnam to the hills of Hollywood, Sheldon's life has gone from one extreme to another while always trying to maintain his integrity. The man who developed these insane action masterpieces also happens to be a beloved husband and father, avoiding the personal destruction and deceit so many people in Hollywood fall in to. Sheldon and I have spent many hours collaborating to bring this book to the masses. Our hope is to entertain, inform, and hopefully inspire our readers to keep these films alive.

Brooklyn to Beverly Hills

The story of Sheldon Lettich starts in the winter of 1951 when he was born in Brooklyn, New York. His parents, Max and Sonja, were refugees from Eastern Europe, who had met at a Displaced Persons Camp in Munchberg, Germany after the end of the war. Max was from Bukovina, an obscure province of the former Austro-Hungarian Empire, which after World War Two became absorbed into Western Ukraine. His mother was from Wolbrom, a small town in central Poland.

As with many immigrants during that time period, they left Europe by booking passage on a ship, which transported them across the Atlantic Ocean to New York City. They were processed by the Immigration authorities at Ellis Island, and then found themselves a small apartment in a six story Brownstone tenement building in the Bensonhurst neighborhood of Brooklyn. The building itself was filled with recent refugees from Europe as well, most of them Jewish, and most of them unfamiliar with the English language. The language most commonly spoken in the building was Yiddish, and apparently that ended up being Sheldon's first language as well. In fact, Yiddish would be the only language he knew for several years since it was all he heard spoken around him both day and night. Sheldon's relatives who knew him at the time said he didn't speak or understand English until he was about five years old. He's still able to understand a small amount of spoken Yiddish, but with the comprehension of a five-year-old.

When it comes to extended family, the war really took its toll on his. "Very few of my parents' immediate family survived the war. I never met any of my grandparents, all of whom perished in the Holocaust. The same was true for most of my aunts and uncles. Out of nine children in my mother's family, she and her sister, Eva, were the only two to survive. From my father's family, only he and one sister, Dora, survived the war." His father found employment in New York's garment district, working with a noisy machine that knit sweaters, while his mother stayed at home taking care of him and, eventually, his two sisters, Yvette and Melanie.

There were a few other relatives, cousins on his mothers' side, who had also survived the war and had migrated to America. Among them were Nathan and David Schpelski, two brothers from his mother's little town of Wolbrom, who eventually changed their family name to the more Americanized version, Shapell. They had made their way to the other side of the country, to Los Angeles, California. Both were very smart, motivated, energetic, and they very quickly found for themselves some golden opportunities in the Golden State. Specifically, they had foreseen a massive postwar need for housing, and very slowly, one by one, they began building houses. Nathan and David, and Nathan's brother-in-law, Max Weisbrod (changed later to Webb), started a small house building company, S&S Construction, which eventually expanded to become Shapell Industries, one of the major builders of tract homes throughout California. They convinced Sheldon's parents that there were much better opportunities to earn a living in Los Angeles. In 1956, his entire family boarded a plane and left New York for California. His parents remained in Los Angeles for the rest of their lives. His father and another uncle ended up buying and managing a millwork plant in Watts, in South Central Los Angeles, where they manufactured all the doors, windows, and cabinets for the newly constructed S&S homes. It was a successful, symbiotic relationship with the Shapell family that lasted for decades, until everyone's dying days. Following Nathan's death in 2007, Shapell Industries was eventually sold in its entirety to Toll Brothers, another major home building company.

The area where the Lettich family first settled down in Los Angeles was Baldwin Hills. Truly, there were real hills in the neighborhood, just a few blocks away from the apartment building they were living in, close enough for Sheldon to ride a bike, or even walk to. On the summit of these nearby hills there was an earthen dam with a water-filled reservoir behind it, and even a small, abandoned World War Two era Army base. Overall, it was an amazing playground for an adventurous pre-teen boy with a fertile imagination, who wasn't shy about getting out and exploring his neighborhood.

Around this same time, Sheldon would begin to discover the movies. There was a nearby theater, the Baldwin, which used to have what were called Kiddie Matinees on the weekends, which was a fixture throughout the 1950s. Many theaters back then used to have these shows every weekend, and they would generally screen two feature films, which were more often than not, Science Fiction. Playwright Richard O'Brian very famously immortalized this concept in *The Rocky Horror Show* (debuted on stage in 1973) with the opening song, aptly titled "Science Fiction/ Double Feature", and which referenced many of the Sci-Fi cultural touchstones from that era. In addition to the feature films, every Kiddie Matinee would also screen a number of cartoons prior to the movies, and usually a black & white serial as well. For those not familiar with them (because they died out due to the popularity of television in the 1950s), serials were multi-episodic stories that were screened over the course of a number of weeks, with each episode being about fifteen minutes in length, and nearly always with cliff-hanger endings that were designed to draw audiences into theaters on a regular basis. Most of them were produced in the 1930s and 1940s, and by the time he was seeing them in the 1950s they were mostly reruns from the earlier period. One of the most memorable was Commando Cody character, who made his first appearance in *Radar Men from the Moon* (1952). He was an ordinary guy who possessed no super-powers, but with the aid of a rocket-pack on his back, he could fly through the air to go after various iterations of evil-doers and bad guys. He was the direct inspiration for *The Rocketeer* (1991) in Joe Johnston's movie, and is also similar in many respects to the Boba Fett character featured in a few of the *Star Wars* movies and *The Mandalorian* (2019-) TV series. It wouldn't be a stretch to conjecture that George Lucas and Joe Johnston were also captivated and influenced by these serials during their childhoods in the 1950s.

One double bill Sheldon saw numerous times was *Journey to the Center of the Earth* (1959), paired with *The Lost World* (1960). They were 20th Century Fox releases, based on classic Sci-Fi novels from the 19th Century, and both featured various species of lizards and other reptiles that were enlarged on-screen via a special effects process known as the travelling matte, which made them appear as though they were huge dinosaurs, menacing the likes of James Mason and Claude Raines. Other Sci-Fi and Fantasy favorites from that era include *The Time Machine* (1960), and the Ray Harryhausen masterpiece, *The 7th Voyage of Sinbad* (1958). There was no such thing as home video back then, so you had to see these films up on a big screen in a movie theater. There were only three nationwide television networks at the time, and they rarely screened movies of this nature. Fortunately, there were local stations that would screen older Horror and Sci-Fi classics, which is how he was able to become a fan of *Kong Kong* (1933) and some of the old black & white Universal Horror classics like *Frankenstein* (1931), *The Wolf Man* (1941), *Dracula* (1931), and *The Mummy* (1932). There was a magazine that catered to fans of these sorts of movies, called *Famous Monsters of Filmland*, which he devoured regularly. Sheldon had heard a rumor that the editor of the magazine, Forrest J. Ackerman, lived in the neighborhood. He would quickly learn that the rumor was true. "Forry serendipitously lived less than a mile from my parents' first house in the Pico-La Cienega neighborhood that we moved to when I started Junior High School. My friends and I would actually be able to ride our bikes to his famous Ackermansion on Sherbourne Street, which was overflowing with decade's worth of memorabilia from monster and Sci-Fi movies of the past and present. By this time I had begun reading Sci-Fi books, and one of my favorite authors at the time was Ray Bradbury, who I actually had the pleasure of meeting in person at Forry's house."

Around this same time he had also been introduced to comic books, and the early 1960s were a particularly fertile time for comic books and their readers, because this was precisely when Stan Lee and Marvel Comics began introducing characters that would go on to become a worldwide cultural phenomenon. Sheldon actually picked up the very first issues of these comics featuring *The Fantastic Four, Spiderman, Iron Man, Thor, The X-Men*, and numerous others from the local drug store or grocery store, where they were available for ten cents on a rotating magazine rack. He and his friends learned which day of the week the latest editions would be put on the stands, and they would be there waiting so they could be the first in line to snatch them up.

The Marvel Cinematic Universe (MCU) would not fully detonate until decades later with the first *Iron Man* (2008) movie, but there were other cultural bombshells about to explode in the early 1960s, all of which affected and inspired him, all of which had an impact on his subsequent career in the movies. The first of these was the release of the initial James Bond movie, *Dr. No* (1962), which Sheldon saw theatrically. This was followed with the second Bond movie, *From Russia with Love* (1963), and then with the blockbuster *Goldfinger* (1964), which set the template for all future Bond movies. "I was a huge fan from my first viewing of *Dr. No*, and my enthusiasm for the character and the franchise only grew with the release of each subsequent film. Of course, I followed up by reading Ian Fleming's novels that these movies were based on."

Another cinematic hero Sheldon began following around this time was actor Humphrey Bogart. "This was pre-home video, so I would just have to be lucky to catch his movies when they showed on television. Like a true fan, I had a few Bogie posters hanging on my bedroom walls. There were a few theaters in Los Angeles that would screen some of the classic films once in a while, and every so often I'd be lucky enough to catch one of Bogie's films on a big screen in an actual movie theater. The one that seemed to be screened more often than others was *The Treasure of the Sierra Madre* (1948), a true classic that was directed by John Huston." Bogie was not an upright, law-abiding movie hero good guy like many of the male stars of that era. In fact, more often than not he would play a villain like Mad Dog Roy Earl in *High Sierra* (1941), or a reluctant hero like Charlie Allnutt in *The African Queen* (1951), or an ambiguous anti-hero like Fred C. Dobbs in *The Treasure of the Sierra Madre*.

"Another actor that I became a fan of during this period was Steve McQueen, who starred in some of my favorite action films of that era, including *The Great Escape* (1963), *The Magnificent Seven* (1960), and *The Sand Pebbles* (1966)." According to Sheldon, McQueen was also a favorite of Van Damme's. The character Chad in *Double Impact* was named after McQueen's son, Chad McQueen, who was a personal friend of Jean-Claude's for a number of years.

In 1964, Sheldon's family moved a few miles west, in order to take advantage of a better high school in Beverly Hills. This worked out well for his sisters, but was not a great move for Sheldon as he had a number of friends that he would be leaving behind. Still, there were opportunities at Beverly Hills High School that would have an impact on him for the rest of his life.

Around this same time, Sheldon acquired an interest in photography, almost by accident when he found an old Voightlander camera hanging from a tree during a trip to the nearby Angeles National Forest. "I took the camera home with me, and began tinkering with it. Then, after I checked a few photography books out of the local library, I began taking photos, and soon found this was a hobby that I both enjoyed and had an aptitude for. It wasn't long before

I combined this new passion with my love of movies, and decided that I wanted to pursue a career as a Cinematographer, a Director of Photography for motion pictures. I subscribed to *American Cinematographer Magazine*, and began following cinematography and prominent cinematographers with an almost religious fervor. I had a few favorites back then, many of whom are still my favorites today. Number One was Gregg Toland, who famously shot *Citizen Kane* (1941) and was also behind the camera of one of my favorite Bogart films, *Dead End* (1937)." Another one of his favorites at the time was Richard Kline, who was nominated for an Oscar for his work on *Camelot* (1967). Years later, Sheldon would have the honor and privilege of actually working with Richard on *Double Impact* (1991).

Sheldon had a favorite teacher all throughout high school, and that was his Art teacher, Mr. Lyle Suter. The school had put him in charge of producing a newsreel, which would showcase highlights of the school year. It was to be shot on 16mm film, and the school actually had a couple of 16mm cameras available. One was a legendary Bolex, which he believes had the capability of recording sync sound along with the picture. The other camera was kind of a primitive, boxy 16mm camera, which may have been manufactured by Kodak, (or at least it had a Kodak label on it). Both of these had rotating turrets with a choice of three different lenses. They also had some editing equipment, which was pre-digital (by many years) and very much old school. Basically, you would cut the film on the frame line, and then attach it to the next shot with a piece of cellophane tape. To screen the film, you'd run it through a projector, and pray that the tape splices didn't break. Sheldon actually worked on a couple of them, which were called *Norman Newsreels*. He would film all kinds of school activities, including some sports events, of course. The school had an outstanding Theater Arts department, which would stage a musical every year. During his freshman year, Sheldon remembers one very excellent staging of *Carousel*. His personal Theater Arts interest at the time was not acting or directing, but Set Design, and in his senior year, Sheldon was actually tasked with designing the sets for the school's quite lavish production of *The Mikado*, which resulted in his life-long obsession with Gilbert & Sullivan.

Of all the events he filmed for the school, the most memorable by far was a yearly event that they called *Jazz Night*, which would generally feature some semi well-known performers who would put on a show for the students in the school's auditorium. During his senior year, Sheldon would hit the jackpot. "On one night they had a few fading stars who had been popular in the 1950s: The Coasters, and The Drifters. Then they scored a rising star named Linda Ronstadt, who was performing that night with her backup band, The Stone Ponies. The school's big coup, however, was booking The Doors, who just so happened to have the nation's number one hit single at the time, "Light My Fire". The school had booked this obscure Los Angeles based band well in advance, before their popularity exploded. To the band's credit, they honored the commitment they had made to give a live performance for the students in this local high school auditorium, at a time when they would have been able to book huge arenas anywhere in the country. I was the lucky guy who was given the opportunity to get up close and personal with them, because I had a professional-looking 16mm movie camera in my hands. I was down in the Green Room with them, filming them while they clowned around, getting ready to put on their show. I was up on the stage with them, getting close-ups while they performed all their latest hit songs. Fortunately for me, I was not a huge Rock 'n' Roll fan at the time; otherwise the excitement of being on-stage with The Doors might have completely overwhelmed me. While I liked The Beatles, The Rolling Stones, and Motown, my musical tastes at the time leaned towards Classical music and Broadway shows, especially those by Lerner & Lowe (*My Fair Lady* and *Camelot*). A couple other favorites of mine back then were *West Side Story* and *Fiddler on the Roof.* I still know the lyrics to every song in those, by heart. My friend, Josh Becker, is also a *My Fair Lady* fan, and the two of us have amazed one another by singing, in unison, "Why Can't the English," and not missing a single lyric." The 1960s were an epochal era for Rock 'n' Roll, but Sheldon found himself marching to a different drummer. To a great extent, he still does. Beethoven, Mozart, Mendelsohn, and Max Bruch are some of his Classical favorites. Thanks to *The Mikado*, he's still a fan of Gilbert & Sullivan, and has CDs of all the G&S shows.

In September of 1966, another cultural bombshell dropped when the first episode of *Star Trek* premiered on national TV. Of course, Sheldon was watching, as he was still an avid Sci-Fi fan. "I was hooked, and probably became one of the first *Trekkies*. Besides loving the show and eagerly watching it every week, I was given a front row seat via a couple friends of mine, Paul and Larry Brooks, whose dad was a production manager on the old Desilu lot at the corner of Gower and Melrose in Hollywood. He didn't specifically work on the show, but he was able to get us in and give us access to the lot, where we were free to wander around and to visit any set that wasn't specifically designated a closed set. I believe the *Star Trek* set was usually designated as one of these off-limits sets, but security wasn't all that tight back then, and nobody seemed to feel threatened by three teenage boys who obviously had some kind of connection or else they would not have been running around like kids in a candy store. We were able to walk right onto the sound stages where *Star Trek* was actually being filmed, and observe William Shatner, Leonard Nimoy, and the rest of the famous cast as they uttered some of their iconic lines of dialogue in some of their classic episodes. I never met the show's creator, Gene Roddenberry, in person, but I went into his office one day and asked his secretary if I could get his autograph. He actually obliged, and signed a black & white still of Kirk and Spock for me, with an inscription which read: '*To Sheldon Lettich. May you one day reach the stars! Gene Rodenberry, STAR TREK.*'"

The following week, Sheldon went even one better than that. He purchased a large, full color poster of Leonard Nimoy, dressed as Spock, holding a model of the Starship Enterprise. On his next visit to the lot, he carried that rolled up poster with him, and then went around to the key members of the cast to ask if they would autograph the poster. "I was warned that Nimoy was generally reluctant to sign autographs for fans, but when I unrolled that big poster for him I got a positive reaction, and even a smile from the famously stoic Mr. Spock. Nimoy signed the poster, and even addressed it to me personally. Then I approached Shatner, who was also happy to sign his autograph (even though it wasn't him on the poster), and the same with DeForest Kelley (Bones) and James Doohan (Scotty). Nichelle Nichols (Uhura) was not on the set that day, but during a subsequent visit I was able to get her to autograph a black & white still of herself. I believe all this made me a bona fide *Trekkie*, probably well before that term had even been coined.

Sheldon's interest in photography continued, never diverging from his goal of becoming a Director of Photography. There were no photography classes taught at his high school, so he managed to enroll in an Adult Education course that taught basic photography in the evenings at an elementary school close to his parents' house. Film schools were not as ubiquitous back then as they are now. Even in Los Angeles, there were only two colleges at the time teaching film courses which led to a degree in the subject, and those were the University of Southern California (USC) and The University of California, Los Angeles (UCLA). After graduating high school, he looked into attending either of those schools, but his high school grades were mediocre at best, and a good academic record was necessary to get into one of those programs at a four-year college. After checking around some more, Sheldon found a local junior college, Los Angeles Trade-Technical College, offering a two-year degree program in Professional Photography, just what he was looking for. A thorough knowledge of photography (cameras, film, lenses) seemed like a good stepping stone towards a career as a motion picture cameraman, so enrolling at Trade-Tech seemed like a good way to get his feet wet. Besides, the grade point averages and the academic requirements were not nearly as rigorous as were required at the four year schools. At this time, Sheldon's plan was to get an Associate of Arts (AA) degree in photography from Trade-Tech, and then transfer to either USC or UCLA afterwards.

He enthusiastically dove into photography classes at Trade-Tech, which were designed to prepare students for careers in Commercial Photography. The students were taught how to work with a big, bulky 4x5 inch view camera, the kind that harkened back to the earliest days of photography, the kind that Matthew Brady toted around during the Civil War. It sat atop a sturdy tripod, had a bellows, and required a shroud draped over the photographer's while focusing the image on a ground glass with the aid of a loupe. The film for those cameras came in 4x5 inch sheets which had to be manually inserted into plastic film holders. All this had to be done in complete darkness; a far cry from the convenient 35mm film cartridges that he was used to. They were taught to develop this film by dipping the film sheets by hand into some very foul and caustic chemicals, and then afterwards to make black & white prints from these negatives, again working with even more foul-smelling chemicals, which were corrosive enough to slowly eat into your skin if you didn't wear proper gloves. This was all done in a darkroom, which was dimly illuminated by red-tinted light bulbs.

In addition to film chemistry, they would learn about the optics of lenses, and about lighting; how to light a person, how to light a shiny reflective object, how to light a transparent glass object, how to light for texture. They were also taught the basics of architectural photography; how to straighten the lines of buildings with the aid of the swing & tilt features unique to a view camera. This was not the sort of photography that focused on creative expression, but on hard-nosed, rigid commercial photography, skills one could actually earn a living with. There was room for creativity, but that was not the emphasis. There was no Bachelor of Fine Arts degree to be conferred at Trade-Tech. Years later; he was able to utilize these skills to earn a decent living for himself as a professional photographer, which became his day job while struggling to gain a foothold as a screenwriter.

"I was seventeen years old at the time, having skipped Third Grade in Elementary School because somebody at the school thought I was a little smarter than average. As much as I was enjoying my studies at Trade-Tech, there was a restlessness gnawing at me. I felt a need to escape from my safe, cloistered, and comfortable life and to insert myself into the wide and dangerous outside world which I had only read about in books and seen in movies. I was feeling a need to test myself, and to gain some maturity which I felt I was sorely lacking at the time." Maybe it was the influence of War movies Sheldon had seen and admired in the mid-60s, especially *The Dirty Dozen* (1967) and *The Devil's Brigade* (1968). There were John Wayne and Audie Murphy movies before those, along with contemporary TV shows such as *Combat* (1962-1967) and *The Rat Patrol* (1966-68). There also was *The D.I.* (1957) with Jack Webb playing a hard-nosed Marine Corps Drill Instructor, decades before R. Lee Ermey took his own memorable shot at that role in *Full Metal Jacket* (1987).

The war in Vietnam was at its height, and Sheldon was feeling that if he didn't jump on that bandwagon, the conflict might be over before he had the opportunity to be a part of that unique and life changing experience. "I didn't discuss this with my parents, who I knew would be appalled. They were already scheming to get me a doctor's note to excuse me from the Draft, citing my childhood allergies as an excuse. Prior to turning eighteen, I would have needed their permission and a parental signature to enlist, so I kept mum until my eighteenth birthday. I had told a few very close friends that I was already talking to a Marine Corps recruiter. My semester at Trade-Tech ended just before my eighteenth birthday in January. I informed the college of my plans and said I wouldn't be returning when the new semester began. I'd already signed my enlistment contract, so all that was left for me to do was show up at the military induction center at the end of January." Not long afterwards he checked in at the induction center in Downtown Los Angeles, then found himself on a bus with a motley assortment of other recruits, all headed towards whatever fate awaited them at the Marine Corps Recruit Depot (MCRD) in San Diego, California.

The Marine

What transpired upon Sheldon's arrival at MCRD is a scenario that's been seen in so many movies and TV shows that it's pretty much become a cliché. First, Drill Instructors (D.I.) yelling at recruits to get off the bus and to find themselves a pair of yellow footprints. Then it's followed by hair being shorn off into high & tight skinhead haircuts before moving on to the ill-fitting green uniforms and black leather boots. Then they're soon herded into a barracks by still shouting D,I.'s for a fitful, sleepless first night as a Marine Corps Boot. "This was so very much different than anything I had ever experienced. I certainly got that change of scenery I had been pining for. Be careful what you wish for, right?" The following weeks were filled with unique learning experiences: how to march, how to properly wear a uniform, how to clean a barracks; fairly mundane stuff for the most part, not much having to do with war fighting.

There was also Physical Training (P.T.), which was mostly calisthenics, pushups, sit-ups, and an exercise they called Side Straddle Hops, known to most of us as Jumping Jacks. There were also three-mile runs, in combat boots. They had chants to accompany these runs, such as "If I die in a Combat Zone, box me up and ship me home!" along with "One-two-three-four, I love the Marine Corps!" The chants made these runs a lot more fun for them. In the Marine Corps, running was not quite the same as jogging. They were seriously running. Guys would drop out, huffing, puffing, and sometimes puking. There was no respite for the dropouts; the D.I.'s would force them to do a hundred side-straddle-hops, or a hundred pushups, or, rather than a finite number, they'd say "Do 'em 'til I get tired!" Most of them, Sheldon included, were getting into the best physical shape of their lives. "I didn't have much enthusiasm for exercising or running in high school, but the Marines changed that mindset for me for the rest of my life. I've been fervent about exercising ever since, hitting the gym at least three times a week, and going on long runs through whatever neighborhood I was living in. In the last few years, however, I've had to change my cardio routine to either a stationary bicycle or an elliptical machine instead of a run, mainly because of problems with my knees, a medical issue I can attribute to the Marines and the many hills and mountains I would be going up and down during my tour of duty in Vietnam and subsequent training in Ranger School and as a Recon Marine after that."

The recruits eventually moved on to the rifle range, where they were taught how to aim, fire, and maintain a rifle, skills Sheldon was woefully unacquainted with. Unlike many of the other recruits in his platoon, his parents never kept any firearms in the home. Having had horrendous experiences with World War Two, they had an aversion to firearms and weapons of any sort. His dad never took him to a shooting range, bought him a BB gun, or took him out hunting, which for many of the other guys seemed to be a standard rite of passage for American boys.

The rifle they were introduced to was the M-14, which was like a supercharged version of the famous M-1 Garand which had been the workhorse for American troops during World War Two. The major difference between the two was that the M-14 could fire on fully automatic as well as single shots. It also fired a different bullet, which was the 7.62 caliber NATO .308, which all the NATO countries had adopted as their standard military round. The lightweight M-16 was in the midst of being phased in to replace the heavier M-14. Fortunately for Sheldon, the M-14 was a better rifle for an introduction to marksmanship, especially for someone who had virtually no experience at all with firearms. Unfortunately for him, the heavier bullets gave the weapon a serious kickback when fired, something he wasn't quite prepared for the first time the trigger was pulled and firing a live round at a target. After firing a few more, his shoulder ached for a week. Despite that, they were back on the range the next day, and the day after that. He would learn to lean his shoulder into the buttstock before firing, to prevent the recoil from slamming that heavy piece of wood and metal into the soft, fleshy shoulder (which was what he was instructed to do in the first place). Little by little he would start to get it, to grasp the basics of marksmanship. Sheldon didn't do quite so well with his marksmanship in Boot Camp, not like many of the other guys who'd grown up handling and shooting firearms, eventually he would become reasonably adept with a rifle.

Boot Camp should have lasted for nine weeks, but they'd managed to accelerate it down to eight in order to get guys over to the war zone a little quicker. The year Sheldon graduated was 1969, when the U.S. had the highest number of troops in Vietnam, five hundred fifty thousand. After graduating, his entire platoon was packed into buses, shipped about forty miles north to the Marine Corps Base at Camp Pendleton, California to commence a few weeks of infantry training. Camp Pendleton was a huge, sprawling base that encompassed about seventeen miles of prime Southern California beachfront real estate, following along the shoreline of the Pacific Ocean, and for another ten miles inland. Established in 1942, marines would be trained there for amphibious landings, which would become their primary means of insertion for their island-hopping campaign across the Pacific in World War Two.

For Sheldon and the rest of the guys in his training platoon, Camp Pendleton became the place where they started feeling like they were really marines. Instead of marching in a neat, orderly formation across an asphalt parade deck, they were humping up and down hills, learning basic combat tactics, learning how to fire and maintain exotic weapons like M-60 machine guns, anti-tank rocket launchers, and M-79 grenade launchers, oftentimes with live ammunition. They also had to arm and throw live fragmentation grenades. They now were doing the cool stuff they had only previously seen in all those old John Wayne movies. It was a lot more than just fun & games. Their D.I.'s and tactical training instructors, nearly all of whom had already served in Vietnam, kept warning them to pay attention to what they were teaching because very shortly, "Y'all are goin' to Vietnam!" In mid-1969, around the time he was going through infantry training at Camp Pendleton, there were over two hundred Americans dying every week in Vietnam, a very sobering statistic.

After completing infantry training, they were bused back to MCRD where everyone was told what their primary Military Occupation Specialty (MOS) was going to be. Most of the guys in Sheldon's platoon were assigned 0311, which was a Rifleman, a basic ground-pounding grunt, the backbone of the infantry. He would be assigned the MOS of 2533, which was a Radio Telegraph operator. Telegraph is not an anachronistic misspelling; 2533's were actually expected to learn Morse Code. Surprisingly, even as late as 1969, the Navy was still transmitting messages from ship to ship using Morse Code, and since the Marine Corps was a part of the Navy, they needed to have operators who could transmit messages via Morse Code while serving aboard Navy ships. Sheldon felt it was totally unnecessary for marines to learn Morse Code in the late 1960's; he never used it once during his entire time in the Corps. Eventually the higher-ups came to the same conclusion; Sheldon's class was one of the last to ever be taught Morse Code. From then on all marine communicators were simply 2531 Radio Operators, which was his job in Vietnam and afterwards.

The small class plowed ahead and learned all the various dots and dashes that make up the Morse Code alphabet. "I was amused to see it unearthed for a scene in Christopher Nolan's *Interstellar* (2014) where two of the main characters use it to furtively communicate with one another. In addition to Morse Code we were also taught touch typing, which is something that actually did come in quite handy for me, but later in life, when I became a screenwriter, not at all while I was in the Marine Corps. We were introduced to the Prick-25, the PRC-25 field radio, and were taught how to use it and maintain it. It was a simple and very rugged piece of electronic equipment, which weighed about twenty five pounds. Depending on the type of antenna used and atmospheric conditions, it could reliably communicate with a similar piece of equipment that was within a radius of about three to four miles. With a longer antenna, the range was supposedly good for around eighteen miles. We practiced carrying these on our backs, communicating with one another at the nearby Marine Corps Air Facility at Miramar."

Finally they were assigned to what would be their first duty stations. Not surprisingly, nearly everyone was going to Vietnam, as had been promised (or warned). They were given a week's worth of Leave, so they could say goodbye to families, or to girlfriends. Sheldon didn't have a girlfriend at the time, so he just visited with his immediate family and a few close friends for a few days. "I was actually chomping at the bit to get overseas, to whatever fate or adventure awaited me. Movie nerd that I was, there was only one thing I wanted to do before leaving for Vietnam: I wanted to watch *2001: A Space Odyssey* (1968), up on the big Cinerama screen one more time. That was my wish, my last request, so to speak. That wish was granted. I got to see *2001* up on that vast curved screen at Warner's Cinerama Theater on Hollywood Blvd., where it had been screening since the day it first opened, and where I had already seen it three or four times. To this day, it remains one of my all-time favorite movies, and I've seen it in movie theaters at least a dozen times." Ironically, the premiere of *Bloodsport* (1988), a couple of decades later, was in that very same movie theater.

It was September 1969 when Sheldon boarded a chartered civilian plane which was packed with Marines heading to the Southeast Asian war zone. After a long flight over the Pacific, with one stopover in Hawaii for refueling, he arrived in Vietnam at the military air base in Da Nang, and it was sweltering hot outside. "When I stepped out of the plane, the heat hit my face like I'd stepped inside a blast furnace." The temperature was hovering near one hundred twenty degrees Fahrenheit and the relative humidity was around one hundred percent. He would soon learn that this would be the norm throughout Vietnam for the entire summer. Under these severe climate conditions he would soon be humping up and down hills and through triple canopy jungles with roughly a hundred pounds of radio equipment and other gear on his back.

Richard Nixon was now the president of the United States, and the number of American troops in Vietnam was at its highest level ever. He had missed the bloody Tet Offensive of that year, which happened around February. The previous year, the 1968 Tet Offensive had seen vicious and coordinated attacks on Americans and American bases throughout South Vietnam, by the combined forces of Viet Cong (VC) and the North Vietnamese Army (NVA). Those attacks triggered a strong retaliatory pushback from American forces, resulting in massive Vietnamese casualties. By the time he arrived over there, the entire country was relatively pacified. The VC and the NVA had pretty much had their asses kicked during both Tet Offensives, and during the desperate siege of Khe Sanh, facts that seem to have eluded much of the general public. South Vietnam was not quite the hellish war zone that it had been in the previous couple of years. It was still a long way from being Disneyland, and battles were still being fought all over the country, but the VC and NVA had come to the realization that their smartest strategy might be to just hunker down and wait, surmising correctly that the American public would grow weary of being mired down in a Southeast Asian war, and would eventually withdraw the troops. That is exactly how the events would eventually unfold. A few decades later, the same scenario played out in Afghanistan. Americans simply don't seem to have the patience and stamina of the Vietnamese, or the Afghans.

Within a day or so, all the newly arrived marines had been assigned to various units dispersed throughout I Corps, which encompassed the northernmost provinces of South Vietnam, and was where most of the Marine Corps units were located. "I was assigned to the Third Battalion, First Marine Regiment, of the First Marine Division. The Battalion headquarters was located on a hill alongside the meandering Song Vu Gia River. That location was named nothing more exotic or colorful than Hill Thirty Seven, which was simply the elevation of the hill. Many of the places where I would be temporarily bivouacked over the next year had similarly mundane and uninspiring names, just the elevation of a piece of terrain and nothing more." A couple kilometers away from them was Hill Sixty Five, which is where the First Marine Regiment was headquartered. There was a ridgeline nearby that the marines would bombard with artillery fire every night, which had been nicknamed Charlie Ridge. A jungle-encrusted valley a few miles away had a more colorful and evocative name, Elephant Valley. Sheldon ended up going on a number of patrols there, but never once saw an elephant. It might have been named after the plentiful Elephant Grass that grew along parts of the valley floor. The grass may have earned that name because it was verifiably as high as an elephant's eye.

As a radio operator, Sheldon was first assigned to Headquarters and Service Company (H&S) for the battalion, which meant he spent most of his days in the Combat Operations Center (C.O.C.), where he would make and receive calls for the officers who ran the battalion. There were three companies that comprised the battalion: India, Kilo, and Mike, and they were all spread out at various locations in the field near the battalion H.Q. He would end up spending a number of months at Hill Twenty Two with India Co., serving as their company radio operator.

Since the Viet Cong were laying low after their defeats during Tet and at KheSahn, it fell upon the American units to seek out and destroy the enemy, which meant they were constantly sending out patrols to try and engage the enemy. Every one of these patrols needed a radio operator. Sheldon went out with a number of squad-sized patrols, usually eight to twelve men. These small patrols would generally go out at night, after darkness fell. "We would find a spot to quietly hunker down for the night, and then we would lay low and wait to ambush any passing enemy patrols. There were larger versions of this concept as well, platoon-sized or even company-sized. When I was with India Company, the unit actually struck pay dirt one night, and ambushed a large contingent of VC ferrying equipment and provisions south towards Da Nang, possibly in preparation for a future attack on the city. I wouldn't doubt that there was some timely intelligence that tipped us off; otherwise it would have been extremely fortuitous that we had an entire company of Marines waiting at the right place and at the right time. Nevertheless the Viet Cong unit was completely decimated by small arms fire – M16 rifles and M-60 machine guns – without one single Marine casualty that night. There were around a hundred dead bodies on the ground afterwards, along with the weapons and the supplies they were transporting. I was the radio operator who was in contact with battalion headquarters that night, informing them of what was transpiring. The Viet Cong were wiped out so quickly and completely that I didn't even have to call for artillery or air support to help them out. I read about it in the military's *Stars & Stripes* newspaper a day or two later; apparently that was the biggest engagement of the entire night."

The night ambush patrols were rarely that successful. Generally, the only casualties were the mosquitoes that were biting on them, which they would quietly swat away. Nevertheless, the danger of their circumstances was always present. If one of the eight-man ambush patrols would have encountered a hundred-man contingent of VC at night, they could have been in a world of shit had they stumbled upon them. A few months after the previous incident, Sheldon found himself in a situation which was close to the realization of that frightening scenario.

There was a specialized unit attached to the S-2, the Intelligence section of the battalion, and that was the Scout Snipers. This was very much a Recon unit, which went out on small patrols with around ten Marines, at the behest of the battalion commander. They conducted reconnaissance missions in the immediate area of operations for the battalion, and they had a secondary mission as snipers. Instead of the standard M-16's they carried the older M-14 rifle, which fired a larger bullet and was more accurate, although it was decidedly heavier than the M-16. An M-14 with one hundred twenty rounds of 7.62mm ammo loaded into magazines weighed nineteen pounds, whereas an M-16 with one hundred twenty 5.56mm rounds weighed just a little over 11 pounds. The M-14's barrel is heavier and longer, which will also explain the difference in accuracy, and why it could be utilized as a sniper rifle. The guys in the unit had a newer version of the rifle, which had a pistol-grip stock, and was designated the M-14 E1. The unit leader was Sgt. Buck Webster, a stand-up guy who hailed from Bakersfield, California. The unit also had about four Kit Carson (KC) Scouts, Viet Cong defectors, who were now working with the Marines, and who were invaluable in the field.

They needed a radio operator so Sheldon volunteered his services, and became their attached radioman for a while. "Honestly, going out on patrols with the Scout Snipers was my best time in Vietnam. I felt very comfortable with them, more than I did with many of the other guys, who were the standard issue grunts that made up the majority of the Marine Corps infantry. I would feel the same way a few years later when I hooked up with an even more elite unit, which was Force Recon."

"One of the first patrols I accompanied them on was in Elephant Valley. No elephants spotted, nor were any expected, but we did notice something moving very quickly and noisily through the dense underbrush. Everyone was quickly pointing their rifles at whatever it was. The source of the noise turned out not to be enemy soldiers, but a small herd of wild boars, about eight of them. The Kit Carson's were quite excited by this, as they were no fans of what passed for food among the Americans. To be quite honest, most of the Americans were no big fans of military C-rations either, but for the Vietnamese this was an opportunity for some fresh meat. They pointed to the boars and excitedly exclaimed, "Number One Chop-Chop!" Which can be loosely translated as, "That's some good eatin'!" Buck gave them the go-ahead to take down a couple of boars. We were still out in the open, near a running stream, and hadn't yet made our way into the dense triple-canopy jungle further into the valley, which was the area we had been tasked with doing recon. One of the KC's had an M-79 grenade launcher; he took careful aim, and then fired off a 40mm HE (high explosive) grenade. I visibly saw it land in the middle of four boars. It exploded, and an instant later all four of the animals were on their backs, legs kicking helplessly at the air. The KC's ran to them, then picked out the biggest boar. The four K.C.'s each grabbed a leg, hoisted the still squirming boar off the ground, and very quickly ran down to the stream with it. They all pulled knives, and very quickly the boar was slaughtered and butchered, right on the spot."

Sheldon, as well as the rest of the Marines observed, and stood security as the KC's gathered wood and started a small campfire, then they would fill some cooking utensils with water from the stream and started boiling it over the burning wood. "Each of them was carrying small sacks of rice, some of which was tossed into the boiling water. Their noontime meal was very quickly coming together. The roasting pig meat began to smell very appetizing, but our Medical Corpsman prohibited us from eating any of it, on the good chance that it could very well be full of exotic parasites, which the Vietnamese had grown accustomed to, but which might put us Americans down with a serious case of diarrhea, or worse."

A few weeks later back in Elephant Valley, they were tasked with going deep into the valley, which was covered overhead with dense triple canopy jungle. The battalion had received some intelligence reports that there was a VC base camp somewhere further up. The Battalion Commander wanted them to check it out and see if those reports were true. A small tracked vehicle transported them to the mouth of the valley where they were dropped off. There was no way to do a helicopter insertion there due to the thickness of the overhead canopy and the steep canyon walls on both sides. Despite the name, this was really more of what Sheldon described as a canyon rather than a valley. "I began having some misgivings about this mission, fearing that the line-of-sight FM radio signal might not make it beyond those canyon walls, and that we might not be able to call for help should the shit hit the fan. But worse than that, how would we get the hell out of there if we ran into a large enemy force? There was no way for a helicopter to land in the canyon, and we were not prepared to be yanked out with a Special Patrol Insertion and Extraction (SPIE) rig, which required each patrol member to be wearing a special harness."

"The officers who thought this mission up did not give much consideration to what our predicament would be should we encounter a large hostile force. Most of the patrol members had their M-14's, but those only had twenty round magazines. What we were sorely lacking was an M-60 machine gun. Two M-60's would have been even better. Air support would have been flying blind and shooting blind because of the thick overhead canopy in this steep narrow canyon. This was back in the days well before laser-guided smart bombs. There was no estimate of how many VC might be in this alleged base camp, but if there were more than a few dozen, and if they had machine guns and Rocket-propelled Grenades (RPGs), we would have been outgunned as well as outnumbered, with nowhere to run and no way to get air support before we started running low on ammo."

That was just speculative rumination on Sheldon's part, until their point man actually did come face to face with a small VC patrol, which was headed right towards them on that very narrow jungle trail. "Suddenly, all hell broke loose! I don't know if the Cong got many shots in, but the point man and Buck Webster blasted quite a few rounds at the VC, who were apparently just as surprised as we were. I crouched down and called it in right away. It took a few tries, but finally I was finally able to get through to Battalion Headquarters (HQ). All I could say was that we were in enemy contact. I'm sure they could hear the loud gunfire in the background which verified what I was saying. I couldn't say much more than that, because I could only see the Marine in front of me, and no further than that on this narrow single-file trail. The gunfire stopped, and the VC took off running up the trail towards this phantom base camp. What they left behind was one dead body, surprisingly, a female. She was dressed in the typical black pajama VC uniform, and had a look of utter shock frozen on her face. There were blood trails heading further up into the canyon, sure signs that she wasn't the only one hit. There was a satchel full of documents, which I believe she had been carrying. "

After consulting with Buck, Sheldon called in all this new information. "More than anything else, the officers back at the Battalion HQ wanted to get their hands on those documents. They said they'd get back to us, but meanwhile the orders were to just hunker down where we were. There was nothing said about getting us out of this canyon, which we could have done by just turning around and retracing our steps. One thing for sure, our presence had been announced very loudly to the enemy. We were no longer a clandestine recon patrol. Standard operating procedure for a scenario of this sort, as I learned later in Force Recon and in Ranger School, was to get that small patrol out of harm's way as quickly as possible, especially if they couldn't be supported by either more troops or artillery or air support. Basically, it's Recon's job to find the enemy, and to be quiet about it. It's Infantry's job to kill them, with the help of artillery and aircraft. "

"Those officers at Battalion HQ were smelling blood, and seemed to either be unaware or dismissive of typical Recon protocols. Even though our presence had been compromised, they wanted us to continue the mission, to go deeper into the canyon to see if we could uncover this base camp, or make contact with the enemy troops who were holed up there, which without a doubt would have entailed a firefight. Well, we just proved that there was indeed an enemy presence in this canyon." Sheldon found himself in a very deadly situation with an outcome that could possibly end in death. "That just wasn't enough for them. They wanted this lightly armed recon patrol to turn itself into an assault force, even though we had just completely lost the element of surprise. Had one of them actually been out there in the bush with us, I'll bet he wouldn't have been so gung-ho; either that or he would have been trying to set himself up for a Medal of Honor."

"Buck and the others guys were taken aback. There was no talk from Battalion of sending a reaction squad to bolster our strength. More than anything, the officers wanted those documents, and they came up with a novel way to get a hold of them. The plan was to have a helicopter lower a rope to us through the triple canopy. There would be a bag at the end of the rope, and we were supposed to put the documents inside. I was the radioman, so I'm the one who was in contact with the helicopter pilots. We sent them grid coordinates of our approximate location. There were no electronic GPS devices back then (in fact GPS didn't even exist yet), so we had to ascertain our exact location by the skillful use of a map and a compass. Somehow we guided the helicopter to our vicinity. It was a twin-rotor CH-46, noisy as hell. In case the VC didn't know we were still in the canyon, they sure did now, and they knew our position as well. That chopper hovered right over our position for a good ten to fifteen minutes. The rope was lowered, and we had to chase after it and grab it. Then the documents were placed inside the bag, and I informed the pilot they could pull the bag back up. The bag disappeared through the overhead canopy, and as soon as it was safely on board, the helicopter took off." With one task completed, this left the soldiers in their current position and Sheldon knew it wasn't over yet. "Now that the documents were safely on their way back to Battalion HQ, we figured the Battalion honchos would thank us for a job well done and order the patrol to extract ourselves from this valley as well. But no, they wanted us to stay where we were, to hunker down for the night and await further orders in the morning. Needless to say, none of the guys were happy to hear this. These Marines were not chickens; they were all combat vets who had been in the shit before and were not afraid to confront the enemy, but not when the odds were stacked against them like this. In addition to all the other factors, we had killed one of the VC and wounded a few others. That woman we killed might have been the girlfriend or even the wife of one of the other Viet Cong in the patrol. For them, this had become personal now. They would be out for vengeance. And we were sitting ducks, with a limited arsenal of weapons."

Fortunately for Sheldon, the Marines he was with were not amateurs. A few of them had been through formal Recon training in Vietnam, and they had picked up a few clever strategies that would hopefully get them through the night. "Buck waited until the sun had set, and then he moved the entire patrol to a different spot to hunker down. We waited anxiously in place while it grew pitch dark, and then he had us move again. We took great pains to make no noise whatsoever. Then Buck picked another spot, something that was inconspicuous, not a spot that was an obvious place to settle down for the night. The patrol then moved into a Wagon Wheel formation, feet touching in the middle, with all the guys pointed outwards, like spokes in a wheel. This way we had a 360 degree field of vision; we could see and hear whatever was creeping around outside our small perimeter. Since our feet were touching, we could silently communicate with our feet, just by touching the other guy's foot to alert him that something was amiss, a message that could easily be passed along to the others as well. Sure enough, people were looking for us. We could hear them quietly moving around, not saying a word, not even whispering. They knew we were out here someplace, and they were out for blood. Our weapons were all loaded, and pointed outwards, so we were as ready as we could be in case we were discovered. Had that happened, it would have been quite bloody and quite chaotic. We didn't know how many additional enemy troops might have been holed up in this base camp. Quite possibly they might have all been out, scouring the jungle searching for us. For the VC, help might have been within reach once the shooting started. For us, we had very little in the way of options, besides just trying to shoot our way out of it."

Once they settled down into their Wagon Wheel, Sheldon would radio Battalion and whisper the grid coordinates. Text messaging would have been a blessing in this situation, but they were decades away from that and GPS was just Science Fiction at this point in time. "We did our best to give Battalion a precise fix on our position, just in case the shit hit the fan and we needed air or artillery support. Artillery would not have been my first choice, since we stood a good chance of being blasted apart by our own cannon-fire if those grid coordinates were off by even a fraction. Air support would have been the better option, especially a C-130 gunship (nicknamed either Spooky or Puff, the Magic Dragon), because that weapons-filled cargo plane could have slowly circled overhead, dropping flares for illumination, and blasting away at everything outside our small perimeter with machine guns and six thousand round-per-minute Mini-guns. In the darkness of night, underneath triple canopy treetops, and with less than precise grid coordinates, we could have easily been chewed apart by our own air support; the pilots didn't have high-tech night vision goggles back then either. Fortunately, it never came to that. The Viet Cong searched for hours but they never found us. They may have had their own fears and misgivings as well, since we had killed one of theirs and wounded a few others. Bottom line, the sun rose in the morning and we were all still breathing. I don't think any one of us slept a wink that night."

"Buck had us move to a different spot, where we set up another perimeter. Once we felt safe enough to speak in a normal tone of voice, I called in our situation to Battalion, explaining that the enemy had been searching for us during the night, and requested to them that we be allowed to extract ourselves from this canyon. Very shortly afterwards we received their reply, which was to continue our patrol further up into the canyon. Everyone in the patrol was dumbfounded. We were being ordered to go on what could possibly be a suicide mission, unless the VC had been as spooked by us as we were by them, and had moved their base camp to another area." Bottom line, there was a small number of Marines, and possibly many more Viet Cong. The Marines had killed one and wounded a few more. They needed reinforcements, plus more weapons and ammo, if they were to continue on with the mission. All of that was denied.

The motto of the Third Battalion, First Marines was ostensibly "*Find, Fix, Finish.*" They had found the enemy, and now it was up to the Infantry to fix and finish them. That's the way it was supposed to work. If they had been part of an actual Recon Battalion or a Force Recon Company, the commanding officer would have told the Infantry commander to go fuck himself. The Battalion honchos of 3/1 were expecting this small Recon unit to do it all by them-selves, even though they were under-armed and had lost the ele-ment of surprise. Granted, it was daylight now, so they could have called for jets to support them with five hundred pound bombs and napalm if they came face to face with the enemy again. There were no jets or even Cobra attack helicopters circling overhead, ready to unleash their loads on a moment's notice. Sheldon and the rest of the patrol had no idea how many VC were supposed to be holed up in this base camp. If the numbers were sufficient, maybe they would have enough time to call for air support before they were decimated.

"Basically, we were nothing more than pawns on a chessboard for these officers. I wasn't thinking about the movie at the time, but we were like those French soldiers in Kubrick's *Paths of Glory* (1957) who are ordered to take the Anthill even though the odds against them are impossible. Buck and the rest of the guys in the patrol had serious misgivings about following these orders. Buck was a courageous Marine, but he didn't want to assume the responsibility or the blame for telling Battalion that we were not going to follow this order. I was the guy with a radio handset in my hand, so I took it upon myself to tell Battalion that we were not going back to search for that base camp. Not this morning, not without reinforcements." It wasn't necessarily an easy call to make but it was something Sheldon had to do. "The guy I was talking to on the radio was one of the other radio operators in the Combat Operations Center. I was not conversing with any of the officers directly, but my voice would have been heard on the squawk box, which was military jargon for loudspeaker. After a few tense minutes, Battalion called us back. The new orders were to extract ourselves, on foot, out of Elephant Valley, and to await further instructions. Everyone breathed a sigh of relief, and we got the hell out of that canyon as quickly as our tired legs could carry us. That same small tracked vehicle that deposited us at the mouth of the canyon was waiting there to pick us up. Within an hour or so we were back at Hill Thirty Seven. Every one of us headed straight for our tent-like hootches, and we spent the rest of the day catching up on sleep. Buck, however, was debriefed by the officers. All I was told about that debriefing was that I wasn't going to be the radio operator for the Scout Snipers any longer. I don't know if Buck told them, or if they had figured it out on their own, that I had taken it upon myself to speak for the patrol when I communicated that we were not going back to search for the base camp."

The eventual outcome of all this is unknown, if someone else was tasked with checking out that particular base camp. Sheldon does have a theory, or opinion he feels is the most logical. "With the trove of documents that was put into their hands, and with the firm knowledge that there really were Viet Cong further up in that valley, they should have contacted Regimental or even Division headquarters, so that somebody else could have sent a properly equipped team from either the Recon Battalion or Force Recon to follow up."

Sheldon was back in the Battalion Combat Operations Center for a while, communicating messages over the radio to units in the field, most likely rubbing elbows with those same officers who had tried to send him on that suicide mission. He did end up getting attached to the Scout Snipers again, and went out on a few patrols with them. "It was at their request. According to what Buck and a couple of the other guys told me, I was the best radioman they had worked with so far, who was actually able to keep up with them as they humped through the boonies. I felt the same about them. I liked being with a small elite Recon unit much better than working with a larger group of regular Infantry." Later, when he was back at Camp Pendleton, this helped solidify his desire to volunteer for Force Recon, which was the Marine Corps' equivalent of the Navy SEALs.

The year was 1970, and President Richard Nixon had begun pulling American troops out of Vietnam, intending for the Vietnamese to take over the war-fighting tasks, pretty much the same strategy that was followed in Afghanistan decades later. The First Marine Division was one of the first units to begin withdrawing, and they redeployed to Camp Pendleton, the base that had been their home for decades. This coincided with Sheldon's own rotation back to the United States. "I was sent to Camp Pendleton as well, assigned initially to the Third Amtrac Battalion, which was based in the Del Mar area of the base, close to the ocean. Amtrac is short for amphibious tractor. These were basically armored troop carriers that could operate on land and in the ocean. They weighed thirty seven tons each, but amazingly were able to float on the water and swim through the ocean. They were designed to move Marines from the inside of a ship and get them to the beach, where they could drive up and deliver Marines to the battlefield." As in Vietnam, he was a radio operator, although with this unit he never carried a radio on his back. The radios were inside the vehicles, but their job here was not to communicate with higher-ups and other units. These vehicles were ostensibly water-tight, an absolute necessity when a vehicle weighs thirty seven tons and is supposed to float. "Seawater would always find a way to come gushing in, especially when these vehicles were entering the water, either from the back of a ship or while crossing from land to sea while traversing the surf zone. This necessitated constant preventive maintenance, which basically meant cleaning the seawater off the radios, and that task, fell to the radio operators. Radio Maintenance Man was not what I had signed up for when I joined the Marines. I wanted to get out of this unit as quickly as possible."

Around the same time, the rest of the First Marine Division had been redeploying, piecemeal, to various parts of Camp Pendleton. The First Force Reconnaissance Company was part of that massive redeployment, and Sheldon had heard that they were moving to barracks in the Las Pulgas area of Camp Pendleton, which was not all that far from Del Mar. "I got in my car and drove the short distance to Las Pulgas and managed to track down the current Commanding Officer of this unit, who was a mere First Lieutenant. The company was a shadow of its former self. Some of the Recon Marines that served with the unit in Vietnam had deployed to the Second Force Recon Company, on the other side of the country at Camp Lejeune in North Carolina. Many of them had simply rotated out of the Marine Corps completely, having finished their enlistments. The Lieutenant seemed happy to have a volunteer, who would help to start repopulating the unit. By the time I formally transferred over, there were a few more volunteers. Within a few weeks three of us had been given orders to attend the U.S. Army's Jump School at Fort Benning, Georgia. I was going to be trained as a Parachutist."

During their first week at Fort Benning, Sheldon and his colleagues were taught a lot of basic stuff, the most important of which was how to execute a Parachute Landing Fall (PLF), so that they wouldn't break their legs or ankles when hitting the ground. Despite that, and plenty of hours practicing, jumping off four foot high platforms, there would still be plenty of leg injuries once jumping out of planes started. "A military jump, out the side door of a big, fast-moving cargo plane from twelve hundred feet in the air, is actually quite scary the first couple of times you do it. The strong prop blast from the propellers is buffeting against you, and you have to make a strong leap to get your body fully out of the door without the prop blast pushing you back in, or even worse, slamming you into the side of the plane once you've made it out. I've seen it happen to a couple of guys. The injuries can be serious, and I saw a few guys wash out of the military altogether because of their injuries. There were Army Medics standing by during our first five jumps at Benning, and they were kept quite busy picking up casualties off the drop zone. I later on had a few bad landings myself, and even got knocked unconscious when I slammed into a concrete foundation during a low altitude night jump at Camp Pendleton."

After graduation from Jump School, Sheldon was back at Camp Pendleton for about a day before he had to turn around and head right back to Fort Benning, this time for Ranger School. "Honestly, I had never heard of Ranger School, but it was one of the toughest courses to get into, in the entire U.S. military. The school lasted for two months, and basically taught patrolling and small unit tactics. It was tougher and more physically and mentally demanding than Marine Corps Boot Camp, by far. It was on the same level of difficulty as Navy SEAL training and Green Beret training; in fact, some other students going through the program already were Navy

SEALs or Green Berets. Most of the other students were commissioned officers and non-commissioned officers. I was a mere corporal at the time, but I lucked out because the school had openings for a couple of Marines, and since the numbers were so meager for the Force Recon Company at the time, I pretty much got the opportunity more by default than anything else. I really didn't know what I was getting myself in to when they sent me there, but I managed to make it to the end and graduate the course." Among other things, in northern Georgia they taught mountaineering, climbing up sheer rock walls with the use of pitons and ropes, or rappelling down steep cliffs. In the Florida Everglades they taught them how to patrol through jungle terrain on foot and with inflatable Zodiac boats. Much of this patrolling was done at night, oftentimes in almost complete darkness.

The entire course was two months long, and the culmination was a week-long patrol at Eglin Air Force Base in the Florida pan-handle, with Sheldon and the other men receiving no breaks for sleep or for meals. "By the end of that sleepless week-long patrol, I was actually hallucinating; my sleep deprived mind was seeing tall trees looking like crystalline fairy castles. They had Aggressors stalking us too, firing blank bullets at us, forcing us to return fire and maneuver around them or take them as prisoners. This was the ultimate in realistic combat simulation. I had actually served in Vietnam and had patrolled those mountainous jungles, with real enemy aggressors stalking me and my patrol. The only difference here was that the bullets were blanks, and these Aggressors were not shooting to kill. Even so, there were real casualties in Ranger School; every year one or two students would die during the course, or would permanently wash out of the military due to injuries sustained."

"During my two-month absence, the Force Recon Company's roster had filled up. We now had quite a few Marines, a few of whom were Vietnam vets, but most of whom were not. Many of them were fresh out of infantry training at Camp Pendleton. They all were gung-ho volunteers who had heard tales about the legend-ary Force Recon, and had wanted to be a part of this elite unit. I had an affinity for guys like these, who did not just want to be part of the ordinary herd. While I was away at Ranger School a num-ber of them had been put through Jump School, so we had enough jump-qualified Marines to fill up the interior of a CH-46 helicop-ter for training jumps at Camp Pendleton. Now that I had gotten my feet wet with parachuting, this became something that I would eagerly look forward to." Parachuting was essential to Force Recon because it was one of the principle means for inserting Recon teams behind enemy lines. The Marine Corps, unlike the Army, did not look for ways to pin all kinds of badges and patches all over our uniforms. They only had one emblem that's worn above a pocket on their shirts, and that's the Navy & Marine Corps Gold Parachut-ist Wings, which would be earned after a total of ten jumps. Once awarded, they would wear those wings proudly, as they were the only authorized emblem that outwardly indicated Recon Marines. In the Army they had Silver Jump Wings. They also have Ranger tabs and Combat Infantryman badges, in addition to a number of others, almost like Boy Scout Merit Badges. "Since I had graduated from Ranger School, if I had been in the Army I would have been wearing a Ranger tab on my shoulder, but the Marine Corps did not authorize it. As far as the Marines were concerned, if you were a Marine you were special enough. I had a few Army guys even ask me, if you can't wear the Ranger tab, why in the hell did you even go through the torturous training? My answer would be, if I'm wearing the Marine Corps eagle, globe, & anchor, why would I need any-thing else?"

The other specialized training that Force Recon Marines received was scuba diving, which was another way of clandestinely inserting behind enemy lines. Sheldon was sent to Pre-Scuba School, which prepared him for going through the rigorous Scuba School down in San Diego. "I did have a few opportunities to go underwater with scuba equipment, and even took a test in a decompression chamber to see if my eardrums could handle the extra pressure underwater. Unfortunately, I found out they couldn't. I was only able to go down to one atmosphere, thirty three feet, before my eardrums would feel like they were caving in." To be qualified as a Marine Corps Diver (and receive a gold Bubble emblem) one had to be able to descend to twice that depth, at least, and he learned it just wasn't physically possible for him.

"I made some very good friends in Force Recon, a few of whom are still friends of mine today, all these many years later. I have visited their homes, and they have visited mine. I've celebrated the Marine Corps Birthday with a few of them, and vacationed with others. These guys were risk takers, crazy enough to jump out of an aircraft in flight or go on a five mile ocean swim in the dead of night. Conversely, I haven't stayed in touch with anybody I knew in Boot Camp or even in Vietnam; we all simply scattered to the winds after we came back home from 'Nam. It was different with those elite Force Recon guys. Many of us have stayed in touch, even if it's only via email and Facebook nowadays."

In 1972, Sheldon began noticing some shortness of breath when he went on the near daily five-mile runs. He thought it might be a respiratory problem, so he went to see one of the Navy doctors who listened to his lungs through a stethoscope and took some chest x-rays. Afterwards, the doctor informed him that the problem was not with his lungs but with his heart. Sheldon had a heart murmur. "The doctor could clearly hear the murmur through his stethoscope, but wasn't sure about the location or seriousness of it, not without further tests. This wasn't the first time that a military doctor had put a stethoscope to my chest, but the problem had not been detected before. So the assumption had to be that I developed the problem while I was in the Marines. This led to a medical discharge, a full half year before my enlistment was scheduled to expire. So the bad news was that I had a serious heart defect, but the good news was that I was getting out of the Marines early, and because this was a service connected disability, I would be eligible to get free healthcare from the Veterans Administration for the rest of my life. This came in very handy about thirty five years later when I had my aortic heart valve replaced at the VA Hospital, and didn't have to pay a dime for it."

This recent development wasn't exactly what Sheldon would be hoping for, regardless of the benefits. "I was actually a little disappointed with this early discharge, simply because I had been enjoying my time with Force Recon and with all the friends I had made in that unit. It was really time for me to move on with the rest of my life. Helping me to do that was a sizeable (at that time) sum of severance pay, which that military would be handing to me on my way out the door."

Film School and the Girl Next Door

Sheldon had not been the most conscientious of students while in high school, but during his three and a half years in the Marine Corps, he had met a lot of guys who were undereducated, and in many cases just plain ignorant. He would strive to be better than that. "I was still interested in pursuing my goal of becoming a cinematographer, and realized I had some serious catching up to do. I enrolled in a local junior college in the San Fernando Valley, to begin accumulating the prerequisites I would need to get into the Film programs at either USC or UCLA. Prerequisites aside, I began taking my education seriously as I had never done before. Eventually I re-enrolled at Los Angeles Trade-Tech to continue my photography education. While I was there, the school informed me that there was an Architectural photographer named George Szanick who was looking for an assistant." Mr. Szanick was actually somewhat renowned among photographers in his field in Los Angeles. He had photographed a number of celebrity homes, like Gregory Peck's and Dean Martin's, and had his work featured regularly in magazines like *Architectural Digest* and *House Beautiful*. All this work was done with a 4x5 view camera, which was the only way to photograph Interiors and Architecture because of its unique ability to keep vertical and horizontal lines straight, even when using an extreme wide angle lens. The wide angle lens (the wider the better) was oftentimes the only way to capture an entire room in a single shot.

Sheldon became George's assistant for a while, and it would eventually morph into something that would feel more like an apprenticeship, learning all the tricks of his trade. All the while he was still attending classes at Trade-Tech, and becoming more assured of himself and his abilities as a photographer. Eventually he decided to try venturing out on his own. "I had my own 4x5 view camera, plus various accessories. I didn't own a lighting package at the time, but I would be able to rent whatever I needed. I didn't try to poach any of George's clients, but just by using the phone book I began cold-calling Architects and Interior Designers throughout Los Angeles. My prices were very low at first; I began having some luck with people who needed their projects photographed, and were willing to take a chance on a newcomer. This ended up being my day job for the next eleven years, until I was finally able to start earning a living from my screenwriting." Sheldon was photographing houses, apartments, office suites, office buildings, and every so often a mansion or two, not just in Los Angeles but in Palm Springs, San Francisco, and other cities throughout North America. His work started ending up in magazines like *Interior Design*, *Los Angeles Magazine*, and like Szanick, *Architectural Digest*. Eventually, the magazines themselves began to hire him. He was doing all right for himself as a professional photographer.

Sheldon was able to accomplish something on his own that so many people strive to do but are never quite able to. "My entire life, I have never had to rely upon a nine to five full-time salaried job to make ends meet, unless you count the Marine Corps, but that was more like a 24/7 job. I did have some tough times along the way where I struggled to pay the rent and put food on the table, but I always managed to find a way to earn a living on my own without having to punch a time-clock."

This was the era before VHS tapes and DVDs. There were no streaming services, not even HBO or TCM. There was no way to see older movies, unless they happened to be playing on one of the local televisions stations, and even so you'd have to catch it precisely when it was scheduled to run, not at your leisure. What they did have in the 1970s were revival theaters, they screened older films on a daily basis, generally two or even three films with similar themes on the same day. The theaters themselves would print out calendars of upcoming bills; there was no Internet at the time to look up the schedules. Sheldon was living in Venice, California at this time while attending classes at nearby Santa Monica College. Just through serendipity, the house he was renting with a couple of friends was only one block away from the best of the revival houses, which was the Fox Venice Theater. "It was walking distance for me, and I would go there at least one or two times a week and catch up on whatever was playing there on any particular night. This broadened my knowledge of Cinema tremendously as they would regularly screen foreign films, experimental films, and quirky cult films like Jodorowsky's *El Topo* (1970) or Robert Downey's *Putney Swope* (1969). In addition, they screened older mainstream movies that were no longer playing in the commercial movie houses. A few times they grouped *The Godfather* (1972, 1974) Parts One and Two together, which totaled about seven hours of movie viewing at one sitting. Nevertheless, I sat through that lengthy double bill a number of times. Science Fiction and Horror would sometimes be on the menu as well, which is how I ended up seeing *2001: A Space Odyssey* up on a big (non-Cinerama) screen a few more times. I saw my first couple of Fellini films there, which is how I first became an ardent Fellini fan. *8 ½* (1963) and *Juliet of the Spirits* (1965) are still a couple of my all-time favorites. It's also where I was introduced to the Japanese action and martial arts epics of Akira Kurosawa, like *Seven Samurai* (1954) and *Yojimbo* (1961)."

There were a couple of Cinema classes being taught at Santa Monica College; nothing hands-on practical, but more about film history and film appreciation. One of them was an appreciation class about foreign films, which would open up an entire new world for Sheldon beyond just Fellini and Kurosawa. There was a proper screening room, with a projection room in the back so the class wouldn't hear the noise of the 16mm projector while watching the movies. The professor who taught the class gave them terrific

SHELDON LETTICH • 43

insights into the films that she screened, and would talk about the filmmakers who made these movies. In this class he would be introduced to the films of Antonioni, Bergman, Bertolucci, Wajda, Visconti, and many others.

One particular film from this era should be mentioned, and that's *Billy Jack* (1971). The story was about the title character, a former Green Beret and Vietnam Vet, who's also an expert in the martial art of Hapkido. He now sees himself as a pacifist, and he's made it his altruistic mission to protect a progressive school that's located on an Indian reservation, on the outskirts of a small conservative Arizona town. Billy Jack ends up tangling with and physically taking down the local sheriff and various deputies who want to close down the school. The students are mostly Native Americans, and Billy Jack himself is a half breed of Native American and Caucasian parentage. Curiously (maybe it's a little more than a coincidence), the novel *First Blood* which introduced former Green Beret and Vietnam Vet John Rambo, was first published the following year. *Billy Jack* was a very low budget movie which starred an obscure actor named Tom Laughlin, who also co-wrote the script and directed the movie. It was actually a sequel to a movie titled *The Born Losers* (1967), in which Laughlin plays the same character, Billy Jack, who single-handedly takes on and defeats a biker gang. Although *Billy Jack* was made on a shoestring budget, it went on to do huge business, grossing nearly $65 million in the U.S. alone. It subsequently spawned a few sequels: *The Trial of Billy Jack* (1974), *Billy Jack Goes to Washington* (1977), and *The Return of Billy Jack* (1986).

For Sheldon, the first film and that book by David Morrell had more things in common than some would expect. "I saw *Billy Jack* a few times in theaters, and also read *First Blood* before it was turned into a movie. The movie plays like an early template for the action movie heroes that followed in the 1980s. All that was missing was the huge bulging muscles of those 80s action heroes. I would not hesitate to admit that I was impressed and influenced by *Billy Jack*, well before I or anyone else had heard of John Rambo. Perhaps David Morrell, who authored *First Blood*, was influenced by *Billy Jack* as well, either consciously or subconsciously. There are just too many overlaps, not just the Vietnam Vet Green Beret, but also the mixed parentage and the Arizona background. I saw *The Trial of Billy Jack*, but wasn't all that impressed with it. As I recall, it was mostly talk and very little action, especially compared to the first one, which I saw a number of times."

It wouldn't be until the mid-1970s when Sheldon would reach the end of his photography studies at Trade-Tech. He received an AA degree from that school, and then one from Santa Monica College as well. Ready to take the next step, he applied to the UCLA School of Film and TV Studies. Disappointingly, he was turned down. He was accused of having accumulated too many credits, and since UCLA was a state-run school, they had some stringent rules about the number of credits that a prospective student could accumulate from other state-run institutions in order to be accepted in as a Junior. In their estimation, he had already accumulated enough credits to be considered a Senior, and the state of California was not going to foot the bill for continuing his education any further. The fact that Sheldon was a military veteran didn't seem to count for anything, and may have actually worked against him.

In the early 70s, there was still a lot of animosity towards the Vietnam War and towards military veterans, especially on California college campuses, where many of the faculty and staff were notoriously Left Wing and anti-military. There's no proof that his status as a veteran factored in, but the excuse given to him made very little sense. He also tried to enroll in the USC program, but was rejected there as well. With the price of their tuition being so high, Sheldon probably couldn't have afforded it at that time and had exhausted the very meager G.I. Bill by this point. He was left in a quandary.

Sheldon heard about the American Film Institute Center for Advanced Film Studies (AFI), which was located very close by, inside the famous old Greystone Mansion in Beverly Hills. It was technically a post-graduate institution that had four disciplines one could apply for: Writers, Directors, Producers, and Cinematographers. He would apply to be a Cinematography Fellow, and submitted some of the photographs he had been taking during that time, including tear-sheets from magazines, and wrote an impassioned letter about his years-long desire to become a Director of Photography. The academic prerequisites for a Cinematography Fellow were far less stringent and cumbersome than those at the other schools, plus the tuition was quite reasonable, especially compared to USC. He was quickly accepted into the program and began his studies there in the fall of 1977.

The AFI was really the ideal spot for Sheldon, because rather than focusing on classroom academics, the focus there was hands-on production. "We may have been shooting on half-inch video but we were making movies. The way it was supposed to work at the institute was that the Writing Fellows would write the scripts, the Directing Fellows would work with actors to bring those scripts to life, and also work with the Cinematography Fellows, who would light the sets and operate the cameras. There was editing equipment available. The Director Fellows would afterwards edit their short movies together, and then screen them for the entire class, who would then offer critiques."

There were also classes with industry veterans like George Folsey, a working cinematographer who had shot *Forbidden Planet* (1956). According to Sheldon, these weren't detailed hands-on classes with reading assignments or tests, but were more like lectures. There were similar professionals lecturing about Screenwriting and Directing. The Screenwriting Fellows were expected to work on short scripts and turn them in to be critiqued. Their scripts were also made available to be read and critiqued by other

Fellows in the various disciplines. "I got my hands on a few of these short scripts, expecting to be impressed; after all, most of these writers had advanced degrees in disciplines like Creative Writing, Playwriting, and English Literature from prestigious universities. I found the majority of their scripts to be dull and unimpressive. I had always had some interest in writing, and took a few stabs at short screenplays and comic books in the past, but I didn't feel confident that I could compete against writers with impressive credentials like those others at the AFI. The proof is on the page, and the proof I was reading from the Screenwriting Fellows made me feel I could maybe do just as good, if not better. I started monitoring the Screenwriting lectures, and then I gave it a shot with my own short original screenplay. I turned it in, and to my surprise the instructor liked it. I can't remember his name, but he was an old timer in the business, with many produced film and TV credits to his name. He gave me a few pointers, and encouraged me to continue following this path, to see where it might lead."

Sheldon ended up being one of the few members of that particular AFI class (1977-78) who actually forged a career as a working screenwriter. One of the Directing Fellows, James Orr, also found success as a screenwriter on *Three Men and a Baby* (1987), *Father of the Bride* (1991), and *Sister Act 2* (1993). The class had a bumper crop of Cinematography Fellows who had successful careers as Directors of Photography afterwards, including Robert Elswit, who shot a few films for Paul Thomas Anderson and George Clooney, and has been nominated for two Academy Awards. Kees Van Oostrum, a Dutchman who went on to shoot *Gettysburg* (1993) and *Gods and Generals* (2003) and eventually became the President of the American Society of Cinematographers (ASC) in 2016. Kees and Sheldon would reconnect a number of years later when Kees shot the movie, *Christina* (2010), for Larry Brand (a close friend of Sheldon's). Another successful Cinematography Fellow from that same class was Jon Kranhouse, who went on to shoot one of Van Damme's most beloved movies, *Kickboxer* (1989).

In order to attend the AFI without having to navigate a punishing commute across town, Sheldon relocated from Venice to the centrally located Miracle Mile area of Los Angeles. It was there he would meet his future wife, who was his upstairs neighbor in a two-story apartment building. You could almost call her "the girl next door". Toni Williams was originally from Dallas, Texas, and had moved to California a few years earlier with a couple of her cousins. The two cousins found themselves not feeling comfortable with Southern California or its fast paced lifestyle, and they eventually moved back to Texas. Toni managed to tough it out and forge her own way, eventually enrolling at Los Angeles Trade-Tech College where she studied Architectural Drafting. Ironically, and coincidentally, her future husband was also attending the same college at the same time, but that had nothing to do with how they first got together. Toni had a somewhat wild roommate named Gilda, and the two of them were constantly throwing noisy dance parties in their upstairs apartment. Sheldon and a couple of movie-nerd roommates lived directly below them, and they were throwing parties as well, but of a completely different nature. Sheldon would rent a 16mm projector from time to time, along with some older movies and cartoon short subjects, so he and his roommates could throw movie-viewing parties. They would project these movies on a blank white wall and crank up the sound, which made their parties nearly as noisy as the ones upstairs. Toni and Gilda would sometimes wander downstairs to watch the movies that their neighbors were projecting, while conversely, Sheldon and his roommates would sometimes wander upstairs to join the dance parties.

Eventually Sheldon and Toni would come to realize that they had a few important interests in common. Toni aspired to eventually become an Interior Designer, and her upstairs neighbor just happened to be taking photographs for some of the most prominent and highest end Interior Designers in Southern California. Sheldon invited Toni to accompany him on some of these shoots, where she assisted him as a stylist, helping with flower arrangements and accessories, basically serving in the capacity of a Set Decorator or Prop Person. Much of the time she simply helped him haul cables and lighting equipment, not much different than a Grip or an Electrician on a movie set. It wasn't long before the two of them began dating. A couple of years later, Sheldon proposed, and they were married the following year.

Toni has been right alongside her husband for over forty years, visiting movie sets, meeting actors, movie stars, celebrities, and traveling to distant locations. The first time Sheldon met Jean-Claude Van Damme face to face was at the apartment he shared with his bride, also in the Miracle Mile area of Los Angeles. At that very first meeting, Jean-Claude brought along his wife, the former Gladys Portugues. By an amazing coincidence, Toni and Gladys were both pregnant at the time, both with big bulging bellies. It's no wonder the two of them hit it off almost as famously as Sheldon and Jean-Claude. That friendship between the two wives has endured for many years as well. Toni and Gladys flew together to Hong Kong to visit their husbands on the set of *Double Impact* (1991).

Around this same time, Sheldon met a young filmmaker who had relocated from Detroit to Los Angeles. His name was Josh Becker, and he had been friends with a number of other young filmmakers in Detroit, specifically Sam Raimi, Bruce Campbell, Rob Tapert, Scott Spiegel, and a few others. Josh had his own Super 8 epics, but his ambition was to become a studio director like his idol, William Wyler, so he decided to head west and try his luck in Hollywood. Josh would eventually go on to direct cult classics such as *Running Time* (1997) and *Alien Apocalypse* (2005) both of which starred Campbell.

Josh was new to the area and he had left his friends back in Michigan. As luck would have it, he would eventually meet some-

SHELDON LETTICH • 49

one with a mind like his. "There was a long gone theater in Los Angeles that was having an Akira Kurosawa festival, his early films, and after the first film I was out having a cigarette in the lobby as was another fellow. I asked him if he liked the movie and he told me no. I told him it was too bad but he said he knew a bunch of people who loved it and told him to go see it. He wrote these names and some phone numbers on the back of a card and since I liked the film, he told me I should get in touch with any one of them. I was seventeen and just moved to Los Angeles nor did I know anybody. A week later I found the card and dialed the number. The guy answered and I started naming off names from the card. When I asked if Sheldon was there, he said it was him. It turns out the guy who gave me the number was his carpenter friend and Sheldon had recommended the movies to him. We talked on the phone for months before we finally met. He was hosting a party for the Academy Awards that year and he invited me over. It was many months later and that's when we finally met for the first time. It was sort of a weird meeting."

When Sheldon and Josh met, he had only been back from Vietnam for a short period of time. Once Josh learned a bit more about him, he learned something very important. "He's a tough motherfucker! He would get up every morning and do five hundred sit-ups, five hundred push-ups, and then run five miles; he was just one intense motherfucker. I'd never get in a fight with him; he'd beat the shit out of me. He went from the G.I. Bill to Los Angeles Trade Tech College and became an architectural photographer. I was actually his assistant on a lot of his stuff which was a great gig. Photographers, unlike movie people, don't lug around a whole lot of equipment with them. It was like a tiny little shoot and Sheldon was really, really good at it. At a certain point he decided to leave it behind and make movies instead."

"Josh and I had a lot of similar tastes and sensibilities, and we quickly became close friends. My career goal was still to become a cinematographer, and after seeing some of my photography work Josh decreed that I would be his Director of Photography when we had both achieved our respective goals." While still striving to meet those goals, both men decided it was time to work with one another in a creative capacity. "Josh was also a writer, and we had discussed writing a script together, but so far had not come up with an idea we both liked. Then one day Josh came to me with what sounded like a really kooky idea: A small group of Marines return from Vietnam; they run into the Manson family and wipe them out. I was momentarily taken aback, and wasn't quite sure if he was serious. "

Josh's recollection of the story is very similar to how Sheldon remembers it. Josh, however, has a much deeper understanding of how the idea was born. "I was sitting in my apartment wondering who would make good bad guys that have never really been used before. Everyone uses Nazis or terrorists, and then I thought about the Manson Family. I thought it was pretty cool; it was going on in 1969, right when the Vietnam War was happening. What if some Marines came back from the war and wiped out the Manson Family? The next day I pitched the idea to Sheldon and he thought it was the stupidest thing he had heard. I wasn't really in love with the idea but Sheldon called me the next day after thinking about it and he didn't think it was so stupid after all. Shortly after, he and I wrote the first draft together."

Sheldon had been taken aback by the absurdity of Josh's idea but that didn't stop him from suggesting a title. "Honestly, I wasn't quite sure if he was serious. I responded, half in jest when I suggested the title *Bloodbath*. Josh didn't laugh, or flinch. He was serious. We both agreed that *Bloodbath* would be an appropriate title, and not a bad one for what promised to be a violent action movie." The two struggling filmmakers started work on the first draft and Sheldon would start things off. "We very quickly came up with our core group of main characters, and then we just started writing. Actually, I'm the one who started writing, since the story began with these Marines in Vietnam, and because I was the one who had actually been a Marine in Vietnam it made sense that I would lay down the template and then Josh would fill in behind me. That was how it was supposed to work, but Josh got fed up with Los Angeles and headed back to Detroit, leaving me alone with the material, and the task of filling in the rest of the story on my own."

This all took place during the mid-70s so the idea of email or even faxing was essentially science fiction. The only option available to them would be the standard postal service. Instead of forging forward with the template they had originally laid down, Sheldon plowed ahead on the screenplay until he ended up with a massive script clocking in at one hundred and eighty pages. While the script was filled with great moments, it was just too massive for them to tackle at the time. Josh could have moved forward and attempted to shoot on Super 8 or 16mm in its current state, except the script was just too much to handle and finding investors was extremely difficult.

The two friends moved on to other projects. Josh, however, wrote a completely new version of the screenplay with Scott Spiegel and titled it *Stryker's War* (1980). The two of them filmed it, with Josh directing and Scott producing. Josh's parents put up the budget. They cast Bruce Campbell in the lead role as Sergeant Stryker and shot it in Super 8. Sam Raimi was cast as Charles Manson, and Scott played one of the Marines. Sheldon received a co-story credit, which he shared with Josh, Scott, and Bruce. A few years later they produced what could be characterized as a remake and told the same story again. This time they shot in 16mm, but by then Bruce Campbell had joined the Screen Actors Guild (SAG), so he could not star in the movie this time. The only way it would be possible was if the producers/financiers (Josh's parents) signed a contract with SAG and agreed to abide by their rules and their pay scales. Sam Raimi was not a member of SAG, so he was able to reprise his Charles Manson role. Josh recalls filming the feature on a shoestring budget, only spending money when necessary. "Sam Raimi is such a ham when he's in front of the camera. The only money we really spent on the movie was Sam's damn wig. I told him that no matter what he did he had to take care of it because it cost like $100. The very first take, Sam starts screaming like a madman, reaches up, and starts pulling huge hunks of hair out of the wig. We later had to glue those back in and it never looked right after that. I guess I should have kept my mouth shut."

In 1983, Sheldon had produced a short film called *Firefight* which dealt with a firefight during the Vietnam War. Scenes from the short were used during the opening war sequence in *Stryker's War*. Because Josh used those scenes, he would then honor him with the screen credit: Second Unit Director, even though he was never physically there. When the film was completed, Josh found a distributor, Irvin Shapiro, who had also distributed the original *Evil Dead* (1981). As with *Evil Dead*, Irvin wanted a more salacious title. He would be the one who suggested *Thou Shalt Not Kill... Except* (1985).

While not exactly a massive hit, *Thou Shalt Not Kill ...Except* has gone on to amass quite the cult following. Sheldon would learn the film had an admirer in one of Hollywood's most celebrated filmmakers. "Curiously, when I first met Quentin Tarantino, back in 1989 when he was working for Imperial Entertainment, the first words out of his mouth to me were "Wow, you're Sheldon Lettich, you co-wrote *Thou Shalt Not Kill... Except*!" He was obviously a big fan of the movie, which he'd probably watched numerous times while clerking at a video rental store. Then, nearly three decades later, he made a movie with a premise that was similar in so many ways, In *Once Upon a Time in Hollywood* (2019), Brad Pitt's character was a recent war veteran, same as Sgt. Jack Stryker, and of course the insane ending where they brutally wipe out the Manson family. Quentin's version of the story was nominated for a number of Oscars, and won a couple of them. So in retrospect, Josh Becker's original idea wasn't so kooky after all."

Sheldon had met Bruce Campbell when one of his photography clients flew him to Chicago to photograph an office. Bruce and Josh drove down to Chicago, picked him up and then drove him from there to Detroit, where they hung out for a few days. Sam Raimi was out of town, putting the finishing post production touches on *Evil Dead*, but it wouldn't be long before Sheldon met him and Rob Tapert in person. "While I was in Detroit, Josh screened for me a Super 8 film that Sam had made, titled *The Happy Valley Kid* (1977). It starred Rob Tapert, and it was about a kid who's bullied in high school, and fantasizes about taking revenge on all his tormentors in the guise of a heroic cowboy named *The Happy Valley Kid*. At the end of the movie he actually does gun down his tormentors, with real guns. I mention it only because it was the best student movie I had ever seen, far better than anything I had seen at the AFI, and when the movie concluded I asked to see it again. This Raimi kid had some talent. When *Evil Dead* was fully completed, Sam, Bruce, and Rob all flew to Los Angeles, where I finally had a chance to meet the entire Detroit crew, all of whom had known Josh for most of their childhoods." Sheldon let them all stay in his one bedroom apartment in the Miracle Mile neighborhood for a couple of weeks while they ran around town screening and selling their low-budget movie, which has gone on to become a cult classic, spawning sequels, remakes, and a TV show.

When the Detroit crew made their way to Hollywood, Josh couldn't wait to introduce them to his new pal Sheldon. "Once the rest of the guys (Bruce, Sam, Rob) came out to Los Angeles, the first place I took them was Sheldon's. I'd known Sheldon for maybe three or four years before those guys came out so I introduced them. They brought *Evil Dead* with them when they came to Los Angeles." Shortly after their arrival, it's not hard to figure out they would make history with that little horror film.

Sheldon's association with Sam Raimi, Renaissance Pictures, and the Detroit Guys continued for a number of years. They hired

Sheldon to do a rewrite on a script titled *The XYZ Murders*, which became the movie *Crimewave* (1985) after Joel & Ethan Coen did a rewrite on it. He also did a draft of a project titled *Evil Dead 1300 A.D.*, which became *Army of Darkness* (1992) after Sam and his brother, Ivan, did a final rewrite on it. He also introduced Sam to Jean-Claude Van Damme, and they hit it off. This would have been prior to *Bloodsport* being released, so Jean-Claude was pretty much an unknown commodity at the time, but Sam was quite impressed by him. He must have seen those movie star qualities radiating through as clearly as Sheldon could, and the two of them did end up working together eventually on *Hard Target* (1993) and *Timecop* (1994).

In the late 1970s, Sheldon met another Marine Corps veteran, who had also served in Vietnam. His name was Eric Emerson, and he was an aspiring actor as well as a photographer, so they had a lot in common. "I mentioned to him that I was also an aspiring screen-writer, and I let him take a look at my magnum opus, the *Blood-bath* script. Eric followed a local newsletter called *Drama-Logue*, which posted casting calls for non-Equity plays and low-budget non-SAG movie productions. One day he spotted something in the newsletter that he thought might have been of interest to both of us. An actor named John DiFusco, who was also a Vietnam vet-eran, was searching for other local actors who were Vietnam vets as well, with the intention of putting together a theatrical piece about the Vietnam experience. He wasn't specifically looking for a writer, but apparently there was nothing down on paper yet. He wanted to get a group of vets together then try to develop something tangible and stage-able based on improvisations and psychodramas." John had been teaching Drama classes to inmates at a local prison, and had segued from classes to improvisations about their prison expe-riences, and had then used some of that improvised material to put together a theatrical piece, which he staged at the prison with his students basically portraying themselves. Based on that, he had an epiphany about doing something similar, but it would specifically be about the Vietnam experience and would feature actors who were actual Vietnam veterans.

"I arranged a meeting with John and his wife, Lupe Vargas, and explained to them that I was a Vietnam veteran, but not an actor. Furthermore, I had no desire to be an actor, but I was a writer, and I felt I could be of assistance to this endeavor by listening to these actor-veterans tell their personal stories, and also by transcribing their improvisations. I felt I could then boil down the essence of this raw material and fashion it into dramatic scenes, which I would structure into something that looked like a play, and then put it all down on paper, neatly typed. I gave John a copy of that bloated one hundred eighty page version of *Bloodbath*, which, despite being a bloody over-the-top genre piece, actually had some good dramatic material where I explored (in way too much detail) the lives of my Vietnam vet characters." Sheldon was excited to learn John and Lupe went for it; they asked him to be the Writer-Member of this little theatrical ensemble they were putting together. They also asked Eric to be part of the group, as one of the actors, and possibly their first recruit. It was John's intention to be the director of this piece, with his wife serving as a producer. Of course there was no money involved, not at this early stage of the game. They were doing it mostly because they had a story that needed telling, about Vietnam veterans. It hadn't been done yet, and there were a lot of false and distorted ideas about Vietnam vets that were running rampant in that immediate post-war period.

John and Sheldon would begin to audition actors. They didn't really have a proper venue to do this, but went ahead nonetheless and just started holding try-outs in Sheldon's first-floor apartment. "We were vetting these actors not just for their acting abilities, but we also wanted to make sure that they genuinely were Vietnam vets. A couple of phonies tried to slip through, but we tripped them up by asking questions that only a real vet would have been able to answer. John wasn't looking for professionals who made a living as actors, since this was all very speculative and there was no promise of money on the horizon. He wanted people who at least had some acting potential, and were willing to put themselves out there for however many months this process was going to take. Needing a larger space to do our workshops and rehearsals, John and I contacted the Veterans Administration (VA) and explained to them our intentions. We got lucky with them, because the VA had a huge campus in West Los Angeles, where their main Veterans Hospital was located on acres of prime real estate that the VA had owned for decades. Most of the decaying old wooden buildings across the street from the hospital were empty and hadn't been used for decades, probably since World War Two. They gave us the ground floor of one of these buildings, which had a huge open area that might have served as a dining hall in earlier decades. This became our workspace for the next several months."

They added Vincent Caristi, Richard Chaves, Rick Gallivan, Merlin Marston, and Harry Stevens to the core group, and they were ready to get to work. John knew his business when it came to acting, and he was very good at imparting acting lessons to the group, most of whom had very little in the way of formal training. Sheldon never had much in the way of acting lessons, aside from a short introductory course taught by the father of a girl he was dating at the time. He would learn a lot from John and his techniques, which came in very handy when he would begin directing actors himself, especially actors like Van Damme or Paco Prieto, who'd never had any formal training either.

They didn't have a name for their *Vietnam Vets Piece* yet, but had begun the process by sitting in a circle and introducing themselves one by one. They would talk about where they came from, family backgrounds, and professional experiences, which were quite minimal at the time. They eventually started getting into their reasons for joining the military, or the circumstances that pushed them into the military, including Sheldon. "We started relating to the others our personal experiences in Vietnam. Just in the small group we had guys who had served in all four branches of the military. John had served in the Air Force, Richard and Vinny in the Army, Sheldon, Eric and Merlin in the Marines, while Harry served in the Navy. No two experiences were quite the same, although there were experiences which were common to every one of us, such as Boot Camp." There were tears shed a few times, and personal stories were revealed which had not been told to anyone else, stories they kept bottled up. There was a level of trust and comfort between the group due to their shared experiences. It would allow them to dig deeply, and to eventually share this experience with an audience.

John had the guys doing improvisations, giving them a topic such as drugs. They learned that half the guys in the group were stoners, who at the very least had smoked marijuana while they were in 'Nam, and a few who had done harder drugs, such as heroin. The other half, Sheldon included, were juicers, who stuck to alcohol to get high. This led to one of the best sequences in the play, which was titled *Every Day's the Fourth of July*. "The improvisations could drag on for a while. I would watch and listen, and take notes. I would then take these notes home and work the improv into scenes. I would bring the scenes in a couple days later, and the guys would attempt to act them out. Generally these scenes would need a lot more work afterwards, and sometimes I would just toss them in the trash, although a few times they played out just as I had written them, and I would get a round of applause from the guys. We would meet at our VA workspace a couple times a week, and this process continued in similar fashion for many months."

Eventually they had enough material accumulated and finally felt they could begin calling it a play, or a theatrical experience. They also arrived on a title – *Tracers* – which is the name given to phosphorous-filled bullets that mark a trail when they're fired. In Vietnam, they would sometimes load one or two tracers into the bottom of their ammo magazines, so when they would see a streak of red, they would know the magazine was out of ammo and would have to reload. They attached all sorts of meanings and symbolism to the notion of knowing when you're running low on ammo, though in all actuality, it was just a short, catchy title that everyone in the group agreed upon.

Tracers wasn't meant to be your typical play, with one main protagonist and a three-act structure. Instead they used a core group of characters, all of whom were given nicknames that were common or typical to the Vietnam experience. The audience follows these characters, sometimes singly, sometimes as a group, through a range of experiences which were common to anyone who had served in Vietnam. There was no plot, but there were stories, some of which had a beginning, middle, and an end. Some were simply vignettes, small slices of life featuring two or three characters. *Professor and Doc* was basically a two-person scene between our resident bookworm, who was of course nicknamed Professor, and a similarly intellectual Army medic who treats him for a rat bite while discussing Nietzsche and Pirandello. Not wanting to impose double duty on one of our other actors, we all voted to give that single scene role of Doc to John DiFusco.

One of the scenes that Sheldon had dramatized and wrote had enough story and enough drama for a short film. It had even been rehearsed by actors. John decided not to use it in the play because it was too big and unwieldy to put up on a stage, plus it had a helicopter as a main character. A few years later he turned this scene into a short 20-minute film he would also direct titled *Firefight*.

John was acquainted with Ron Sossi, who was the Artistic Director of the Odyssey Theater Ensemble in West Los Angeles, a renowned Los Angeles theater company. He had been telling Ron about this theatrical piece he'd been developing with a small group of Vietnam vets. When he finally felt comfortable enough with the material, he staged a private viewing for Mr. Sossi in their makeshift workspace at the VA campus. Sossi was impressed, and agreed to stage the play at the Odyssey. A few months later a work-in-progress performance was presented at the Odyssey before an invited audience on July 4th, 1980. Sheldon was in that audience, as was Ron Kovic, the author of *Born on the Fourth of July*, and a few other Vietnam vets as well. "From the moment the play began, it was one of the most memorable, electrifying experiences I have ever had in a theater. The audience hit all the beats perfectly, laughing at the antics of the Drill Instructor played by Eric Emerson, and gasping at the harrowing Blanket Party scene where the soldiers pick up pieces of blown-apart bodies and lay them on a blanket. Since then, I don't believe I've seen another performance of the play that was quite as perfect and quite as mind-blowing." At the play's conclusion that evening, the audience went ballistic with cheers and applause. It may have been an invited crowd, but the enthusiasm was palpable. The play worked, beyond their wildest expectations.

The play formally had its opening night on October 17, 1980 at the Odyssey for a sold out performance. Critics were in the audience, and in the next days they all published glowing reviews. The Los Angeles Times called it "a five finger exercise written and performed by eight actor-veterans with immediacy and a rigorous absence of self-pity." The play ran for nine months at the Odyssey. It was next produced at the Steppenwolf Theater in Chicago, directed by Gary Sinise in a new production with a new cast. It was produced at Joseph Papp's renowned Public Theater in New York City, followed by productions at the Royal Court Theater in London, and productions in Sydney and Melbourne, Australia. It is still being performed on college campuses and at theatrical venues throughout the world.

After working on *Tracers* with a group of Vietnam veterans for the better part of the year, Sheldon now had Vietnam on his mind. "I wanted to write a screenplay about Vietnam, and I wanted it to be a classic war movie, something in the vein of *The Dirty Dozen*

(1967) or *Patton* (1970). We were still five years away from *Platoon* (1986), which in my estimation is still the best Vietnam War movie made thus far. There had been a couple of meager attempts, like *The Boys In Company C* (1978) and *Purple Hearts* (1984) both written by Rick Natkin and directed by Sidney J. Furie, neither of whom were military veterans. Then I saw an amazing British film called *Zulu* (1964) at a revival theater. It was about a small group of British soldiers at an isolated outpost in South Africa, which is surrounded and attacked repeatedly by thousands of Zulu warriors. This gave me an idea, which was to transpose the story to Vietnam, and to have an isolated fire support base surrounded and besieged by thousands of Viet Cong guerillas and North Vietnamese Army soldiers. A simple but iconic title popped into my head: *Firebase.*"

Through an old high school friend, Sheldon was introduced to Bruce Melson, who was also a Vietnam vet. Bruce had served in the Army, roughly around the same time Sheldon had served in the Marines. Bruce had been an Army Medical Corpsman with an Artillery unit. "In Vietnam, I had briefly witnessed the setting up of a small, temporary firebase on a remote jungle hilltop, but this was not a typical firebase with 105mm or eight inch howitzers for fire support to infantry units in the field; it only had three Four-Deuce's, or so-called heavy mortars, which were only effective at a very short range, for self-defense more than anything else. Bruce, however, had been stationed at a more typical firebase with full contingent of artillery pieces and a crew of cannon-cockers to load and fire the weapons. At first, I was just picking his brain for technical details about artillery, but the more we talked the more I realized he might better serve me as an actual co-writer." Bruce also had a lot of knowledge and sometimes-gruesome details from his service as a Medical Corpsman, and they worked a lot of this material into the screenplay. The two of them spent about seven months working on the script, which was a total labor of love because they had no idea what to do with it after it was completed.

Bruce didn't stick around to complete the screenplay, in large part due to some serious substance abuse issues, which, he had relayed to Sheldon, were a consequence of his service in Vietnam. After he left Los Angeles, Sheldon finished writing the screenplay by himself, though Bruce was still awarded a co-story credit.

"Once the screenplay was completed, I showed it to a few friends, and got some enthusiastically positive reactions. A couple of the first people I showed it to were Sam Raimi and Rob Tapert. They were in no position at the time to get a big-budget war movie like this made, but it did lead to them hiring me to do that draft of *Army of Darkness*, which, in the third act, pretty much became a massive war movie, though in a completely different and non-realistic era. I also showed it to an acquaintance named Travis Clark, a talent manager who had my friend, Freeman King, as a client. Travis was also a Vietnam vet, who had been a crew chief on B-52 bombers. Travis loved the script, and he gave it to a friend of his named Harold Moscowitz, who was a literary agent at the time." Based on that writing sample, Harold took Sheldon on as a client. Since the subject matter was Vietnam, Harold introduced him to another client of his, Frank Dux, who claimed to be a Vietnam vet, and had written a thousand page Vietnam novel titled *The Last Rainbow*. A few years later, Travis and a writing partner, Steve Duncan, went on to create and produce the Vietnam-based TV series, *Tour of Duty* (1987-1990).

For Sheldon, the *Firebase* script would end up being the equivalent to a great car; he was able to get a lot of mileage out it even though it never came close to going into production. "I like to call it "The greatest War Movie never made". Director Walter Hill read it and fell in love with it. I had a meeting with Walter and his producer at the time, who was Joel Silver. Walter had just directed *Another 48 Hours* (1990) for Paramount, and he told the studio that he wanted *Firebase* to be his next movie with them. They nixed the idea with their excuse being that nobody wanted to see a movie about Vietnam. This was before *Platoon* (1986) had opened in theaters. The following year at the 1987 Academy Awards, Oliver Stone's Vietnam film won Oscars for Best Screenplay and Best Director, after earning a shit-load of money at the box office. I ran into Walter at a Director's Guild event shortly afterwards, and he lamented to me 'If Paramount wouldn't have been so short-sighted, that would have been us taking home those Oscars.' The *Firebase* screenplay also earned me an interview with Sylvester Stallone, who had read it while searching for a screenwriter to do *Rambo III*. He loved the screenplay, and promised me he was going to get it produced, with himself playing one of the lead roles. First, however, they would have to write *Rambo III*." This is where the next phase of Sheldon's story begins.

Russskies

It was November 6, 1987 when the New Century Vista Film Company released the film *Russkies* into theaters around the country. It's the story of three military kids Danny (Leaf Phoenix), Adam (Peter Billingsley), and Jason (Stefan DeSalle) who discover a Russian sailor named Mischa (Whip Hubley) who has found himself stranded on American soil. Set during the Cold War and in a time when Americans had a negative view of Russians, the film takes an amusing and heartfelt look at how these young boys begin to form a friendship with the sailor. They all begin to learn that their perceptions of the two cultures isn't quite what they originally believed. *Russkies* was not a financial success but is still notable for several reasons. One of those reasons was the fact the film starred a young actor named Leaf Phoenix, the younger brother of River. Leaf would later on in his career drop the stage name and begin to use his birth name, Joaquin.

While the film was totally fictitious, there's a pinch of reality to the origin of the story. Many years ago, a friend of Sheldon's was posted at the Naval Radio Station in Cutler, Maine, a very remote part of the state. One day on a nearby beach, sailors from the base found the remnants of a raft that had washed up on the beach, a raft with Cyrillic writing on it. The obvious conclusion was that Russians had been spying on the base, and ran into difficulties when they tried to return to their submarine. His friend was told to keep things hush-hush, but it was too good of a story to keep completely under wraps. Years later, Alan Jay Glueckman and Sheldon were tossing around some story ideas, and a light bulb went off. He mentioned the true incident to Alan. The two writers became excited about the concept, shortly after, everything began to fall into place.

This led them to think, "What if some American kids had found that raft, then took it for safekeeping to their secret "clubhouse"? One idea led to another, and they had very quickly concocted an entire screen story, which had these kids also discovering a washed up Russian sailor, and making him their prisoner (?).

The Cold War had been raging for decades but it was during the 80s when the conflict had come to a head. Even though the end was near, you couldn't hide from the constant headlines, Sheldon and Alan didn't plan their script to be so timely, it was a coincidence. "We just knew we had a really cool idea for a movie, that's it. The fact that it may have been timely or controversial at all made the premise even more interesting, and possibly more enticing to a production company. We even upped the stakes by making these kids jingoistic anti-Communists, who would take perverse pride in capturing a "Commie spy." Nowadays, they all would have been wearing MAGA hats."

Alan and Sheldon went to town on a treatment and began to shop the idea around Hollywood. Once producer Herb Jaffe fell in love with the story, the film began to move forward. "Alan was a genius when it came to pitching a story to producers and studio executives. That's what happened with *Russkies*. We wrote up a treatment for ourselves, but never sent it out. Instead, we went around town and pitched the story to all the studios and to a lot of producers. Eventually, Herb optioned the idea from us and we were paid to write the screenplay. There were a lot of "development deals" like this happening with original ideas at the time; not so much anymore." Once the screenplay was completed Herb shopped it around to various production entities, and found an ambitious new "mini-major" called New Century/Vista, whose executives loved the script, had the cash to produce movies, and also had their own distribution arm.

Once the film was in pre-production, the producers brought in filmmaker Rick Rosenthal, best known for helming the horror classic *Halloween II*. The writers fashioned a script and things were moving forward rather quickly. Rick brought in a third writer, Michael Nankin, who would take a pass at the script to do a dialogue polish. The film would then go into production with a cast that included the names above as well as actors like Leo Rossi, Patrick Kilpatrick, Susan Walters, and Vojo Goric. While Sheldon was strictly a writer on the film, he did approve of the casting decisions. "I had very little to do with the film other than the script, but was very impressed with that kid the director chose to play the lead character, Danny Kovac. We all knew he was good, especially for his age, but none of us could have guessed he'd eventually be an Oscar winner for Best Actor. I'm thinking that Josh Wiggins, the kid who had the lead role in *Max* may one day find himself on a similar trajectory." Joaquin Phoenix wasn't the only actor who left an impression on the filmmaker. Vojo Goric is most recognizable to action movie fans for his role opposite Sylvester Stallone as Yushin in *Rambo: First Blood part II*. Sheldon ran into Voyo a few years later when he was working for Stallone's company. Coincidentally, Voyo was working for Stallone too, except he was his personal bodyguard. "We hit it off right away, and I specifically asked my casting director to call Voyo in to read for *Lionheart*. Jean-Claude liked him so much that he ended up requesting him for a few more movies, specifically *Universal Soldier* (1992) and *Nowhere to Run* (1993)."

Russkies turned out to be a pretty solid film once completed. Sheldon and Alan appreciated the final product but had an issue with a decision that director Rosenthal made. They wrote a massively expensive third act, with the kids and the Russians flying around and battling one another with jet-packs. As fun as that setpiece may have been, it would have cost a fortune. In hindsight, the producers were correct in re-thinking it completely, although that was not how they felt about it at the time.

Upon release, *Russkies* received a very lukewarm reception. It was a staple on cable for many years and was released on VHS and

DVD but as of this writing has not made its way to Blu-ray. Had audiences at the time known that Leaf Phoenix would eventually morph into Oscar-winner Joaquin Phoenix, the producers would have had his name at the top of the poster. Unfortunately, he was no kind of a star at the time, and there were no other movie star names in the movie. During an early screening, Sheldon had brought Jean Claude Van Damme with him to see it. After it was over, Van Damme felt that he could have been awesome in the lead role of Mischa, the ship wrecked Russian sailor. Now take a moment to think about this if it had been a reality. One thing sure, if Joaquin Phoenix and Van Damme had starred in it together, the movie would have had an amazing ancillary shelf life.

Dux, Lies, and a Firefight

Frank Dux was a former Marine and martial artist who claimed to be a covert agent for the Central Intelligence Agency (CIA). His stories of fighting in underground tournaments were legend, the amount of titles and records he's held was unbelievable. In fact, his whole life story was so outlandish it had to be true, right? Well, not exactly, much of Frank's story appears to be falsified. Either way, Frank is an integral part of Sheldon's early career and *Bloodsport*'s evolution.

Sheldon was looking for someone to represent the *Firebase* screenplay and was introduced to an agent named Harold Moskowitz, who owned a small agency on Sunset Blvd. in West Hollywood, called *The Associates*. He read the screenplay, saw that he had some writing talent, and also knew that Sheldon was a Vietnam veteran. It just so happened that he had another client, who had written a novel that took place in Vietnam. It was titled *The Last Rainbow*, and was authored by Frank W. Dux, who also claimed to be a Vietnam veteran. The novel was nearly a thousand pages long. Harold felt he could sell it to a publisher, but only if it was cut in half, and he was wondering if Sheldon might be interested in undertaking this task. He sent him the manuscript, which he immediately read through. According to Sheldon, it wasn't bad. "Dux was not a bad writer, although he had a tendency to ramble on and on, and doesn't quite know when to quit, which is why the book was so long and over-written. The details about Vietnam were for the most part accurate; Frank had done some extensive research about Vietnam, much like Tom Clancy had researched the United States military and the CIA. As accurate as his books were, Tom Clancy had never claimed to have actually served in the military or the CIA, unlike Frank."

Harold would go on and show Sheldon the resume of Dux, which was quite impressive. The introductory page was written by none other than the editor of *Black Belt Magazine*, John Stewart, who vouched for Dux's bona fides as a genuine non-oriental Ninja, one of only two in the world. Among the achievements mentioned in this resume were all the statistics listed at the end of *Bloodsport*: *Most Consecutive Knockouts (56): 1975. Fastest Knockout: 3.2 seconds. Fastest Recorded Kick: 72 mph. Fastest Recoded Punch: .12 seconds.* It also mentioned that Dux was the 1975-80 World Heavyweight Champion, Full-Contact Karate, Nassau; 1975, and that he was the first non-Japanese to be awarded the exalted title of *Shidoshi*.

As if all these martial arts boasts weren't quite enough, Dux went on to make claims about serving in the U.S. military and with various U.S. government agencies, including the Federal Bureau of Investigation (FBI), the National Security Agency, and the Defense Intelligence Agency. Dux also claimed to have been an Anti-Terrorist Consultant for Nicaragua in 1976, and an instructor of Special Tactics for the United States Marine Corps in 1975. The next one should have been a red flag for anyone who was a Marine, including Sheldon. "He claimed to have been an Instructor of Special Tactics for the Royal Korean Marine Corps. I knew that American troops had served alongside ROK Marines in Vietnam, but I also knew that the ROK stood for Republic of Korea. There's nothing *royal* about South Korea, because it's a constitutional republic, like the United States. There is no king or queen, unlike in Thailand, which actually is a constitutional monarchy." Sheldon shined that on, assuming it may have been an unintentional error, possibly made by an employee the agency had assigned to type up the resume.

From what I've gathered from Sheldon as well as those close to him that I've spoken to is that he's basically an honest, upfront person. He's the kind of guy who assumes that most other people were basically honest as well. As a military veteran, he simply could not imagine someone making up stories about serving in the military, and especially about having served in Vietnam. Having spent nearly four years in the Marine Corps he was quite sure he would be able to see through anyone's bullshit if they were lying, if they were fabricating war stories. He had actually met a few examples over the years. Working with John DiFusco, the Director of *Tracers*, the Vietnam War theatrical piece that Sheldon co-authored, they managed to weed out a few phonies when they were auditioning actors for their piece, all of whom were supposed to be genuine veterans of that war. Much later on he would learn that there was an actual epidemic of people making up claims about serving in the military, serving in Vietnam, and even being awarded medals for valorous heroics, none of it true.

It wasn't until 1998 that the term "Stolen Valor" was even coined, in a book of that same title, written by B.G. Burkett and Glenna Whitley, which detailed this phenomenon in nearly six hundred well-researched pages. Frank Dux is included in this book on pages 411-417. There are even a couple photos of him, one with him posing next to a huge trophy he was allegedly awarded after he won the Kumite, another with him dressed in a Marine Corps uniform with a chest full of ribbons which were allegedly awarded to him for valor in combat, including the Medal of Honor. Sheldon met Dux in 1981, so it wasn't until seventeen years later that Burkett's book would be published, and the truth about Dux and all those other phonies would be laid bare.

There was something else in the resume that would catch Sheldon's eye: an article about Dux titled "Kumite: A Learning Experience", which was written by John Stewart, the same editor of *Black Belt Magazine*, who had written that glowing introductory endorsement about Dux. This article detailed Dux's experiences in the secretive martial arts tournament known as the Kumite. It ended up becoming the source material for what would eventually become a movie called *Bloodsport*.

Sheldon wasn't particularly schooled in martial arts or know much about the martial arts world at the time. He had never even seen one of the greatest martial arts films of all time, *Enter the Dragon* (1973). All he knew about martial arts was what he had seen in a few Chuck Norris movies, the *Kung Fu* (1972-1975) TV series, and a small amount of training he'd received in the Marine Corps and in Ranger School. Who was he to question or dispute the editor of *Black Belt Magazine*? Stewart said Dux was legit, so he simply accepted that as Martial Arts Gospel. In 1981, the Internet had yet to become visible or usable to the general public, not until the early 1990's, so without Google, Yahoo, Facebook, or a host of others, there was no way to do a quick Internet Search to check up on any of these claims, short of hiring Private Investigators. Why would that even be necessary if the editor of *Black Belt Magazine* was vouching for Dux and his stories about the Kumite? If a bona fide and licensed literary agent like Harold Moskowitz was confident handing out Dux's resume, with its many amazing claims and purported accomplishments, he was in effect also legitimizing Dux, saying that this guy was the real deal. Sheldon found himself Intrigued by all this, asking Harold if he could get Frank's phone number, to have a beginning conversation with him about tackling *The Last Rainbow*. That's how Sheldon Lettich met Frank Dux.

After reaching out to Frank via telephone, they had their first face to face meeting, which took place at Frank's martial arts dojo, called Dux Ninjitsu, on Magnolia Blvd. near the corner of Whitsett in North Hollywood. There was a class in session, and the students were all attired in white martial arts *ghi's*, going through their *katas* in unison under Frank's tutelage. It was like a scene right out of *The Karate Kid* (1984), which was further proof of Frank Dux's legitimacy, at least as a martial artist. Dux himself looked quite impressive at the time, like everything he was claiming to be. He was around six foot two inches, and probably weighed in the neighborhood of two hundred pounds. He wasn't exactly muscular like Van Damme, but had a lean sportsman's physique which only helped to lend to his commanding presence in class. The students looked up to him, and listened to him attentively. He was very much like the Martin Kove character, Kreese, in *The Karate Kid*. He had brochures for his school on a counter near the entrance, which reiterated the claims made in his resume: that aside from being the *World Heavyweight Full Contact Karate Champion* in 1975, he was the first and only Occidental to be taught the ancient and arcane secrets of the Koga-Yamabushi Ninja clan. That his teacher was a wizened old Japanese Ninja master named Tiger Tanaka, descended from many generations of Koga-Yamabushi Ninja's. Also, Frank Dux himself was one of the *most decorated veterans* of the recent Southeast Asian Conflict. Impressive credentials, to be sure, and for Sheldon, watching him lead the class through their *kata* exercises, there was no inkling he might be full of shit, nor did he have any convenient or credible way of vetting those claims. After all, the editor of *Black Belt Magazine* gave him a solid endorsement, so who would want to dispute it?

What solidified the friendship between Dux and Lettich were a few important pieces of background information, which happened to dovetail together with his. First of all, Frank was Jewish, and so is Sheldon. He had served in the U.S. Marine Corps, a branch of the military in which Jews are few and far between. Dux's parents were Holocaust survivors from Eastern Europe, and so were Sheldon's. "I had met Frank's mom and dad a few times, and they definitely had the Yiddish-flavored Eastern European accents, same as mine. Beyond that, there wasn't much else about their wartime experiences. His mother was Hungarian, same as one of my aunts. I saw photos of Frank's dad wearing the uniform of the Jewish Brigade, a unit that was formed by and served with the British military during World War Two, mostly in the British Mandate of Palestine." Frank would later on spin wild tales about Alfred Dux being some kind of a super-secret spy for the British military in the Near East, but no one has ever seen any confirmation of that.

Sheldon's father was from the former Austrian province of Bukovina, which is currently part of Ukraine. After the Nazi's invaded in 1940, he and a few other local Jews hid in the attic of a barn for a number of years, until the Soviet Army rolled in and pushed the Germans out in 1944. After that he was drafted into the Soviet Army for a short period of time before he made his way to a Displaced Persons camp in Munchberg, Germany, where he met Sheldon's mother. Most of his family did not survive the war.

Sheldon's mother was from a little town in Poland called *Wolbrom*, which was invaded by Germany in 1939. Most of her family was murdered by the Nazi's, and a few of her cousins were sent to concentration camps. She and one of her sisters managed to escape to Central Asia, where they spent much of the war years picking cotton and plucking chickens, anything to survive. After the Nazi's were defeated in 1945, the two of them migrated to Munchberg, Germany, where the American military authorities helped reunite them with the last few remnants of their family.

The first hint that Frank was full of shit came just a couple months after *Bloodsport* first opened. It was in the form of an article published in the *Los Angeles Times* on May 1st, 1988, titled "Ninja Hero or Master Fake?". The article featured a photo of Dux proudly posing in front of a *Bloodsport* billboard. The secondary headline was "Others Kick Holes in Fabled Past of Woodland Hills Martial Arts Teacher." It was researched and written by John Johnson, a staff writer for that paper. What Johnson uncovered was that most of what Dux had been telling to Sheldon and to other people was nonsense. The article mentioned that Dux "never ventured any closer to Southeast Asia than San Diego." His only known war injury occurred when he "fell off a truck he was painting in the motor pool." Johnson went so far as to track down and interview a few local Marine Corps officers, all of whom said Dux was lying about any medals he may have been awarded by the Marines, and especially about his secret Medal of Honor. Johnson also tracked down a recognized Japanese Ninja Master named Shoto Tanemura, who said he had never heard of either Frank Dux or Senzo Tanaka. He said there was no Tanaka in the history of Ninja families. Johnson even tracked down the source of that spectacular trophy that Dux said he'd been awarded for winning the Kumite. Apparently it was manufactured at a local trophy shop in the San Fernando Valley. They even had a receipt, which Dux claimed was a fake because his name was spelled "Dukes" instead of "Dux," even though the trophy itself had the correct spelling of his name.

Frank always felt he was movie star material. Back in the 80s he used to compare his looks to Tom Selleck. When Sheldon decided he was going to try and turn one scene from *Tracers* into a short movie, he asked Dux if he might want to get involved and play one of the Marines. He was very interested, to say the least, and even invested a small amount of money towards the budget.

We're going to take a step back in when Sheldon was attending the American Film Institute's (AFI) Center for Advanced Film Studies as a Cinematographer Fellow. This meant he would be doing the camerawork for the Directing Fellows who were making short movies. There were also Screenwriting Fellows and Producing Fellows. He was accepted to the school based on a portfolio of his photography work. This would be his day job while attending college; he was a professional photographer for eleven years. Sheldon's career goal up until that time was to become a Director of Photography. While attending the AFI, he was bit by the Screenwriting bug and the Directing bug.

Sheldon read some of the scripts being written by the Screenwriting Fellows, many of whom had a Master of Fine Arts (MFA) in Creative Writing from prestigious universities, and found most of these to be disappointing. He began monitoring the Screenwriting classes, and decided to try writing a script of his own. Simultaneously, he was being utilized as a Cinematographer on some of the short student films that were being helmed by various Directing

Fellows, shooting them on ¾ inch tape with video equipment. In many cases, he found himself giving these directors far too much help, and realized that many of them didn't have a clue with regard to knowing where to place the camera, nor having any idea which shots were necessary to put a sequence together in the editing room. Sheldon decided to give directing a shot as well. The school gave every student, no matter the discipline they were following, the opportunity to make a short film of their own. He took the opportunity to write, direct, and edit a little Science Fiction piece that was based on an Arthur C. Clarke short story. It ended up being a bit of a magnum opus, and ran 45 minutes long, but afterwards felt he had found his calling, and was no longer pursuing his previous goal of becoming a Cinematographer. Sheldon began to pursue Screenwriting, which had a lot of stops and starts and bumps in the road along the way, until he finally began to get projects optioned by producers, and eventually began getting paid (very small amounts) to write scripts for some low budget producers.

Getting back to Frank Dux's acting debut, in the early 80s, the way you would put out a casting call for low-budget, no-pay, non-SAG movie productions, or for non-Equity plays, was through a weekly newsletter called *Drama-Logue*. That was how Sheldon would find the cast for the play *Tracers*, and similarly how he found the actors for *Firefight*, a little seen short he would use to help launch his filmmaking career. Frank Dux had came on board with him as a producer (Sheldon had promised him a lead role), and they simply ran an ad in *Drama-Logue* seeking out young actors for a no-pay production that was going to film at the Marine Corps Base at Camp Pendleton, California. They had a twenty four page script Sheldon had written, based on the one omitted scene from *Tracers*.

Thanks to the fact that Frank and Sheldon were both former Marines, and because the story itself was about Marines, he had managed to convince the base authorities to allow him to film a short student movie on location at Camp Pendleton. In addition, he told them he would also like to have a twin-rotor CH-46 helicopter for a couple of hours; a CH-46 that was actually flying in the air, and performing a few maneuvers in support of the story. Amazingly, they acquiesced to both requests. The one major caveat was that they would have to reimburse the Marine Corps for the costs of the fuel expended by the helicopter during its brief appearance in the film.

They ran their ad, which called for seven male leads, 18-25, all races and types, and Vietnamese males, 16-40 (to play the Viet Cong adversaries). They also advertised for male extras 18-30, and for stuntmen. Very shortly they began receiving photos and resumes, lots of them. After sifting through these and making selections, the duo began setting up auditions for actors who were interested in this little production. The actors were promised very little except for the chance to acquire some on-camera experience (most had never been in a movie before), and possibly a small snippet of film demonstrating on celluloid their acting abilities.

Sheldon had an office on the eleventh floor of an old Art Deco building at the corner of Wilshire and La Brea, and that's where they set up their casting office. The actors started coming in and one of the first to walk through the door was Brian Thompson. He was a college student at the time, and this would be his first film role ever. Within a few years the two of them were both involved with Sylvester Stallone, Sheldon co-writing *Rambo III*, and Brian playing Stallone's main nemesis in *Cobra*, as a psychopathic killer called The Night Slasher. At the end of the film, Stallone's rogue cop character famously impales Brian on a meat hook.

Brian Thompson has a very distinct recollection of his first real acting role, as well as the start of a lifelong friendship. "I'd just finished my second year of the Masters of Fine Arts Acting Program at the University of California – Irvine (UCI). I'd been submitting myself on Drama-Logue to a few projects but then along comes this ad advertising a project about Vietnam done by Vietnam veterans. I was really interested in reading about Vietnam at the time so I submitted my picture and resume and got an audition. I met Sheldon and Frank Dux and eventually they gave me the part in the movie. There's a wonderful picture of me in a foxhole holding up a cupcake with a candle in it because I celebrated my twenty fourth birthday on set August 28, 1983. It was at Camp Pendleton with Sheldon and he gave me a ride in a Huey helicopter for my birthday. That really was the start of our friendship. They also mentioned they were looking for investors, I don't think I received a producer credit, but I lent them some money to finish the movie. I had some money saved and I believe I loaned them four thousand dollars total. I've loaned a lot of money to friends and family and Sheldon was one of two people who actually paid me back."

Brian went on to star in many movies and TV shows, oftentimes playing a villain, frequently meeting a horrible death. Shortly after *Firefight* and before *Cobra*, Brian was also cast in *The Terminator* (1984), as one of the three punks who encounter a naked Arnold Schwarzenegger in one of the movie's opening scenes. He was one of the first character's to meet an untimely demise at the hands of Schwarzenegger's T-800 cyborg. This would mark two down for Brian; first he was terminated by Arnold then hooked by Sly Stallone. Not a bad start to what would become a very long and solid acting career. Sheldon would use Brian quite a few more times, casting him as the henchman to the duplicitous Cynthia (Deborah Rennard) in *Lionheart* (1990). Then a few years later as the villainous CIA crony of Robert Englund in *Perfect Target* (1997), then a third time as a villainous (what else?) religious cult figure in *The Order* (2001), which was filmed in Israel and Bulgaria, and which gave Brian the opportunity to be terminated by yet another action star, Jean-Claude Van Damme.

Frank Dux, via his martial arts connections, knew a number of stunt people and wannabe stunt people, and was very helpful in gathering together a number of stuntmen for the film. In particular he found some Asian stunt guys who were willing (and anxious even) to play Viet Cong in the movie. Among them he brought Korean brothers Philip Rhee and Simon Rhee to the shoot. They had their own martial arts dojo in Los Angeles, and would go on to produce and star in their own action movies, the *Best of the Best* (1989) most prominent among them.

Firefight was filmed over the course of two consecutive hot-as-hell weekends in August of 1983. The first weekend was devoted to dialogue and character scenes. The second was the action weekend, where they filmed most of their battle scenes, explosions, and the grand helicopter finale. It was in every way a non-professional student film, with no assistant directors, no lighting technicians, no grips, no costumers, etc. The cast, crew and director pretty much did everything, starting with using shovels and entrenching tools to dig out the foxholes on the hilltop that would become their set for the next couple of weeks. For wardrobe, Sheldon just dumped a few loads of Vietnam-era surplus military uniforms on the ground, and he told the cast to pick out some shirts, trousers, boots, helmets, and web gear, just whatever fit them. Then he went around and made adjustments to assure accuracy, based on his recollections from a year with the Marine Corps Infantry in Vietnam. They also had a couple of Marine Corps advisors, who were active duty Marines and had been assigned to keep an eye on them, but were also a big help as well. They also had a small arsenal of M-16 and AK-47 assault rifles, which they had rented from Stembridge, a prop house that specialized in weapons for movies. All of these were movie props and had been adjusted to fire blanks. They actually had one guy who worked as both their Prop Man and Armorer, and had been hired to keep an eye on the weapons and make sure they were working when they needed them to work. None of them were adjusted to fire full auto, but with prop guns sometimes it's a chore to get them to even fire a single round, a problem Sheldon would encounter many times later on while working on big budget movies.

Brian was one of the cast members who wasn't afraid for a second to get down in those trenches. In fact, he had a shovel and put himself to work. "Being a newbie, I had a film acting class at Irvine, which I really enjoyed, so I had a bit of familiarity of the more intimate approach and how the camera amplifies, which was much different than stage work. We had to dig our own foxholes too. Where we ended up on the hill was not vehicle accessible so we had to hike all the equipment up the hill. At the time, I was in amazing shape so I helped a lot getting things up and down the hill. I dug my foxhole, I dug other people's foxholes, so the sweaty, grinding type of work we did for the film was all part of the process, part of the production. Just think about all the sweat, grinding, and hard work all the soldiers went through setting up their bases and camps. Of course, what we went through was nothing compared to them but it certainly helped seeing it from their perspective. I really had to get in the mindset that I was acting in a life and death situation and my whole motivation was not to get killed. It was the first time I ever had to act out a scenario like that."

They managed to complete all of their scenes in the two allotted weekends, including the battle scenes, explosions, as well as the big helicopter finale. It was grueling for everyone but the feeling of excitement was worth it when the project was complete. Sheldon had an editor assembling the film back at his office in Los Angeles while they were shooting, and after looking at the cut scenes, he realized that he needed some pickup shots. "I was not about to go through the effort and paperwork of asking for permission from the Marines at Camp Pendleton once again, especially after everything they had granted us so far, so I managed to secure permission to use a location that was much closer to home, in Chatsworth, California, on a large parcel of land in the Santa Susana Mountains that had been set aside for future construction of tract homes. I brought together our main cast at the location in Chatsworth, with costumes, cameras, a few weapons and a few props, and we managed to finish all our pickup shots in one day."

The film would then go into post-production to finish things up. After it was edited, Sheldon turned to his old pal Josh Becker to take care of sound. "I did all the sound cutting on *Firefight*, the foley, and post sound stuff. I was the entire sound department by myself. There was a scene with a platoon of guys storming over a hill and here I am in the sound studio with helmets on each hands, a belt with canteens, knives, and guns strapped to it, all while wearing combat boots just trying to shake all this shit so it would sound like a platoon of guys." Josh nailed his part as well and the film would be used for years as a showcase for producers so they could see for themselves just what Sheldon was capable of.

After the completion of *Firefight*, Sheldon and Frank had cemented a friendship along with a solid working relationship. Getting back to their meeting, Harold Moskowitz had introduced them for the stated reason of getting him to edit down Frank's Vietnam novel, it was only logical that they would begin their conversations by discussing their experiences in Vietnam. Sheldon was quite straightforward with Frank. "I told him I had spent one year in Vietnam as a radio operator with an Infantry unit, the Third Battalion of the First Marine Regiment. Afterwards, when I returned to Camp Pendleton, I spent a few months with the Third Amtrak Battalion, and then transferred over to the elite First Force Reconnaissance Company, where I spent the remaining two years of my enlistment. Force Recon is the Marine Corps equivalent of Special Forces, akin somewhat to Navy SEALs in their missions and their training. As part of my Recon training I was sent to the U.S. Army's Jump School at Fort Benning, Georgia, where I was schooled in the basics of being a military parachutist. I made five jumps there, and earned my silver Parachutist wings. Almost immediately afterwards I was sent back to Fort Benning to attend the Army's Ranger School, where I spent two grueling months learning small unit tactics, climbing steep mountains in the middle of the night, trudging through mangrove swamps and patrolling through dense jungles in Florida; basically learning how to be a military badass. Most of the elite Special Forces in the U.S. military pass through these two schools. Ranger School especially has a very high attrition rate. Those were the basics of my short military career."

Frank, unlike Sheldon, is someone who always wants to one-up the other guy's accomplishments, although it had not been realized at the time. Sheldon figured Frank would have been as straightforward with him as he had been with Frank, but instead Frank had to prove to him that he had been far more badass than Sheldon could have ever hoped to be. According to Frank, the military sent him straight out of Boot Camp to a very specialized unit, which he told Sheldon was called the Special Operations Group (SOG), and that was where he spent the bulk of his deployment in Southeast Asia. Sheldon had never heard of this SOG unit, even though he had spent time with a number of elite and specialized forces. With Force Recon, he had rubbed elbows with Navy SEALS on a number of occasions, and had met plenty of Green Berets and Army Rangers at Ranger School, but he figured this SOG unit must be so special and clandestine that their existence somehow eluded even Sheldon. There was no Internet to reference to, but eventually he was able to research it, and learned that this special unit Frank had claimed to be a part of really did exist, and was called MACV SOG. The acronym stood for Military Assistance Command, Vietnam, and the second part was either Studies and Observation Group or Special Operations Group. The unit itself did exist, and nowadays it's quite easy to hit a Search button and look up information about their history and exploits, which are formidable to say the least. What's also easy to verify nowadays is that Frank Dux was never any part of this unit. In fact, he never even set foot anywhere in Southeast Asia.

Brian Thompson was there from the beginning of Sheldon's friendship with Frank and experienced many of the same stories he spun. "Frank is a prolific storyteller. He had taken me to his house shortly after *Firefight*, and he lived nearby in the valley. He took me there and showed me all his medals. Because of Sheldon's authenticity, I totally bought in to Frank's at the time. He'd written a book about his experiences in Vietnam, he actually gave me a copy of it. I'd visited his studio and we all bought in to him. He really has a prolific imagination which is a great asset to have for screenwriting." This would only be the beginning of Frank's stories and he would continue to spin tales for many years to come which will be explained in some detail later in this book. Brian pretty much sums him up best. "Frank's a fantastic character and it's remarkable how a person can survive being so out of touch with reality for so long."

During his year in Vietnam, Sheldon had seen some combat action. His small squad-sized unit had gotten into an intense firefight with a Viet Cong patrol on a steep, jungle-covered mountain trail. He witnessed a small bus packed full of Vietnamese completely obliterated by a roadside bomb. He saw dead bodies, bloody and torn apart, and with freshly opened wounds. He never received any medals or commendations for military heroics his entire time in Vietnam, and never claimed to have received any. He was basically the guy on the radio calling for airstrikes or artillery support, or for a medevac or an extraction. The other guys did most of the shooting; that wasn't his job. John Rambo was a guy he wrote about years later, and that was not Sheldon. Frank, on the other hand, always had a ready supply of war stories about his military exploits and heroics in Southeast Asia.

Sheldon eventually met the woman who was Franks's wife at the time, whose maiden named had been April Fleser. Frank had started to feel comfortable enough with him so he took him to meet and visit with April's parents' at their comfortable middle class house in the west San Fernando Valley neighborhood of Woodland Hills. There Sheldon saw on the in-law's living room wall the now infamous photograph of Frank attired in a Marine Corps "Dress Greens" uniform, his chest bedecked with military ribbons for valor in combat. There was a Silver Star, a Bronze Star, a Navy Cross, and the highly coveted, rarely-awarded Medal of Honor, the highest award for valor that the U.S. military can bestow. Little did Sheldon know at the time that Frank did not earn a single one of those ribbons. "The rank insignia on the side of his sleeve can't be seen, but he wears no officer bars on his epaulets, so he was not pretending to be a commissioned officer. Years later, when his actual military records were pulled up via the Freedom of Information Act (FOIA), it was revealed that he never rose above the rank of Lance Corporal. One more thing: in the photo he's also wearing gold jump wings, which for the Navy and Marine Corps denote at least ten military jumps. I proudly wore those same gold wings myself. As far as I know, Frank never made a single military jump in his life."

Years later, after the bullshit about his background became exposed; Frank would start explaining away that photo as a Halloween costume which he wore to a college fraternity party. That it wasn't meant to be taken seriously, that he wasn't trying to pull the wool over anyone's eyes. The alternate explanation he resorted to was that it was a costume for a student movie. Then why was it so prominently and proudly displayed on his in-laws living room wall, where it could serve as a conversation starter to brag about their heroic son-in-law? Were they in on the joke, or were they naively swallowing the bullshit story that their son-in-law was a certified war hero?

Bloodsport

It was very easy for Frank to segue from tales about his military heroism to equally heroic tales about the secret Kumite tournament. In both cases, he claimed to be revealing highly confidential secrets to Sheldon. "SOG was so secretive and clandestine that I hadn't heard about it even though I was in an elite military Reconnaissance unit. Similarly, the Kumite was so secretive that most martial artists did not have a clue that it even existed, and so were not aware that Frank Dux was the first Westerner to be awarded accolades as its "World Heavyweight Kumite Champion" in 1975." Both SOG and the Kumite had one thing in common, in the early 1980s, sans Internet: there was no convenient or credible way to verify either of these stories, or to verify that Frank Dux was an actual participant. The only verification was supplied by Frank himself: that photo of himself posing with his Kumite trophy, and that photo of himself with all those ribbons for valor pinned onto his Marine Corps uniform." At that time, Sheldon was acquainted with his wife and his in-laws, and they seemed to be fully onboard with his claims as well. How could he possibly say he thought Frank was full of shit?

Believing Frank's claims, Sheldon would begin to lay the groundwork for *Bloodsport* by introducing Frank to producer Mark DiSalle. He started the screenplay in June of 1985, and delivered the first draft in October of that same year, so it took about four months to complete. Mark is the one who got it to Cannon, via a financier named Lew Horwitz, who he believes was a friend of Menahem and Yoram, and knew they'd been doing well with low budget martial arts movies like *Enter the Ninja* (1981) and were constantly on the lookout for more projects in a similar vein.

Screenwriters Mel Friedman and Christopher Crosby were brought in to do a dialogue polish, before the film went into production. As a writer, Sheldon will be the first to tell you he's very good with structure, figuring out how to tell a story, and is very good with action. "Dialogue is my weakest attribute, which is why I generally team up with another writer, someone who's great with dialogue, when I'm working on a screenplay, especially when it's a spec script. I didn't work with another writer on the initial *Bloodsport* script, and the director (whom I never met) probably felt the dialogue needed some punching up, so those two guys were brought on board to basically do that." There were also some sequences in the script that were quite elaborate and would have been expensive to film (training sequences, for example) and they found less expensive ways to get those story points across, keeping in mind that the budget for this movie was quite modest.

Newt Arnold would eventually be hired to direct the film but he wasn't the only person approached to take the reins. Sam Firstenberg was quickly becoming Cannon's go-to guy for martial arts action films. After the success of *Revenge of the Ninja* (1983), he was tapped to shoot a small action picture in the Philippines called *American Ninja* (1985) with rising action star Michael Dudikoff. "When I returned from the Philippines after *American Ninja*, the producer, Mark DiSalle was introduced to me and he had a script, it was *Bloodsport*. I don't remember the details, I don't think Van Damme had been attached at the time, maybe they were interested in Michael Dudikoff, I'm not sure. He offered me the script and I read it but I was still so busy with *American Ninja* and then I realized most of the script took place in a single location. That's when I made up my mind, I liked to travel around, so I met again with Mark and told him no thanks." It would have been a much different film had Firstenberg directed. "In hindsight, that may have been a huge mistake. Sheldon tells the story best but I had no idea why *Bloodsport* sat on the shelves at Cannon for two years. I don't understand why they didn't believe in it. That was such a huge mistake, when it was released; it was such a huge hit. I know it went through another editing later on, and eventually it just blew up."

Sam may have turned down *Bloodsport* but there's still a connection between him and Arnold which is quite interesting. "Newt Arnold was hired to direct and he was a very famous first and second unit director for a very long time. In fact, I was Newt's assistant on the William Friedkin film *Sorcerer* (1977)."

The Screenwriter is usually the low man on the totem pole, the last one to be invited to visit the set. Especially on a low budget production filmed on the other side of the world. So Sheldon was not invited to visit the set in Hong Kong, unless he was willing to do it on his own dime. "Regrettably, I never did get an opportunity to meet with Newt Arnold, who in my opinion did a terrific job directing the movie."

The first time he met Menahem was through Blacksploitation star Leon Isaac Kennedy. Leon had starred in a very low budget but successful prison movie titled *Penitentiary* (1979). Cannon got into business with him by producing a sequel, *Penitentiary II* (1982), which did very well for them. Around the same time Leon co-starred in an action movie titled *Lone Wolf McQuade* (1983), which starred Chuck Norris and David Carradine. Leon received third billing behind Chuck and David, and the film did reasonably well at the box office. David's character dies at the end of the movie (at the hands of Chuck Norris, of course!), so he would not have been included in any sequel, but Leon would have been, so Leon set out on a mission to convince Chuck Norris to make a sequel. Chuck was not interested, but Leon would not let go of this idea. Sheldon had written a few scripts for him, generally at about $2,000 per script, so Leon came to him with an offer to write a sequel to *Lone Wolf McQuade*. Leon did not have the rights to that title, so Sheldon would have to write a sequel that used a different title and different character names, but could be swapped back to the original names if Leon managed to talk Chuck into doing the movie.

Around the same time, *Bloodsport* had already been shot, but was lying dormant in an editing room at Cannon. Menahem had seen the first cut of the movie, and hated it. Sheldon had seen the exact same cut. "I don't blame him completely, because the first cut of the movie was actually quite bad. Not until it was re-cut by a different editor would Cannon consider releasing the film, but we didn't know that. Meanwhile, I had introduced Leon to my new friend, Jean-Claude Van Damme. They hit it off right away, and I suggested to Leon that if he couldn't talk Chuck Norris into starring in this sequel, maybe we could substitute Van Damme into the lead role of this project we were now calling *Stryker'sForce*." This made a lot of sense because Jean-Claude had already starred in a movie for Cannon, and also had a deal with them to star in two more movies. At this point, Leon had made two movies for Cannon so it seemed a no-brainer to team up these two Cannon stars into an action buddy-movie. Both of them knew Sheldon personally, and felt comfortable with him directing the movie, so now they had a package: a script, a director, and two movie stars. Leon sent the script to Cannon, along with his proposal for a production package. Sheldon may have sent over a 35mm print of *Firefight* as well, which would serve as his Director's Reel. Shortly afterwards, he and Leon were invited to have a meeting with Menahem Golan, in his office on San Vicente Blvd. Sheldon told Jean-Claude the good news, and then the two were off to meet with Mr. Golan.

That was to be his first meeting with Menahem Golan, and in some ways it could not have gone better, but in other ways it could not have gone worse. The good news was that Menahem liked the script, liked Leon, and liked Sheldon's little movie. What he absolutely rejected, however, was Jean-Claude Van Damme. Menahem's word for Jean-Claude was "poison". Based on what he had seen in that first cut of *Bloodsport*, he felt Van Damme was a terrible actor and had no on-screen charisma. According to Menahem, this guy would never make it as a movie star. He also felt the movie itself was terrible, and was planning to release it straight to video, this at a time when even the shittiest, most low budget Cannon movies would get a theatrical release. Leon and Sheldon were flabbergasted! They tried to lobby him to change his mind about Jean-Claude, but he just wasn't hearing it. Menahem still wanted to make the movie, but told us he wanted a real movie star alongside Leon, and that movie star would be Michael Dudikoff! They went back and forth with him for a long time, but Mr. Golan would not budge. Basically there was an offer on the table: Cannon would finance the film, with Sheldon directing and with Leon playing the co-lead opposite Michael Dudikoff, who at that time had starred in a number of Cannon's roster of *American Ninja* movies. That was the deal, take it or leave it!

Sheldon decided to take a risky long shot with Menahem. At that time, their big upcoming release was *Braddock: Missing in Action III* (1988), which starred Chuck Norris and was a sequel to two previous *Missing in Action* (1984, 1985) films, both of which had done quite well at the box office. Menahem was confidently expecting that the third iteration would be Cannon's most successful movie ever, and would pull in box office numbers similar to the *Rambo* movies. Sheldon politely disagreed. He then predicted that when *Bloodsport* was released in theaters, it would pull in more money than *Braddock*. Menahem laughed, and proclaimed "You're dreaming, my friend!" He wasn't angry, just amused by Sheldon's naiveté. Of course, in retrospect, and with 20/20 hindsight, it appears that his prediction was not off the mark at all. Not by a long shot. *Bloodsport* actually did make more money that year than *Braddock*. Years later, taking into account the ancillary markets worldwide, it may have actually been Cannon's most successful movie ever. *Braddock* still has its fans, but *Bloodsport* has become iconic and a classic, especially among martial arts and action movie fans. President

Donald Trump even cited it as one of his favorite movies. Just a few years later, Andy Vajna and Mario Kassar (of Carolco, the company that produced the *Rambo* films) offered producer Mark DiSalle $5 million for the sequel rights. The only caveat was that Van Damme had to be part of the package. Van Damme declined, and the sequel rights eventually went to producer Alan Mehrez, who went on to produce three sequels with former model Daniel Bernhardt in the starring role.

Despite Sheldon's contrariness with Menahem, Cannon's offer to produce *Stryker's Force* was still on the table. They showed the script to Michael Dudikoff, which led to the two of them having an actual meeting. Michael politely told Sheldon he wasn't comfortable with the screenplay. For him, there were too many social and racial issues in the material. Part of the plot dealt with racists developing a weapon that would only affect Blacks and other minorities, and this turned out to be too controversial and divisive for Michael's sensibilities, even though he had already made *Avenging Force* with the late, great, Black action star Steve James, touching upon some similar elements.

Cannon, however, still wanted to be in business with Sheldon. While *Bloodsport* was still locked away in an editing room, unreleased, they next offered him a re-write of a movie that was about to go into production: *Delta Force II* (1990), which was to star Chuck Norris, and be directed by his brother Aaron Norris. "Aaron and his crew were already on location, in Israel, prepping to shoot the movie. The basic storyline was that an element of the elite American *Delta Force*, led by Norris' Colonel Scott McCoy, would find them in a situation where they reluctantly have to team up with a group of Soviet Spetsnaz commandoes, their Cold War Russian counterparts, to overcome a common adversary. This led to my first trip to Israel, at the behest of Cannon Films, which would be the first of many trips to Israel, nearly always on the dime and at the behest of a movie production."

"The first time I met with Jean-Claude was on the telephone. He and Frank Dux called me from Hong Kong, to lament the fact that Mark DiSalle was making a lot of changes to the script, changes that they were not happy with. Jean-Claude and I seemed to hit it off, and we promised to meet one another face to face when he got back to Los Angeles." True to his word the day after he got back, Jean-Claude and his wife, Gladys, came over to my apartment." Jean-Claude and Sheldon got along right away, but their wives got along even better. Coincidentally, they were both pregnant at the time, so they had plenty to talk about!

Sheldon didn't get an opportunity to meet Bolo Yueng at the time that *Bloodsport* went into production. A few years later, when he and Jean-Claude were prepping *Double Impact* (1991), he was their first choice to play Raymond Zhang's murderous henchman, Moon. The actor who played Zhang in that movie was Philip Chan, another holdover, who played Inspector Chen in *Bloodsport*.

"I first met Michel Qissi in Los Angeles, around the same time I first met Jean-Claude. Both of them had been good buddies back in Brussels, and they both were trained at the same martial arts dojo by Claude Goetz. I used Michel in *Lionheart* (1991) to play one of the Legionnaires who's pursuing Lyon to Los Angeles, and in the same movie I used his brother, Abdel Qissi, to play the fighter Atilla." When they couldn't find a suitable Thai fighter to cast as Tong Po in *Kickboxer*, Jean-Claude got a local make-up artist to do some heavy work on Michel's face and hair, and the disguise was so perfect that he fooled Mark DiSalle, who thought he actually was Thai (instead of Moroccan) when he saw him in all that make-up. Michel ended up playing one of Van Damme's most memorable villains in that movie. Jean-Claude and Sheldon used Abdel again in *The Order* (2001), and Jean-Claude used him a final time in *The Quest* (1996), a movie he directed himself.

With the film being based on Frank Dux's supposed true life experiences; he found a way to ingrain himself even more in the production. Frank negotiated the position of fight choreographer for himself, and actually ended up doing a damn good job. That's why Jean-Claude and Sheldon used him again to help choreograph the fights in *Lionheart*. Sheldon would hire him again for the next movie he directed, which was *Only the Strong* (1993). Unfortunately, Frank ended up being a big disappointment to everyone on that movie, and to Sheldon personally because he had talked him up so much when selling him to the producers.

As mentioned earlier, the first cut of *Bloodsport* was a disaster. It was edited by Carl Kress, an old timer who had won an Oscar for *The Towering Inferno* (1974), but did not have the correct sensibility for putting together a martial arts action movie in the mid-80s. *Bloodsport* was actually quite fresh and innovative for its day. There hadn't been a movie quite like it before, a tournament movie that had martial arts fights and more martial arts fights, from start to finish. One producer who had read an early draft of the script disparagingly described it as "*Fight, fight, fight, and more fight, fight, fight!*" For everyone involved up to then, that was their entire intention. It wasn't *Rocky* (1976) and it wasn't *The Karate Kid* (1984). It wasn't even *Enter the Dragon* (1983) though the two films do share some minor sensibilities. An entire sub-genre of movies, plus video games, was built from that concept. Menahem and Yoram totally got it. Sheldon has worked for other Israeli producers as well, Avi Lerner and Moshe Diamant in particular, and when it comes to action and fights they believe in putting the pedal to the metal and holding it down for ninety minutes.

Cannon had an editor on payroll named Michael J. Duthie, who had cut a lot of their *Ninja* movies and other low budget action movies. He was like an in-house film surgeon for them. Michael could see what was wrong with a movie, pull out his scalpel, his saw, and his stitching thread, and then get to work. He would pull the movie completely apart, before putting it back together again in much better shape than before. Michael was brought in to fix *Blood-*

sport, and he worked some miracles with it in the editing room. Jean-Claude helped him make sense of the fights, and together they got those working. They brought the excitement that the fights had been lacking before. Then the really terrific music score by Paul Hertzog was added, and also a few songs by Stan Bush, and suddenly the movie transformed into everything it was supposed to be. When Jean-Claude, Michel Qissi, Frank Dux and Sheldon saw a screening of the new cut, they were euphoric! Menahem and Yoram must of saw it as well, because the rumor is that Yoram was the one who convinced Menahem to give the movie a test screening on the west coast of America: California, Oregon, and Washington. They opened it on thirty screens, one of which was on Hollywood Blvd. at the Pacific Theater. Cannon even gave the film a little mini-premier at that theater. They advertised it in local newspapers, promising free posters to the first fifty people who showed up. Surprisingly, a big crowd did show up. Jean-Claude was in the lobby, autographing posters until his hand went numb.

The premiere was a special event for everyone, especially Sheldon. "I was there, and so was Frank Dux, Mark DiSalle, and Michel Qissi. Forest Whitaker was there too; not any kind of a movie star yet. I introduced myself as the writer, and did manage to have a brief conversation with him in the lobby. My buddy, Sam Raimi, was there. I had introduced Sam to Jean-Claude a few months earlier, and he had a strong hunch that Van Damme had all the markers to make it as a movie star. On this night, in February of 1988, Sam had yet to see proof if Jean-Claude would deliver, up on the big screen in front of a paying audience. That night he got his proof. The audience loved the movie, and they loved Van Damme!" It would only be a few short years before those two would collaborate.

The reactions Cannon received from all along the west coast, and from the box office numbers, were very promising. Based on that test, Cannon finally opened the movie nationwide. The amount of screens they opened it on isn't exactly known, but the movie became a small sensation. People who'd seen it were talking about it, telling their friends. Cannon found even a few more screens to open it on. They were all on their way to having a small but certifiable hit on their hands.

Josh Becker was on hand to witness the excitement everyone felt that night in the theater. "It was crazy! At the premiere, by the end of the film, the entire audience was chanting, "Kumite! Kumite! Kumite!" I couldn't believe how the audience was just eating it up. At that moment, you could just tell it was going to be a hit movie and Van Damme was going to be a star. I've always had the most fun with *Bloodsport*. I know Newt Arnold directed it but being at that premiere with a huge audience, everyone was just transported into that ring, myself included."

For Josh, meeting Van Damme would be a bit of an interesting experience. "I first met Jean-Claude at Sheldon's apartment. Coincidently, Sheldon would meet Toni there. She lived in the apartment above him and later became his wife. He used to have these little gatherings at his place on Friday nights and Jean-Claude was there with his first wife Gladys. She was a female bodybuilder and put out a book on the sport. Sheldon introduced me as the Director of *Thou Shalt Not Kill...Except*. To everyone there, I was the most important person in the room and a successful filmmaker. Within moments, Jean-Claude was suddenly my best friend. He kept putting his arm around me saying, "You and I make movies together, yes?" It was a little uncomfortable to say the least." If you're a fan of Josh's work, then the fact nothing ever came of this is certainly a disappointment. It could have been a very interesting project.

When *Bloodsport* was wide released in 1988, no one could have predicted the success the film would end up obtaining. Menahem Golan and Yoram Globus were most likely thankful their minds had been changed about releasing it theatrically. While shot on a miniscule budget, the film would go on to earn over $11 million at the

Box Office and audiences began to notice the films' star. The film never would have happened if it hadn't been for that chance meeting between Lettich and Frank Dux.

Rambo III

Sylvester Stallone formed White Eagle Enterprises, his production company, in 1986. It wasn't long after that word began to spread around Hollywood he was looking for a writer to aid him with the script for *Rambo III*. Sheldon's agent at the time, ICM's Linne Radmin, had heard of the search and quickly sent in a script he wrote as a sample. He soon found himself in meetings with arguably, the biggest action star of the time period. Stallone read his Vietnam War script *Firebase* and loved it. He was interested in producing it but sadly it never happened. After a couple of meetings, an offer was sent to his agent, to co-write the screenplay for *Rambo III*, which he readily accepted. This would be the big opportunity he had been waiting for.

Sheldon also worked on a French Foreign Legion screenplay for Stallone's company; that was the project he had come in to pitch when he first visited the office. Sly was also interested in producing a movie about the Legion, however, he wanted it to be about the contemporary Legion and Sheldon wanted it to take place in the past, during the classic "Beau Geste" period. The one he wrote for Stallone never made it past the script stage. A few years later, he pitched a classic Foreign Legion story with Van Damme to producer Ed Pressman (*The Crow*), and that one did eventually get in front of the cameras, with Van Damme in the lead.

When things stalled on the Foreign Legion script, the focus moved to what would arguably be Sheldon's biggest film, *Rambo III*. After Stallone suggested he use a small tape recorder to record their story talks, a practice Sly learned from James Cameron, they began to bounce ideas off one another, shaping the story. They decided to use current events (of the time period) as the backdrop. They both agreed immediately, with no discussion at all, that the story should take place in Afghanistan, which was a perfect arena for a *Rambo* movie. The Russians (Soviets) were in Afghanistan at the time, battling the local Mujahedeen insurgents while attempting to install a puppet communist government. The Americans, via the CIA, were aiding the insurgents by supplying them with weapons, in particular with Stinger missiles that had the ability to bring down a Soviet armored helicopter. This was during the height of the Cold War, when the U.S. president, Ronald Reagan (a friend of Stallone's) had labeled the Soviet Union "The Evil Empire." In the previous *Rambo* movie the enemy was also the Soviet Union, but the arena was Vietnam, with Rambo attempting to rescue American P.O.W.'s. Sheldon and Sly quickly came to an agreement that Rambo would be asked to go to Afghanistan at the behest of Colonel Trautman and the CIA, to deliver Stinger missiles to the insurgents.

Like all partnerships, there will be times when everyone involved doesn't see eye to eye. Sly and Sheldon were no different but everything ended up working out for them both. Sly thought Rambo should willingly accept the mission, where Sheldon felt that Rambo would be hesitant. Since he had actually served in the Vietnam War and heard first-hand accounts from fellow soldiers, Sheldon felt that most of them would have been reluctant, having seen enough war already to last a lifetime, and many of these men who served were afflicted with PTSD. Rambo himself was afflicted by PTSD, which was made abundantly clear in *First Blood,* the first of the *Rambo* movies. Sly would eventually agree, which would lead Sheldon to an interesting plot twist. Trautman goes on the mission to Afghanistan, on his own, with no backup, and he's captured by the Russians. Now they hit another plot point that worked so well in the second *Rambo* film: Rambo has to go in and rescue a P.O.W., not just any P.O.W. – his friend and mentor, Colonel Trautman. Now there's also personal guilt motivating the complicated character because he didn't accept Trautman's plea to go with him, and because of that, his friend and mentor has become a prisoner of the Russians. Those factors gave them some very strong motivation to propel Rambo forward to undertake what might be a suicide mission to rescue his closest friend.

Josh Becker had the opportunity to visit Sheldon while he was working on the script but his plan didn't exactly work out. "I came by Stallone's company while was working there hoping to meet Sylvester Stallone! Of course, he wasn't there. After they finished the script, the pre-production on *Rambo III* took over a year. When MGM was still MGM and Sheldon was working with White Eagle, he brought me along a couple of times with him to the offices but Sly was never around. I'm not sure if he still has them but Stallone would have him audiotape their meetings. Sheldon would bring them back and I'd listen to them, so there was that." At least Josh was able to enjoy the minor consolation prize.

When *Rambo III* eventually moved forward, it wasn't exactly smooth sailing. The production was plagued with issues behind the scenes causing the budget to skyrocket. While it doesn't sound like much, at the time, $60 million dollars was huge and it was considered the most expensive film produced from that year. Filmmaker Russell Mulcahy was originally hired to direct. After being flown all over the world scouting locations and a couple weeks of filming, Russell was relieved from his duties and second unit director Peter MacDonald was promoted. While Sheldon's involvement was strictly with the script, he does have a little bit of insight into the situation. "At the time it was going down, I wasn't aware. I remember the production company sending Russell all over the world, scouting to find an appropriate location to substitute for Afghanistan. Very early on I suggested to Stallone that he might consider Israel, but he was too nervous about the security situation over there and the constant state of war (at the time) between Israel and its hostile Arab neighbors. I learned some of the details about Peter Mac-Donald pushing Russell out when I worked on my movies, *The Last*

Patrol and *The Order*, in Israel with much of the same Israeli crew that had also worked on *Rambo III*. What they told me was that Peter, who was originally hired to be the Second Unit Director, was constantly working to undermine Russell, deliberately campaigning to get him fired so that Peter could step into his shoes. Ironically, Peter MacDonald did the exact same thing to me on *Legionnaire*, with the exact same result. Quite honestly, Peter did a decent job directing both those movies, with some major exceptions on *Legionnaire*, which went straight to video thanks to his mis-steps. Bottom line, Peter MacDonald is a snake and a weasel, who smiles in your face while putting a knife in your back."

With most films, the script is used as a blueprint and things morph and change throughout production. One of the most notable differences from script to screen had to do with its finale. Part of his contribution was an ending Sheldon had written where Rambo and Trautman escape over some very treacherous mountain terrain, pursued by a contingent of Soviet *Spetsnaz* troops. That ending was discarded in favor of a huge *Lawrence of Arabia* (1962) styled battle, with a somewhat ludicrous tank vs. helicopter showdown. A few years later, when viewing *Cliffhanger* (1993), Sheldon saw what looked very much like the same escape scene he had written for *Rambo III*. He wasn't in any way complaining, he was paid to write the scene after all, there was just no denying the similarities. Most of the dialogue should be credited to Stallone, but Sheldon was never aware of *Rambo III* having much humor in it, except for the character Moussa, who was played by an Israeli actor named Sasson Gabai. Ironically, Sheldon would use Sassona a few years later in the movie, *The Order*, where he was cast in a very similar role, playing a semi-comedic foil to Van Damme's character.

The film would eventually wrap production and was released on May 25, 1988. Compared to *Rambo: First Blood Part II*, *Rambo III* was a financial disappointment. Only raking in a little over $53 million domestically, it looked like small potatoes compared

to $150 million the previous chapter earned. While still success-
ful, it wasn't a massive hit when it was released. *Rambo: First Blood
part II* was one of the highest grossing films of 1985 (second place
behind *Back to the Future* though Stallone also nabbed third with
Rocky IV). By comparison, *Rambo III* was a bit of a disappointment,
because it had been expected to gross even more. The problem was
that the pre-production dragged on for far too long. First of all, they
couldn't figure out where to shoot the movie, and wasted a lot of
time sending Russell all over the world to scout potential locations,
until they finally settled on Israel. Then Sly would get cold feet
about having the story take place in Afghanistan, and had Sheldon
spend some time working on a new treatment that would have had
the story taking place in Siberia. By the time they finally moved
into production, the Soviets were already beginning to pull out of
Afghanistan, and when the movie was released they were almost
completely withdrawn, so the story had lost much of its urgency
and timeliness. Either way, it was a huge step up for the writer. "I
was quite overwhelmed that I was working with Sylvester Stallone,
who was the number one box office star in the world at that time,
and also that I was working on a *Rambo* movie. I had been a big fan
of *First Blood* as well as the first sequel, so overall this was a great
honor for me. Sure, the magnitude of the budget was quite impressive, though nowadays, $60 million is just about average for most
studio movies."

The film was exactly what Sheldon needed to really get things
moving forward with his career. There were offers and projects he
had been working on and he hoped this would be the big push he
had been waiting for. Before *Rambo III* was even released, he had
come up with a new idea for an action movie, titled *Warbirds*. It was
going to be about military helicopters, specifically "attack helicopters" like the American *Cobras* and the Russian *Hinds*. The main
characters would have been an American helicopter pilot and his
nemesis, a Soviet helicopter pilot. The finale would have been an

epic aerial battle of American helicopters versus Soviet helicopters. There was a major difference between the two; the American birds were sleek, fast, and agile, while the Soviet version was more of a "flying tank," heavy and cumbersome, but armored and loaded with weapons. Walter Hill had been a fan of the *Firebase* script, so they spent some time talking about working together on something, and he liked that particular idea. It was going to be structured like an old World War One aerial combat movie, like *Wings* (1927), *The Dawn Patrol* (1930) , or *Hell's Angels* (1930).Walter was a Howard Hawks fan, and he saw *Warbirds* as being very much in the vein of something Hawks would have directed.

Hill had just directed *Red Heat* (1988) for Carolco around the same time and had a deal with them to direct another movie or two. They had also produced the *Rambo* movies, and the two principles of the company, Mario Kassar and AndrewVajna, really liked his idea, as well as the idea of Sheldon, the co-writer of their movie, *Rambo III*, writing the script. Very shortly his agent received an offer from them for him to write *Warbirds*, with Walter Hill attached to direct.

It seemed like everything was on the fast track and the project was going to move forward when one of the pitfalls of Hollywood reared its ugly head. Completely out of the blue, Andy Vajna got a call from his friend, Arnold Kopelson, the producer of *Platoon*. Arnold had somehow heard that Sheldon was being hired to write an action movie about military helicopters, and he warned Andy to not proceed any further with this, because he had already been developing an action movie about military helicopters, titled *Wings of the Apache*, about the Army's new AH-64 *Apache* attack helicopters. Arnold said his script was finished, a director (John Flynn) had been hired, and they were gearing up to go into production. If Carolco proceeded, they would be the last horse out of the gate, and Kopelson would release his helicopter movie well ahead of theirs. Not wanting to get into a pissing contest with Kopelson, Carolco reluctantly withdrew their offer. This left both Sheldon and Walter Hill feeling disappointed their film was scrapped.

With the *Warbirds* project dead in the water, Sheldon was left to figure out where he was going to go from there. Well, he didn't have to wait very long and in an unexpected chain of events, he found himself in a curious position. A few days later, his agent would receive a call from Arnold Kopelson and his producing partner at the time, Keith Barish. They wanted to have a meeting with him, about their own helicopter movie. This was a couple days after Christmas and a few days before New Year's, not a time when meetings are generally scheduled in Hollywood, because most everyone is out of town. In this case, there was some urgency because the script for *Wings of the Apache* was far from being "camera-ready." In fact, it was a mess. The script had been written by three non-professionals: a couple of retired Army Colonels, and a retired Marine Captain named Dale Dye, who was a "military advisor" on Kopelson's Oscar-winning *Platoon*. Captain Dye would later go on to be Spielberg's cherished military advisor on *Saving Private Ryan* (1998) and *Band of Brothers* (2001), but a screenwriter he was not, and neither were his two co-writers. While it wasn't exactly what he and Walter Hill were planning with *Warbirds*, it was still intriguing enough to pursue. Kopelson and Barish were not looking for this movie to be an updated version of *The Dawn Patrol* but something more contemporary, like *Top Gun* (1986) with helicopters instead of jets. John Flynn was actually on board to direct, as Kopelson had promised. A deal for Sheldon to re-write the script was very quickly structured and written up, and within a few weeks he was on his way to conduct some research at the U.S. Army Aviation Center at Fort Rucker, Alabama. About a week later, Flynn and Kopelson would show up there as well.

It was an amazing ten days for the filmmaker at Fort Rucker, which was where all of the Army's helicopter pilots received their initial training. There was a super-wide concrete tarmac which was populated by every kind of helicopter the Army had in its inventory, but mostly Hueys, which had been the Army's workhorse in Vietnam. Being a military veteran, he was in his element, with every minute there being filled with excitement. "I didn't count them, but there were literally hundreds of helicopters parked across that tarmac; every hour of the day they'd be either taking off or landing, or hovering around overhead. It was a truly amazing sight."

The AH-64 Apache was the newest addition to the inventory, and also the baddest-looking attack helicopter anyone had ever seen. It also happened to be the subject of the film. The AH-64 made the fearsome Huey Cobra attack helicopters look tame by comparison. Sheldon was able to take a look at them up close, and even had the opportunity to sit in the cockpit to see how that felt. Sadly, none of the Hollywood elites actually had the opportunity to take a ride in one because they were two-seaters, with the pilot taking the backseat and the gunner having an unobstructed view from the front seat. Along with Kopelson and Flynn, he did get a few free helicopter rides while they were there, but unfortunately the AH-64 was off-limits to them.

As the project inched closer to production, once again the shifting wheels of Hollywood would send the movie into another direction. Once he turned in his re-write, and things seemed to be humming along smoothly, John Flynn abruptly exited the project. No one is quite sure what the circumstances were, but this unexpected development brought everything to a halt. Another director was brought on, a Brit named David Green who had directed a movie called *Buster* (1988). Other writers were brought on to re-work the screenplay even further, and Sheldon became busy developing what would eventually become *Lionheart*.

Meanwhile, *Wings of the Apache* went into production, with an amazing cast: Tommy Lee Jones, Nicholas Cage, and Sean Young. Unfortunately, David Green was not the right director for this project, and the movie didn't turn out how everyone had hoped. With

Sheldon's screenplay and John Flynn directing, it had the potential to be an awesome movie, but unfortunately that was not to be. It was renamed *Fire Birds* (1990), kind of similar to Sheldon's title, *Warbirds*, and received lukewarm reviews when it was released in May. It didn't do particularly well at the box office either, which is a shame because the subject matter was so well suited to becoming a long-running franchise.

Saving *Cyborg*

After the success of *Bloodsport*, Cannon Films was hoping to have another hit film when they greenlit the project *Cyborg* (1989). Written and directed by Albert Pyun, the movie stars Jean-Claude as a mercenary living in a post-apocalyptic wasteland, who is hired to protect female cyborg carrying vital information that can save the world from the vicious plague that has destroyed it. The movie opened to large numbers and was quite successful for the company. The fact it was released at all was a bit of a miracle since the original cut of *Cyborg* was a disaster and needed some serious re-tooling to save it.

Jean-Claude was in Thailand filming *Kickboxer* (1989) when the first test screening of *Cyborg* would take place. Sheldon called and told him about the scheduled test screening. "Jean-Claude wanted me to sneak into the screening, which was going to take place in the private screening room at the Cannon Films offices on San Vicente Blvd. I don't recall having any problem getting into the screening, because everyone who worked for Cannon at the time knew me and knew I was a close friend of Van Damme's. I don't recall seeing Albert Pyun at the screening either, he may have been off somewhere working on another film."

The audience would consist of one hundred people who were randomly recruited off the street, the same way most test screenings are. The film was in rough-cut form, which (at the time) meant that it was the 35mm workprint, cut together from 35mm dailies. There were no visual effects whatsoever, fades and dissolves were indicated with lines drawn on the film itself with a Sharpie pen. There was temporary music, produced via synthesizer, which may have been composed by Albert's chosen composer.

What happened during the screening would end up being every filmmaker's worst nightmare. Rather than elaborating on the painful details, we will let Sheldon explain what he had witnessed. "About halfway through the movie the audience started laughing. The movie was not intended to be a comedy, so the audience was not laughing with the film, they were laughing at it. The laughter grew and grew. By the final climactic fight, Gibson vs. Fender, they were in hysterics. The movie ended, the lights went up, and score cards were handed out. The audience members dutifully filled these out and handed them in before they exited the auditorium. The scores were quickly tallied. Out of the one hundred people who had just seen the movie, only one person liked it. The movie was scheduled to open in just a couple weeks. Posters had already been printed up, and theaters had been booked. Based on those audience scores, I saw an epic disaster looming on the horizon, and Van Damme's budding career quickly going into the toilet. I'm not quite sure about the time-line, but I believe at this juncture there were already conversations about me writing and possibly even directing *The Wrong Bet*, which would eventually become *Lionheart* (1990). So there was additional motivation for me to keep Van Damme's career afloat, besides just being a concerned friend."

Not wanting to see his friend failed, Sheldon did what any good friend would do. "As soon as I could get to a phone I called Jean-Claude in Thailand. They had just wrapped on *Kickboxer* (1989), and he was planning to spend a couple of days just relaxing in Bangkok. I advised him to change that plan and get back to Los Angeles as soon as possible; his career was hanging on the line." Jean-Claude was back in Los Angeles the next evening. The first thing he did was head to the Cannon building to watch Albert's cut of *Cyborg*. He would watch the film on a KEM editing machine, and after seeing it, he was livid. "He went straight to Yoram Globus's office and demanded they halt the pending release of the movie. Yoram argued back that he couldn't do that, as the film had already been booked into theaters across the country, and trailers were already being screened. Jean-Claude insisted, and said he would personally pay whatever costs would be necessary to re-cut the movie. As I'd already mentioned, the film's director, Albert Pyun, was not around and off shooting another movie. Menahem Golan was not around either, although I'm sure Yoram consulted with him before making the decision to pull the film and allow Jean-Claude to re-cut it. I'm sure Menahem and Yoram saw those dismal test scores, so to prevent their movie from being totally flushed down the box office toilet Cannon Films eventually acquiesced to picking up a good portion of the costs."

What would follow was a months-long whirlwind of activity. Sheldon volunteered to help in whatever way he could, which would entail re-structuring the movie and finding a way to make sense of what was essentially a non-sensical storyline. He and Jean-Claude knew a couple of editors, who they hired to work with them, as well as recruiting a twenty-two year old writer who recently had his first screenplay produced. *The Punisher* (1989) was written by Boaz Yakin who was a close friend of Sheldon. He asked Boaz for his help, who was happy and eager to oblige. "Sheldon came to me and told me that *Cyborg* was a total mess and Cannon was just going to release it direct to video. He asked if I would take a look at it, so I agreed. I watched some of the movie. The director really knew how to make things look interesting visually but it was a total mess as a dramatic piece. I had the idea of interweaving a flashback structure, which Sheldon and Jean-Claude were on board for. The editor and I went in with two reels and I put together a sequence and they all thought it was great. During the few weeks we worked on it, Sheldon and Jean-Claude worked on their portions in one room and the editor and I worked in another. After we finished it, they took it to Menahem and Yoram and it was soon realized that they had something worthwhile. If Jean-Claude's second film as a leading man would have gone straight to video, he may not have had the career that he did, so this really saved him, I think. The three of us working together with the editors really saved that movie."

The editors did the actual hands-on work of pulling apart the film splice by splice, reconstituting the cut scenes back onto the daily rolls, and then re-cutting the entire movie from start to finish. This was back in the pre-digital era, when movies were shot and edited on 35mm film, when each cut was held together physically by taped splices, when reconstituting basically meant pulling off each tape splice by hand, and then re-taping the cut pieces of film back onto the daily roles. It would be an arduous and time-consuming process, but that was the only way to re-cut a movie when there was no digital media stored on hard drives. That's the way it had been done since the dawn of cinema, and they were doing it splice by splice. Then they set to the task of re-structuring and re-cutting the movie itself. Since Sheldon was a screenwriter, his role in the process would include additional responsibilities. "I took on the task of re-structuring the story, and also writing new dialogue to bridge the gaping holes in the story. Jean-Claude took on the task of re-cutting all the fight scenes. I was in one room with a Czech-born editor named Julian, and Jean Claude was in the room next to mine, with an editor named Ruben Mazzini, whom I had met years earlier when he was cutting pornos for *Bloodsport* producer Mark DiSalle."

Boaz was hard at work on his portion of the picture, a contribution he was really proud of. "It's such a wacky-ass, eighties, post-apocalyptic movie with some interesting things in it. The crucifixion scene in the film was originally just one long shot, no cuts or flashbacks, just Gibson (Jean-Claude Van Damme) looking deep around before kicking it and then it falls down. I had the editors interweave it with the flashbacks and other things; it turned out to be a really cool scene and sort of the centerpiece of the movie."

Once they had locked the picture, the next step was re-doing all of the sound, starting with the dialogue, much of which was the new lines Sheldon had written. This meant doing ADR (Automated

Dialogue Recording, or "Looping") with Jean-Claude and whatever other actors they could round up. Since so much of the dialogue had been re-written, they had to get creative with the ADR as well since the new lines would not have matched the actors on-screen lip movements. For this reason much of the dialogue in the movie is played over the speaking actor's shoulders, or off-screen over another actor's close-up.

They also did some creative re-voicing, using different actors to re-voice every line that had been uttered by the on-screen actors. In the case of Vincent Klyn, who played Fender, Sheldon's choice was to bring in another actor altogether to re-voice all of his lines. "As fearsome as Vincent looked on-screen, in person he had an almost effeminate voice that simply did not jibe with the character he was portraying. I believe this mismatch may have been part of the reason that the test-audience was laughing so hysterically. On top of that, Vincent lived in Hawaii, so we would have had to fly him to Los Angeles and put him up in a hotel while he was looping his lines. Fortunately, I found a local actor named Branscombe Richmond, who had a suitably scary voice, and we used him to re-voice every one of Fender's lines, the new ones as well as the original ones." The result was a triumphant melding of voice and visage, which gave the movie a truly terrifying villain.

Albert had commissioned a music score from a friend of his, Tony Riparetti. Sheldon felt it to be another negative that was dragging the movie down. "Albert had envisioned the movie as some sort of a Rock Opera, and the moody, otherworldly music he'd used in his Director's Cut was completely inappropriate for what was intended to be a Jean-Claude Van Damme action movie. I brought in a friend of mine, Kevin Bassinson, to write and produce a completely new score, something that was appropriate for an action movie." Kevin was a close friend of Alan Jay Glueckman, who Sheldon had co-written *Russkies* with. Kevin had also been responsible for composing and producing the music for his short 16mm war movie, *Firefight*. With very little time and money, Kevin gave them a kick-ass action movie score, produced entirely on a synthesizer, which gave *Cyborg* the appropriate action movie vibe throughout.

The movie was screened for Menahem and Yoram and some of the other executives at Cannon. They were pleased with what they saw, and felt it was much improved, but also felt it needed a better ending. In particular, they felt the audience needed a more decisive and graphic moment when Gibson finally kills Fender. As it stood, Gibson delivers a *coup de grace* to Fender while they're both battling outside in the rain, and the power of Van Damme's kick was partially obscured by the pouring rain. This change would require a re-shoot, and fortunately Albert Pyun was back in Los Angeles, so he was able to see the changes that Jean-Claude and Sheldon had made, and would also be available to direct the re-shoot.

The first time Sheldon had met Albert face to face was at the location in Long Beach which had been booked for the re-shoot. "I don't recall having much of a conversation with him, but he had sent a huge bouquet of flowers to Jean-Claude after seeing the new cut of the movie, so we assumed he was happy with our changes. The new ending entailed Gibson and Fender crashing inside some kind of a work shed, with Gibson eventually impaling Fender on an ominous-looking meat hook that was hanging on a wall. Albert shot the scene, it was cut into the movie, and then we did a proper sound mix, supervised by a young sound mixer named Patrick Cyconne, who was Cannon's in-house sound mixer at the time, and who I would work with again on *Double Impact* (1991)."

Albert has subsequently had disparaging words to say about the work that Jean-Claude and Sheldon did on his movie. "I still maintain that we rescued his film from oblivion. It remains the most successful and most well known film in Albert's entire oeuvre of more than fifty titles." Albert managed to locate an early workprint of his original Director's Cut of the movie, which he had remastered and then released on Blu-ray and DVD under the title *Slinger*. "I've read fan reviews of this release, and there is not a single one that says this version is better than the version which was officially released by Cannon Films back in 1989, if anything, they say it's far worse."

The movie opened in the USA in April of 1989, and did quite well at the box office for a low budget Cannon release. It also did reasonably well all over the world, and has become a favorite among fans of Van Damme's movies. It actually did well enough to spawn a few sequels, including a spiritual sequel titled *Nemesis* (1992) (which also spawned three sequels), was produced by Imperial Entertainment (*Lionheart*) and directed by Albert Pyun.

Lionheart

Riding high on the success of *Rambo III*, Sheldon was ready to take on his next project. Little did he know that this next film would not only be a major stepping stone for himself but also for that of his star, Jean-Claude Van Damme. The journey they embarked on took them around the world, finding a success that neither of them had ever experienced before. *Lionheart* (1990) was the first major studio release for the actor and the directorial debut for Lettich. In case you need a refresher, *Lionheart* is the story of Lyon Gaultier (Jean-Claude Van Damme), a soldier in the French Foreign Legion, who learns of his brother's death and begs his superiors to be released. When they turn him down, with nothing but the clothes on his back, Lyon escapes to the United States where he stumbles into an underground fighting ring. Realizing he has found an opportunity to make major money, he teams up with down on his luck former street fighter Joshua (Harrison Page) to make his way through the ranks, and bank as much money as he can to help his brother's widow and his niece. The head of the organization, Cynthia (Deborah Rennard), has other plans for Lyon when he threatens to leave.

The story of *Lionheart* came from an original idea Van Damme himself had previously titled *Wrong Bet,* which was loosely influenced by the Charles Bronson classic *Hard Times* (1975). Even though his career was really picking up steam at this time, it was a rather long and winding road getting it to where it needed to be. Jean-Claude pitched the idea to Sheldon one night in a coffee shop named *Ben Frank's,* which used to be on Sunset Boulevard in West Hollywood. They decided this fighter should acquire a sidekick, an ostensible Manager like the James Coburn character in *Hard Times.* Right around this time, Sheldon had been working on the previously mentioned French Foreign Legion script for Sylvester Stallone's company, White Eagle Productions. He enlisted Jean-Claude's assistance on that one a few times, to help him come up with some colorful French phrases and expletives to use in the screenplay. This stirred up conversations the Legion, both realizing a French Legionnaire would be an ideal character for Van Damme to play. It made perfect sense their French fighter could be in the Legion, but he's forced to desert when he gets the news his sister-in-law is in trouble, and his commander won't allow him to go on leave in order to take care of the family problem. Okay, now they had a story, and a perfect Van Damme vehicle! Over many cups of coffee (and nothing else) they would flesh out a lot more details over many hours the same night, including the tough-as-nails woman who runs an illegal fight circuit in New York and Los Angeles. Finally, their brainstorming session came to an abrupt end when a Sheriff's Deputy entered the shop and asked the two of them to leave. Apparently the manager of the shop grew tired of them hogging space in one of the booths and ordering nothing but endless coffee refills.

In a recent interview for the MVD Rewind Collector's Edition Blu-ray of *Lionheart*, Jean-Claude had this to say about his idea for the film. "It was kind of my story in a sense. I came from Belgium to L.A. After leaving the Foreign Legion Lyon came here and fought. I fought here when I arrived here to survive before I became famous so that was the concept of *Lionheart*. That's why it felt so real, so painful, and with good drama."

Around the same time, Van Damme was being courted by producer Sunil Shah, who had produced *Black Eagle* (1988). In that particular film, the actor portrayed a Russian villain that would face off with the film's star, Sho Kosugi. Sunil asked Jean-Claude if he had any scripts or ideas that could serve as a starring vehicle for him in a low budget action movie. Jean-Claude pitched him *Wrong Bet*, which Sunil liked, and very shortly they were in business. Jean-Claude asked Sheldon to write the screenplay. At that time, he had already co-written *Rambo III*, which to Sunil was impressive, though it put him outside of his budget range for a screenwriter. He was also now a member of the Writers Guild of America (WGA), which meant that Sunil would have to follow their somewhat stringent labor rules; he would have to pay into the WGA Health, Welfare, and Pension fund, plus he would be obligated to pay residuals to Sheldon for the lifetime of the movie once it began bringing in profits. Not wanting to play by those potentially expensive rules, he opted to hire a much cheaper, non-WGA writer.

Sunil had originally hoped to get filmmaker Eric Carson (who had previously helmed Shah's *Black Eagle*) to direct the new project. Eric was the one who enlisted his friend Stephanie Warren, a non-WGA writer, to tackle a first draft. She had written the script for *Angel Town* (1990) which Eric had directed and was produced for Imperial Entertainment by Ash Shah, Sunil's younger brother. It was the first lead role for Olivier Gruner, who had served with the French military. Coincidently, the producers thought he might be able to help with some technical advice for the Foreign Legion scenes. Sheldon actually knew quite a bit about the Legion already, having penned the Foreign Legion screenplay for Stallone's company. Since Olivier was starring in another movie for Imperial Entertainment, they wanted to get his name out there wherever they could which led to his name appearing in the credits. Stephanie was hired by Sunil and Ash to turn Jean-Claude's idea into a screenplay. A few months later she delivered her draft, and Jean-Claude immediately hated it. Actually, no one except for Eric Carson seemed to like it at all. According to Sheldon, after he read Stephanie's draft, it didn't seem like a screenplay for an action movie at all, and read more like some lukewarm drama you might see on The Hallmark Channel. Not surprisingly, at Jean-Claude's insistence, shortly afterwards Sheldon was hired to write a completely new draft of *Wrong Bet* as an action movie, not using any of Stephanie's material, starting completely from scratch. The only thing kept from her draft was the *nom de guerre* that she had Cynthia give to her new fighter: Lionheart.

Several different factors contributed to the film's success. One such factor, possibly the most important, was how perfect the casting was. Van Damme's characters until *Lionheart* were mostly one-dimensional. It really feels as if the actors he's surrounded by in this particular film helped him to stretch his skills and deliver one of his career best performances. Lettich and Van Damme really wanted to prove that he could be an actor as well as a fighter, and they very deliberately went against many of the current action movie conventions. One of the unwritten rules for action movies at the time was that if a family member is killed or injured in the first act, the protagonist spends the rest of the movie hunting down and violently exacting vengeance upon the people who injured and disrespected his family. In *Lionheart* they didn't do that, not at all. Lyon never even chases after the guys who killed his brother. Also, Lyon's final fight is against an opponent whom the audience had never met before, and who had never even crossed paths with him earlier. If they had been following the typical template, Attila would have been the guy who ordered Lyon's brother to be killed; either that or he would have been the one who tossed the lighted match.

The cast of *Lionheart* filled out rather quickly with familiar faces as well as newcomers. Performers like Deborah Rennard and Ashley Johnson had just begun to get their feet wet in the business but it was the casting of Harrison Page that really added something special to the picture according to Lettich. "Harrison is a very talented and experienced actor, who has no compunctions about ad-libbing lines, especially when they seem to be naturally flowing out of the character he's portraying. He put much of his own self, and of his father, into that role. Many of his funniest lines were ad-libbed on the spot, while the cameras were rolling." With plenty of other roles in need of performers, Lettich relied on his casting director James Tarzia to help him along the way. It may have been the first movie that James helped choose the cast for. He's the one who brought most of those actors in to read for parts. Van Damme and Lettich used him for their next feature, *Double Impact*, which also introduced him to producer Moshe Diamant. He pretty much became the go-to guy for casting Martial Arts movies afterwards. He would be used again on *Only the Strong* (1993) as well as a few other of Sheldon's pictures. James would go on to cast the *Best of the Best* movies, *The Quest*, and many others. Sheldon brought his actor-friend, Brian Thompson, into the mix, and then later used him on a few other movies as well. Voyo Goric, who had been in the movie *Russkies*, which we know Sheldon co-wrote, was happy to join the project. Jean-Claude brought along the brothers Michel Qissi and Abdel Qissi, who were friends of his from Belgium, and had trained in Martial Arts with him. Michel had previously played the villain, Tong Po, in *Kickboxer* (1989). Stephanos Miltsakakis, who was in *Cyborg* with Van Damme (and would later appear in a couple more of his films), came aboard. Frank Dux brought them Jeff Langton, who plays Cynthia's fighter, Sonny, the one who very famously goes down after one punch to the nuts. They found the majority of their fighters, however, by hosting an open casting call at Frank Dux's dojo in North Hollywood. They actually had a thousand fighters come in and try out for the movie. That number wasn't exaggerated either, they had a numbered sheet with the names of every fighter that tried out.

Brian Thompson couldn't have been more excited to have been a part of his friend's directorial debut. It would prove to be another exciting credit to add to his resume. "Sheldon just gave me the part in *Lionheart*; I didn't even have to audition. He did have me come in and read with some of the actresses who were auditioning for the role of Cynthia, which would eventually go to Deborah Rennard. Every actor should be a part of auditions. I've maybe only done it half a dozen times during my forty years and every time it was a learning experience, just witnessing how nerves can cripple or be a catalyst to the energy in the room. I'm not sure I ever told Sheldon just how much I appreciated him allowing me to be a part of those auditions."

We really should point out the fact that two very prominent figures in early 90s action cinema also appear in the film, albeit in very minor roles. In an early scene when Lyon makes his break from the French Foreign Legion, one of the fighters he confronts is Billy Blanks. Billy would go on to star in films like *TC-2000* (1993), *Showdown* (1993), *Tough and Deadly* (1995), with the late Rowdy Roddy Piper, and many more. His greatest success came in the form of the popular *Tae Bo* workout. The other actor who makes an even briefer appearance was Jeff Speakman of *The Perfect Weapon* (1991) fame. For Sheldon, it was a nice bonus to give them a small role on their road to success. "I certainly took note of their career trajectories afterwards, and was pleased to see they were doing well for themselves, Billy especially. Before *Lionheart* was even shot, Jeff Speakman was my reader in the actors' auditions. In other words, Jeff was the guy who read Jean-Claude's lines to the actors who were trying out for the various parts."

On the subject of bringing friends in, Lettich was happy and excited to bring along a couple of his. "I brought along Lawrence Bender and Scott Spiegel, to play minor roles. Lawrence's role was small, but memorable. They were part of my circle of friends at the time, a circle which included the likes of Sam Raimi, Bruce Campbell, Boaz Yakin, Chuck Pfarrer, Rob Tapert, and eventually, Quentin Tarantino. Oddly enough, Quentin was working for Imperial Entertainment at the time, selling their movies to video stores all across the country. That's how I first met him, because his office was adjacent to our production office. I ended up introducing him to Scott Spiegel and Lawrence Bender, and the rest is Cinema history." Bender produced many of Tarantino's early films, including the phenomenon known as *Pulp Fiction* (1994). Spiegel directed and co-wrote *From Dusk Till Dawn 2: Texas Blood Money* (1999) which Bender and Tarantino served as producers on.

Even being surrounded by friends doesn't always mean a shoot will go smoothly. At the time, Sheldon Lettich was known as a screenwriter and *Lionheart* would be his directorial debut and it wasn't easy. He worked with a crew that was constantly testing him, mainly because he was a first time director, and they all assumed they knew more about making movies than he did, especially the Director of Photography, who Sheldon was just an inch away from firing. Maybe he was being too much of a nice guy to them at first, and would have to learn to be more assertive, especially on the films he would direct afterwards. Many of the crew had serious doubts that the movie would turn out to be anything other than a cheap chop-socky, and be nowhere near the box office success or genre-busting classic that it eventually became, or that it would turn Van Damme into a movie star. It was independently produced by Imperial Entertainment. They then sold distribution rights to Universal and to various other distribution companies around the world. Some of these distributors then changed the title of the movie for release in their own territories, to something that would be more appealing and understandable to their particular audiences.

Thompson was along for the ride and he was able to witness first hand Sheldon's ability to work with actors, especially his connection to Jean-Claude. "Van Damme really listens to Sheldon and during *Lionheart*; he had this boyish effervescence, with a hint of devilishness. I really had massive respect for his abilities as a martial artist. It was a bit disappointing to see his reluctance to take acting direction. I'm from the school that the director is the boss, end of story. You can collaborate, make suggestions, but whatever the director says, there shouldn't be any resistance. To Sheldon's credit, he had a way of working past that and work him into an actor. Some of the best acting Jean-Claude has ever done was under Sheldon's direction. I don't think there are many other directors who had a connection with him the way Sheldon did. The amount of time Sheldon spent with Jean-Claude preparing, being together in social situations, I know that their families were really close for awhile. I think that gave him an insight on how to move him in a dramatic, cinematic way." Whatever differences Sheldon and Jean-Claude may have had on set, the connection Brian mentions the two having would be what turned the film into something special.

Two things that have always really stood out in regards to *Lionheart* were the fight choreography and the score. The action scenes were unique and Sheldon will be the first to point out that it was a team effort bringing them to the screen. "I came up with some of the concepts and the venues for the fights, the swimming pool fight especially. I pretty much let Van Damme, Michel Qissi, and Frank Dux come up with the actual fight moves. The fight with Sonny, played by Jeff Langton, was choreographed to be a longer and much more elaborate fight, but Van Damme came up with the idea of just giving him one punch to the nuts, which turned out to be one of the most memorable moments in the movie."

With the exception of the main theme, which the audience doesn't hear in full until the final fight with Attila, and then again over the end titles, John Scott's original score was, for the most part, serviceable but not exactly what Sheldon was hoping for. That main theme, played by a full symphony orchestra, is quite grand and magnificent, once the composer fully lets loose with it. Until then, well into the third act of the movie, we just get occasional glimpses of the melody. Originally, he had wanted a jazz-flavored score for most of the movie, and knowing the budgetary limitations he was prepared to hand the job to a young but inexpensive composer named Steve Edwards. Steve created some temp tracks first, using nothing more than a synthesizer, which was quite pleasing to the filmmaker. Pleased, but not overwhelmed. Of course, those tracks would have sounded much better with live instruments rather than just a synthesizer.

In Hollywood, especially for a young director making his first feature, things don't always work out exactly how they may have wanted and in this case, the producers took over. Once they had a full director's cut of the movie, the producers were so satisfied with it they decided to take a gamble and spend big money to hire an established composer, someone who had a number of feature film credits under his belt. Sheldon had one brief meeting with John Scott, to spot the film for musical cues, and then Scott was off to compose the score and record most of it in Munich with a full symphony orchestra. Quite frankly, the producers decided that they would take charge of the music for the movie, and tried to distance Lettich from the process as much as possible. He was not yet a member of the Directors Guild, and this was not a Directors Guild sanctioned production, so there was very little he could say or do.

He never heard the results of John Scott's efforts until they were on the mixing stage in Hollywood, where they would combine the music with the dialogue and the sound effects into a final mix that would then be optically added to release prints of the completed movie. At such a late stage of the process, there were no options to re-do any parts of the score if Sheldon was unhappy with them, and he was unhappy with a few of John Scott's music cues. One of the cues he was unhappy with was the cue that John had composed for the pool fight. One of the producers, Ash Shah, was on the stage as well, and he agreed with the director's assessment after hearing the cue played against the edited picture. All wasn't lost and Sheldon, thinking one step ahead, had a solution. "Steve Edwards had written a jaunty Reggae-flavored piece for this scene, which seemed to jibe well with Paco Prieto, the Hispanic-looking fighter that Van Damme was up against. And more than any other fight scene in the movie, this one had a colorful Caribbean vibe, taking place in broad daylight, centered around a partially filled swimming pool, with spectators wearing colorful bathing attire. We tried playing Steve's piece against the picture, and it worked amazingly well. Even Ash agreed. I called Steve on the phone, and asked him if he could rush over with a more finished version of that track. Fortunately, he had one, plus he lived nearby in Hollywood." It didn't take long for Steve to reach the stage, business arrangements were made, and the rest is history.

With one obstacle down, Sheldon felt there was one more musical cue that needed attention, one that didn't quite work, and one that could potentially make or break the picture. The cue leading up to the final fight written by John Scott just didn't work and Steve Edwards never wrote anything for that particular sequence. "I'm not sure who made the suggestion, either Ash or the Music Editor, mentioned that we had a few songs available to us, songs already cleared for use, so we were free to try and fit a couple of them into the film. One of those songs was "No Mercy," by Bill Wray. They may have played a few other songs for me, but this one seemed to work perfectly." They tried simply laying the song down against the picture, and uncannily it seemed to hit every dramatic beat right on cue, almost as if it was actually written for the film, but it wasn't. With blessings from Ash Shah, they went ahead and put that song into the Music track, and then left it to Ash to work out the financial arrangements with Bill Wray and his representatives.

When it was released on January 11, 1991, it debuted in the number three slot and cemented Van Damme as a bona fide action star. Much like the underdog nature of the lead character, the modestly budgeted film would go on to gross over $24 million dollars worldwide. He had cross-over appeal, men loved the action and women love the film! Among Van Damme's many female fans, it's consistently a favorite, probably because he shows a tender side of his personality that's not often seen in his films, a side that's not frequently displayed by other action stars either. The scenes with his little niece, Nicole, are particularly heartwarming, without being saccharine or smarmy. It's been documented over and over again from women who love this movie, and who love it above all his other movies.

With the success of the film, not only would it propel the careers of Lettich and Van Damme but serve as a booster for the supporting cast as well, including Brian Thompson. "Anytime you're in a movie that is successful, it's a great credit to have on your resume. It shows that you're a working actor and in current films that people enjoy. Like *Lionheart, Cobra, The Terminator, The Three Amigos* (1986), they were all solid, respected credits. Being in successful films such as those really helped to sustain my resume and lead to further success. I'm really surprised by how often people recognize me from *Lionheart* and talk about it. It happens probably as often as with *Cobra* or *The X-Files* (1993-2018)."

The entire movie exceeded anyone's expectations. It was the first Van Damme movie to be picked up and released by a major studio in the USA, which was more than anyone could have hoped for while they were filming it. It also led to Van Damme starring in a number of subsequent movies for Universal, all of which were released theatrically.

The movie was released in foreign territories before it was released in the US, simply because Van Damme had caught on with foreign audiences before he connected with audiences in the US. The first country it opened in was France, on August 1st, 1990. It was released by *Metropolitan Filmexport*, whose president, Sammy Hadida, was a very early fan of Jean-Claude's. He had released *No Retreat, No Surrender* (1985) in France under the title, *Karate Tiger*, and had done very well with it. Sammy, in fact, had told Menahem Golan that he would be very happy to take *Bloodsport* and open it theatrically in France, if Menahem was reluctant to go theatrical with it. This particular move may have been instrumental in giving the folks at Cannon the impetus to try a theatrical test run with *Bloodsport* on the West Coast.

Sammy flew Jean-Claude and Sheldon to Paris to do publicity for the film ahead of its opening there. He re-titled the movie *Full Contact*, and when driving from the airport, they would see posters for it all over the city and hear ads playing on the radio: "Van Damme! *Full Contact*!" At the time, there were also posters up for the latest Steven Seagal film which was *Above the Law* (1988), re-titled *Nico* in France. There was another Seagal film already playing in Paris, and that was *Hard to Kill* (1990), in France titled *Echec et Mort*. It was playing on the biggest screen at the Lido, a prestigious three-screen theater on the Champs Elysee. *Full Contact* was scheduled to open in that same theater on one of the smaller screens.

While the duo were in Paris, they were joined by a group of Jean-Claude's old buddies, including Michel Qissi and Kamel Krifa, who drove in from Brussels to congratulate the friend who had trained alongside them in Karate classes when they were teenagers, and who had now seemingly hit the big-time. There were lots of interviews scheduled for Jean-Claude and Sheldon to do over the course of a few days with the local press. On the day the movie opened, Michel and Sheldon would manage to sneak away and talk their way into a few of the theaters to see how the movie was actually playing on a big screen in front of a live, paying audience. One of the theaters they checked out was the Lido. The small auditorium where *Full Contact* was showing was up on the second story (formerly a balcony section) and it was packed, standing room only. The audience was falling in love with the movie. Then they made their way down to the big main screen where the Seagal movie was playing, and the crowd was sparse, to say the least. There seemed to be no reactions from the audience either. This was great news for everyone involved except it wasn't over; it was only the beginning for Sheldon and his film. "Michel and I very politely informed the management about this uneven distribution of moviegoers, but they told us this was how the two films had been booked in advance, and nothing was going to change. We thanked them for allowing us inside to see how our movie was doing on its opening day, and then we headed off to another theater. The next theater, to our surprise and delight, had a line of people who had already purchased tickets, and were waiting to get inside. There was only one film showing at this theater, and it was *Full Contact*. While

Michel and I stood there admiring the size of the crowd, an usher stepped outside to inform those who were still waiting to purchase tickets: "*Full Contact*, COMPLET!" Which meant the theater was completely sold out. We were ecstatic!"

Jean-Claude, Sammy Hadida, Sammy's brother, Victor, and a few others went ahead to a somewhat famous old Parisian *brasserie* called *La Coupole,* where they were going to have dinner while Sammy awaited the box office reports from the theaters. The first report came from Michel and Sheldon, telling him they had just been at a theater that was sold out. Needless to say, the champagne was immediately ordered and brought to the table, and the small group proceeded to have one hell of a celebration. While they were imbibing champagne and eating dinner, Sammy was getting updates from various theaters around town. Apparently what Sheldon and Michel had witnessed was not an anomaly. It was official, *Full Contact* aka *Lionheart,* was kicking ass on opening night!

After having such a major success with the opening, Sheldon and Michel went back to the Lido. It was an opportunity to see for themselves if the movie was performing as well as they were expecting. *Full Contact* was now showing on the bigger screen downstairs and Seagal's movie had been moved upstairs to the smaller auditorium. It was a smart move on the part of the theater, because the audience for Jean-Claude's movie was at least twice the size of the audience for Seagal's movie. Maybe it was because Jean-Claude was actually there in France, promoting his movie and conducting all of his interviews in French, and Seagal was nowhere to be seen. Whatever the reason, audiences in Paris were loving Jean-Claude and loving the movie. With success comes celebrity and as Jean Claude's star rose, so did the unwanted perks. They started noticing teams of paparazzi tailing them, snapping photos from the backs of motorcycles, and scores of people were rushing up to Jean-Claude to get autographs when they recognized him on the street. Fortunately, in addition to Michel Qissi, they had a few more of Jean-Claude's old

Karate school pals with them, like Kamel Krifa, who were on hand to step in as bodyguards.

The movie was next scheduled to open in Belgium, Jean-Claude's home country, where he had grown up, trained in Karate, and dreamed of becoming an action movie star. Upon their arrival, a car drove them the relatively short distance from Paris to Brussels, where they hooked up with Jean-Claude's immediate family: his mother, Eliana, his father, Eugene, and his sister, Veronique. Aunts and uncles soon followed, and then Claude Goetz, the teacher from his old Karate school, who had trained him and helped shape him into the ass-kicking martial arts star of the movie that was titled *Wrong Bet* in Belgium. Jean-Claude was the hometown hero, the prodigal son who had gone off to Hollywood, against everyone's advice, and had now come back as the star and co-writer of a Hollywood movie. Since then, he's become one of the most famous Belgians in the world, right up there with Audrey Hepburn and Jacques Brel. Nowadays there's even a bronze statue of him in downtown Brussels, striking one of his famous fighting poses.

As in Paris, there were a lot of interviews scheduled in Brussels, many of them for local TV. The fact that Jean-Claude was fully conversant in French was a big advantage, and because of that, most of the interviews were conducted in French. There were also a few theatrical screenings of the movie in Brussels as well, with Jean-Claude and Sheldon doing interviews and audience Q&A's, either before or after the movie. Fortunately, a lot of the people in Belgium are bi-lingual or tri-lingual (French, Flemish, and English) so Sheldon did have the opportunity to participate in some of these as well. The next stop was Amsterdam, where they did more of the same. Then off to Germany, where the movie had been re-titled *Leon*.

Once the duo reached Germany, their experience was a bit more interesting and exciting thanks to a couple fellas there to protect them. At the airport in Munich, they were met by representatives from Highlight Film, which was the company distributing the movie in Germany. Accompanying them were a couple of local body-guards, real ones (Sheldon has since forgotten their names). One was a very typical-looking German, who had formerly been a police officer. The other guy was a mixed-race Dutch-Indonesian who had served with Special Forces in the Wehrmacht, the German Army. He had previously served as a bodyguard to American General Alexander Haig, when Haig had been the Supreme Allied Commander of NATO forces in Europe. Sheldon described them both as being able to speak English perfectly, and neither had the beefy-burly look you'd expect of a stereotypical bodyguard you'd see in a movie. In fact, they both looked quite normal, and were certainly less muscular and formidable-looking than Jean-Claude. These guys ended up hanging out with them 24/7, the entire time they were promoting the movie in Germany. As a bodyguard, one of the more important aspects of the job is to blend in and they were quite successful at it. Not appearing obvious they were providing security, they looked to any outside observer like they were merely buddies hanging out, like Jean-Claude's old friends who were hanging out with them in Paris and Brussels. They were however very discreetly packing weapons, and knew how to handle themselves and keep everyone safe should any serious problems arise. Thankfully, none ever did. Also, they knew how to safely drive a car at insanely fast speeds, using a technique that required one foot on the gas and simultaneously having the other foot just lightly touching the brake pedal, a technique Sheldon still finds himself using from time to time. Hanging out with those guys for a week while they promoted the movie in Munich and Hamburg, it would plant the idea for another Van Damme movie character, a bodyguard, similar to these two guys. Nearly twenty five years later, they made that movie, titled *The Hard Corps*, with Jean-Claude playing a bodyguard to Vivica Fox.

On June 12, 2018, the MVD Rewind Collection released a massive special edition featuring an extended cut of the film. The Blu-ray that MVD released was very close to the Directors Cut Sheldon had initially turned in to the producers. The *Platinum Cult Edition* released under the German title, *Leon* by Oliver Krekel's company, *Digidreams*, was also very complete. The reason that there are so many variations at all was that the executives at Universal mandated a few cuts and changes for the US release. Along with the title *Leon*, *Lionheart* was also known as *AWOL*, *A.W.O.L*, *Wrong Bet*, *Absent Without Leave*, and *Full Contact*.

From the bonus feature, "Lionheart: The Inside Story" on the MVD Rewind Blu-ray, Jean-Claude discusses in a little more detail why there were so many titles and different cuts for the film. "Those producers, when they sold the movie, sometime, some territories have different tastes then other territories and they want one extra explosion, for example, with a jeep. So we produce an extra one to make them happy. Sometimes you have to be flexible with the buyers because they know the public in their own countries."

Lionheart is a movie from the early 90's that still holds up. While the action draws you in, Van Damme's character and how he relates to the others around him take it to another level. Sheldon made the right move by focusing on character which lent to the success of the film. In early 2018, Van Damme announced that a sequel was in the works and would begin shooting later that year. Nothing every materialized and talks have disappeared. Van Damme has also discussed the possibility with Sheldon, and of getting him involved, but there hasn't been anything concrete on the table, at least not yet.

On the MVD Rewind Collection Blu-ray, Jean-Claude sums up the film and his experience quite eloquently. "The audience loves *Lionheart* because it's sincere with the relationships, brotherhood, friendship, love, betrayal, this is great and it was done in a very high class way." His affection for the cast and crew was apparent as well. "We're all actors, we're all doing a job so sometimes you argue about a shot, have feelings, emotions, but it's a big family. *Lionheart* was an amazing experience where the people go away but, in a sense, they never left."

Double Impact

Menahem Golan wasn't a big fan of Jean-Claude's, until *Bloodsport* opened and did amazing business all over the world. He had a three-picture deal that Jean-Claude had signed with Cannon Films, and there were still two movies left on that contract. The first of those would be *Cyborg*, which, after Jean-Claude and Sheldon completely re-cut the movie, also did quite well for Cannon Films.

Menahem called the two of them into his office to discuss Jean-Claude's next movie for Cannon. At the moment, Sheldon and Jean-Claude had no clue what it would be. Jean-Claude had come up with an idea, which was titled *Atlas* and was basically *Spartacus in Space*. It was a Science Fiction re-working of the classic gladiator movie, *Spartacus* (1960). They pitched this to Sam Raimi, and his producing partner, Rob Tapert. Sam and Rob loved the idea, and took it to Dino DeLaurentiis, with whom they had just made *Evil Dead 2* (1987). Dino had a production company at the time named DeLaurentiis Entertainment Group (DEG). Sam showed *Firefight* to Dino and his daughter, Rafaella, and after seeing Sheldon's short, they agreed to a development deal that would have had Sheldon writing and directing, Jean-Claude starring, and Sam Raimi & Rob Tapert producing. DEG would finance the film, with Dino and Rafaella serving as Executive Producers.

Around the same time, Sheldon would meet Chuck Pfarrer, a writer who had spent eight years in the Navy SEALs, and had written a screenplay titled *Navy Seals* (1990), which was about to go into production with Charlie Sheen and Michael Biehn starring. "Chuck and I bonded very quickly over our military service in elite units. I had read his script for *Navy Seals* and thought the two of us might make a good writing team, so I introduced him to Sam, Rob, and

Jean-Claude. Good chemistry all around. Chuck would go on to work with all of them on a few other projects, most notably *Darkman* (1990), which Sam directed and co-wrote with Chuck, and then *Hard Target* (1993), which Jean-Claude starred in, with Sam & Rob producing. Chuck and I wrote the screenplay for *Atlas*, and after it was finished, everyone from Dino on down signed off on it. Very shortly we were in pre-production. Then we hit a very big snag: DEG filed for bankruptcy! Suddenly all the wheels ground to a halt, and all we had to show for our efforts was a screenplay, which was now bound up in bankruptcy and completely out of our hands and off-limits. Sam, in particular, loved that project, and tried to break it free a number of times, but eventually he and Rob moved on to other projects."

As mentioned previously, Jean-Claude and Sheldon were sitting in Menahem's office, trying to come up with an idea that could serve as the next Van Damme movie for Cannon. Menahem had a wall of scripts in his office; literally, a wall filled with screenplays that Cannon had commissioned, bought, or had under consideration. Sheldon scanned those titles which were written on the spines until one jumped out at him: *The Corsican Brothers*. "I had heard this title before, and knew that the basic story line was about identical twin brothers. Possibly I'd even seen the comedic Cheech & Chong version of the story or the Douglas Fairbanks, Jr. version from 1941. I asked Menahem about that title, and he immediately lit up. One of the reasons he lit up so quickly was because Cannon had already commissioned a British writer named Lionel Lober to write a screenplay for them, which was not based on the original Alexandre Dumas short story, but on that 1941 Douglas Fairbanks, Jr. version. The screenplay for that movie was written by Howard Estabrook (who won an Oscar for *Cimarron* in 1931) and George Bruce. I don't believe Lionel Lober gave any credit to those two writers on his cover page, but if you watch the 1941 version (which I did) you will clearly recognize the structure and characters for what eventually became *Double Impact* (1991). The WGA eventually forced us to give a courtesy credit ("based on story material by") to Lober on the DVD case, but none of the previous writers were ever mentioned. The one exception was the original author, Alexander Dumas, whose distinguished pedigree Jean-Claude would be quite proud to boast about, and also the fact that he was a Frenchman, no less!" The movie's release date would have been well outside the limits of copyright laws, which was possibly another reason Menahem would be so enthusiastic about pursuing the material.

During the "Making of *Double Impact*" Special Feature on the MVD Rewind Blu-ray, Jean-Claude had this to say about the origins of the story, "When I was not successful, I was knocking on the door of Sheldon Lettich, he was more successful than I, but I was driving a limousine at night and had no clients. It was three in the morning and I threw a little rock at his window. He came out and we had a cappuccino. We would talk about life and movies then suddenly it rang a bell for me so right away I ran to Sheldon and said we have to do something and we started to organize everything."

Cannon hired Jean-Claude and Sheldon, as a writing team, to write *The Corsican Brothers* screenplay with Sheldon as the Director. The original version of their story was to be set in Paris and Corsica, settings which later on would become Los Angeles and Hong Kong. The two brothers were originally named Carlo and Marco. Carlo would be the one who was brought up in Paris (he would later become Chad), and Marco would be the brother who was brought up under harsher circumstances on the island of Corsica (he would later become Alex). Sheldon very quickly worked up and turned in a basic Story Outline, and everyone at Cannon seemed to be quite happy with it.

They would next do a photo shoot, with Jean-Claude wearing different wardrobes and holding different weapons to portray the two brothers. The photos were then put together into a poster that Cannon created for an initial ad, which would have run as a double page spread in *Variety* and *The Hollywood Reporter*. Sheldon was able to see the direction they were going with it but it never made it into the Hollywood trade papers. "The ad looked quite spectacular, but unfortunately I never made a copy of it. I still have the Polaroid test-photos, however. The next step was to send Jean-Claude and myself on a scouting trip, since at that time I had never even been to Europe. The two of us were off to Europe, in the middle of summer, August, 1988. It turned out to be quite a spectacular vacation."

The timing couldn't have been more fortuitous because *Bloodsport* had opened in France just a week or so earlier, on July 27th, 1988. The distributor there was Cannon, France. There was no premiere or anything like that, but Sheldon and Jean-Claude were able to visit a few of the theaters where the movie was playing and according to Sheldon, the reactions in France were just as positive as the one they had seen on Hollywood Blvd. earlier that year. "So not only were we scouting for *The Corsican Brothers*, but we were also able to do some promotion for *Bloodsport*, which had been opening all across Europe around the same time. Looking back, this might be why Menahem, who was notoriously tight-fisted, seemed so eager to send us off on a scouting trip to Europe, with all expenses paid. The movie had opened in the United Kingdom on July 8th, distributed there by Cannon International, so during the trip we were able to take a promotional excursion to London as well. Menahem had a spectacular apartment in London, and Jean-Claude and I dropped by to visit with him for an afternoon. He was quite enthusiastic about the business that *Bloodsport* was drumming up in Europe, and very excited about our next movie with him as well."

After returning to the U.S., they finished up and handed in the first draft of *The Corsican Brothers* screenplay. Apparently, the reactions were generally positive at the company, but there were serious misgivings about trying to film the movie in both Paris and Corsica, which would have been prohibitively expensive for a small company like Cannon, especially since the star of the movie, Van

Damme, playing both lead roles, had not yet proven to be any kind of a major box office draw despite the success of *Bloodsport*. Jean-Claude had already finished filming the very low budget *Cyborg* for Cannon before we left for Europe. After returning, he would be off to Thailand to star in *Kickboxer* for *Bloodsport* producer Mark DiSalle, while director Albert Pyun was editing *Cyborg*.

In the interim, before the focus would be shifted back to *The Corsican Brothers*, Cannon had another movie for Sheldon to work on, and that would be *Delta Force 2* (1990). This was to be the sequel to a very successful Cannon film that had starred Chuck Norris and action legend Lee Marvin. "The sequel would not have Lee Marvin (whose health was declining at the time), but would once again have Chuck Norris in the lead role. Chuck's brother, Aaron Norris would be directing, and the movie would be filmed entirely in Israel. Aaron and his key crew members were already over there, doing some early prep work, but nobody seemed to be happy with the script, especially the star, Chuck Norris. I had a brief script discussion with Chuck at his Wilshire Blvd. condo in Westwood, and then I was off to Israel, the first of many trips to that country, which was the homeland of Menahem, also his cousin and business partner, Yoram Globus, and many of the other folks who worked and made movies for Cannon Films."

After Sheldon arrived in Israel, he noticed that Aaron Norris and the rest of his small crew were in a depressed state because the movie had been temporarily shut down while the script problems were being ironed out. "They were all quite happy to see me because I was there to be their savior – the writer of both *Bloodsport* and *Rambo III* – to fix the script and get the wheels of production turning again." The basic storyline was that some of America's elite Delta Force commandoes would, via circumstances out of their control, be compelled to team up with their counterparts and adversaries from the elite Soviet Spetsnaz, to battle a common enemy who was a threat to both America and the Soviet Union.

They had already selected a few key locations, including the ancient Crusader city of Akko (also called Acre), on Israel's central Mediterranean coast. Sheldon would mostly be holed up in a comfortable room in the Tel Aviv Hilton, working on the revisions. "I did get to tag along with Aaron and the crew on a few scouting expeditions. I believe I was there for about a week or ten days, working away on the revisions, showing pages to Aaron when we would go to dinner or for a drink in the evenings. Everything seemed to be humming along smoothly. Then we unexpectedly received some jolting news: the production was shutting down again! Even worse, Cannon had decided to pull the plug on Israel altogether! What none of us had known was that Cannon Films had overextended themselves financially, and they were having some serious money problems. They were actually in negotiations with Italian businessman (and Mafioso) Giancarlo Paretti to take them over completely. Paretti did exactly that shortly afterwards, and renamed the company as Pathe Communications. Pathe was an old French company that Paretti had acquired in a similarly hostile takeover. His next target would be the venerable old Hollywood studio, Metro Goldwyn Mayer, which would be renamed MGM-Pathe Communications after he took it over.

Their immediate problems in Israel were far more mundane: how the hell to get out of Israel and get back home? They were handed the news on a Friday, which at sundown in Israel is *Shabbat*, when absolutely everything shuts down, including the airport and even the airline ticketing offices. They would get around this by booking tickets via ticketing offices in New York City, which had to be arranged via long distance phone calls because there was no Internet back then. Finally, Sheldon managed to book a flight to Los Angeles, but it was on three different flights on three different airlines, and took more than 24 hours, but at least he made it back home. "The nightmare was just beginning for the crew of *Delta Force 2*. The old script was completely thrown out, and a new one with a completely new storyline would be commissioned by Pathe. Thankfully, I was not asked to write it. The new story took place in Colombia, and had the Delta Force going up against a drug cartel. It would now be shot in the Philippines, where Chuck and Aaron had filmed a couple of Cannon's *Missing in Action* movies. At least now they had a new script that Chuck apparently felt comfortable with, and also a familiar location with a crew they had worked with before. Their nightmare was still far from over. While they were filming a shot from inside a helicopter that was in-flight, with one of their key cast members, John P. Ryan, on board, their helicopter crashed. Five crew members died, including the pilot. John P. Ryan survived, as did two other crew members. One of them worked with Sheldon years later as a camera assistant on *The Order* (2001), which was filmed in Israel. "I believe his name was Gaby. Ironically, we needed him to get into a helicopter, which would deposit Van Damme and myself on top of a mountain. He was petrified, and said he had not stepped inside a helicopter since that crash in the Philippines. Somehow we managed to coax him onboard, and we were able to get our shots. He also calmed his nerves enough to take a great photo of me with Van Damme and our cameraman on top of that mountain."

Getting back to *The Corsican Brothers*, it would now be in limbo due to Paretti's takeover. It was a different story with *Delta Force 2* because they had already hired a crew, and they didn't want to piss off their cash cow, Chuck Norris, so they just switched scripts and locations. It wasn't going to be as easy for Sheldon and his project. "The company was strapped for cash, so, as low budget companies often do, they just stopped paying certain bills. Anything that wasn't imperative was simply put on the back burner. They had invested a relatively small amount of money into *The Corsican Brothers*, just the script and the scouting trip to Europe. They were just going to let that one sit on the shelf for a while, unless they received a large infusion of cash from Paretti. Their new owner had grander plans, like purchasing MGM. So our project just seemed dead in the water, for the time being. I managed to get in touch with Menahem on the telephone, and asked him what was happening with the project. He told me they were canceling the movie. I asked why, and he point blank told me (I'm quoting verbatim): 'Van Damme can't play one character, how do you expect him to play two?!'"

Menahem was back to his earlier assessment of Jean-Claude, that's he's not an actor. At least that's how Sheldon would perceive it, not being informed that the company was strapped financially and had been taken over by Paretti. Anything else that required an immediate cash infusion was also left dangling. Since they had already moved forward with *Delta Force 2*, using a completely different script, they saw no reason to pay Sheldon the rest of the money he was owed for the re-write. This didn't sit well with him or his representatives. Granted, it wasn't a huge amount of money, but for the work he had done for them he at least deserved to be paid what was still owed.

They contacted Cannon (now Pathe) a number of times to remind them that Sheldon was still owed this money, but neither Golan nor Globus returned phone calls and very blatantly ignored their obligation to him, assuming he would get tired of waiting for the money and simply walk away. Wrong! "Cannon had a reputation for screwing people in this same manner. We could clearly see what their game-plan was, and we simply refused to go along with it. I did something that I had never done before and hope to never have to do again. I hired a litigator and we sued them, for nothing more than the money that was owed to me. At first they tried to ignore this as well, but the litigator I'd hired, Dan Coplan, was very stubborn and he refused to let this go, serving them with legal papers over and over again. To make a long story short, they eventually came up with what they thought was a cheap and clever way out of this quandary. Rather than paying me the cash I was owed for the *Delta Force 2* script, they offered to give me all the rights to *The Corsican Brothers* script, free and clear, no strings attached."

Sheldon with Forest J. Ackerman, on the front porch of the *Ackermansion*, around 1965, when he was 14 years old. Photo courtesy of Sheldon Lettich

"I" Corps, South Vietnam, 1969. Patrolling past rice paddies.
Photo courtesy of Sheldon Lettich

Hill 37, Vietnam, 1970. Getting ready to go out on a night patrol.
There's a bootlace tied to his rifle instead of a sling, to keep
the noise down at night. Photo courtesy of Sheldon Lettich

Camp Pendleton, 1971. Getting his Gold Jump Wings
literally pounded into his chest after completing his tenth
parachute jump. Photo courtesy of Sheldon Lettich

Training exercise near Payson, Arizona, 1972. Getting ready for
a parachute jump with Force Recon and Green Berets.
Photo courtesy of Sheldon Lettich

Detroit, Michigan, 1977. Sheldon visiting with Josh Becker
and Bruce Campbell. Photo courtesy of Sheldon Lettich

Sheldon with the original cast and crew of *Tracers*, 1980.
Photo courtesy of Sheldon Lettich

Camp Pendleton, California, 1983. Sheldon giving directions to Frank Dux on the set of *Firefight* (1983). Photo courtesy of Sheldon Lettich

Brian Thompson in the foreground, closest to camera. *Firefight* (1983) was Brian's very first movie, and he's moved on to a very impressive career afterwards. Photo courtesy of Sheldon Lettich

Van Damme signs *Bloodsport* (1988) posters in the lobby of
the Hollywood Pacific Theater, at the premiere screening on
February 26th, 1988. Photo courtesy of Sheldon Lettich

Sheldon with Van Damme and Michel Qissi, below a billboard
at the corner of Wilshire and Sycamore, February, 1988.
Photo courtesy of Sheldon Lettich

Sheldon with Van Damme in front of a theater on the Champs Elysee, Paris, France, 1988. Photo courtesy of Sheldon Lettich

Rambo III (1988) Press Book for the UK, 1988. Photo courtesy of Sheldon Lettich, from his personal collection

Sheldon directing Van Damme in *Lionheart* (1990), Downtown Los Angeles, 1989. Photo courtesy of Sheldon Lettich

Sheldon with Van Damme in Paris, beside a kiosk advertising
Lionheart (1990), renamed *Full Contact* for France, 1990.
Photo courtesy of Sheldon Lettich

Sheldon directing *Double Impact* (1991) on the Star Ferry in Hong Kong, 1990. Left to right: Producer Ashok Amritraj, Alonna Shaw, Even Lurie, JCVD, Georges Bejue. Photo courtesy of Sheldon Lettich

Sheldon directing Van Damme on a set built for *Double Impact* (1991). Santa Clarita, 1990. Photo courtesy of Sheldon Lettich

Cory Everson and Sheldon on the set of *Double Impact* (1991), 1990. Photo courtesy of Sheldon Lettich

Taking a break on Lantau Island, Hong Kong, 1990. Top row, left to right: Sheldon Lettich, Gladys Portugues (Mrs. Van Damme), Cory Everson, Georges Bejue ("Chad" stunt double), Kamel Krifa (Bartender at Mah Jong Parlor). Bottom, left to right: JCVD, Christopher Van Varenberg, Toni Lettich. Photo courtesy of Sheldon Lettich

Sheldon on the set of *Only the Strong* (1993), with Mark Dacascos,
Miami, 1992. Photo courtesy of Sheldon Lettich

Sheldon smoking stogies with Paco Prieto, who was the Swimming Pool
Fighter in *Lionheart* (1990), and then played the main villain, Silverio, in
Only the Strong (1993). Photo courtesy of Sheldon Lettich

The two "Loopy Latins" from *Only the Strong* (1993), Paco Prieto and writer Luis Esteban. Photo courtesy of Sheldon Lettich

Puerto Vallarta, Mexico, 1996. Sheldon directing the assassination scene in *Perfect Target* (1997). Photo courtesy of Sheldon Lettich

Sheldon directing an action scene for *Perfect Target* (1997). The Fight Choreographer, Chad Stahelski, is on the far left, wearing sunglasses and a baseball cap. Chad went on to direct all the *John Wick* movies. Photo courtesy of Sheldon Lettich

Sheldon directing Robert Englund and Julieta Rosen in *Perfect Target* (1997). 1996. Photo courtesy of Sheldon Lettich

Sheldon directing Dolph Lundgren in *The Last Patrol* (2000).
Israel, 1999. Photo courtesy of Sheldon Lettich

Taking a break with the cast and crew of *The Last Patrol* (2000), off
the coast of Eilat in southern Israel. On the far right (with white hat) is
Sheldon's daughter Angelique, who played the role of Tamara in the movie.
She's scrunched up next to Dolph's stunt double, Wade Eastwood, who
would go on to be the Stunt Coordinator and 2nd Unit Director of all the
Mission: Impossible movies. Photo courtesy of Sheldon Lettich

Sheldon Lettich, Charlton Heston, and Van Damme, in Tel Aviv, Israel, 1999. Filming *The Order* (2001) in Israel with the actor who starred in *Ben-Hur* (1959) was a peak, once-in-a-lifetime experience for both Jean-Claude and Sheldon. Photo courtesy of Sheldon Lettich

Sheldon with camera operator Ross Clarkson, and Van Damme, on a mountaintop east of Jerusalem. *The Order* (2001), 2000. Photo courtesy of Sheldon Lettich

Viv Leacock and Sheldon Lettich with the *gangsta* posse, on the set of *The Hard Corps* (2006), Romania, 2005. Photo courtesy of Sheldon Lettich

Van Damme and Lettich on the set of *The Hard Corps* (2006) in Vancouver, British Columbia, Canada, 2005. Photo courtesy of Sheldon Lettich

Sheldon vacationing with his wife, Toni, Jean Claude's wife, Gladys, and JCVD in Paris, 2007. Photo courtesy of Sheldon Lettich

Sheldon, Toni, and Jagger, one of six dogs that portrayed hero-dog, Max. On the set of *Max* (2015) in North Carolina, 2014. Photo courtesy of Sheldon Lettich

Toni and Sheldon visiting with Boaz Yakin in New York City, on location for his movie *Uptown Girls* (2003). Photo courtesy of Sheldon Lettich

What Golan and Globus didn't know, however, was that Jean-Claude was being courted by producer Moshe Diamant to star in a movie for him.

Moshe had acquired a Van Damme three-picture deal from another Israeli-born producer, named Shimon Arama. Shimon had produced an earlier Van Damme movie, *Black Eagle* (1988), in which Jean-Claude had played a Russian villain against Sho Kosugi. Realizing Jean-Claude's potential, Shimon signed him to a three-picture deal. This was before *Lionheart*, or *Kickboxer*, or *Cyborg*, and even before *Bloodsport* had been released. Shimon made a good call and signed Jean-Claude to the three films, the first of which was to be titled *Red Fox*, and was vaguely similar to a movie that Dolph Lundgren made later, titled Red Scorpion (1988). Jean-Claude was to play a Soviet agent or spy, who grows disenchanted with the Soviet Union and switches his allegiance to the West, which then sets in motion a plot by the Soviets to either capture or kill him. Shimon had even run a few ads and was making pre-sales, but he could never get the project off the ground.

Shimon had a new wife at the time, considerably younger than him, with a baby on the way. They were living in a small, cramped apartment, which was going to be even more cramped once the baby arrived. Sheldon isn't quite sure how Van Damme connected with Moshe, but they may have known each other from years earlier. "Moshe found out about Shimon's contract with Jean-Claude. This was after *Bloodsport* had been released all over the world. Sensing that Van Damme had the potential to become a major action star and knowing that Shimon was in desperate need of a house, Moshe offered him a swap. Moshe had a very nice, good-sized house in the hills of Tarzana, which he offered to trade Shimon in exchange for his Van Damme contract. That, basically, is how Moshe Diamant got into the Van Damme business, a relationship that lasted many years over the course of many movies. The deal was even more significant for Moshe than it sounds on the surface, because Moshe was able to leverage those three movies into nearly a dozen, by rightfully claiming, for example, to Universal Pictures that he had the next slot for a Van Damme movie, so if they wanted to use Van Damme in *Hard Target* they had to include Moshe on the movie as a producer, without him having to give up one of his slots." Shimon got his house, which worked out great for him and his family, but Moshe scored the big prize by getting what turned out to be a multi-picture deal with rising star Jean-Claude Van Damme.

Moshe had a script for his first Van Damme movie, titled *Night of the Leopard*, and was working on hiring a director. He was already making foreign pre-sales, and had formed a partnership with Michael Douglas's company to obtain the financing to make two movies, one with Van Damme and one with former footballer Brian Bosworth. The *Night of the Leopard* script was owned by another company, although they'd been in serious negotiations to sell the script to the new entity, Stone Group. At one point, Sheldon was even approached to do a re-write on it, and went so far as to have a meeting with the original writer. Then their negotiations to acquire the script unexpectedly fell apart, and Moshe was left with pre-sales he had made for a Van Damme movie, which suddenly didn't have a script. "I had been keeping Jean-Claude apprised of what was going on with my lawsuit against Cannon/Pathe, and now he suddenly became intensely interested to see what the outcome was going to be, because he had a deal with Moshe Diamant, but no script, and was still very much in love with the project and the concept of himself playing twin brothers. I told him about the offer that Cannon's attorneys had made to me, and the wheels started spinning very rapidly."

Sheldon set a date with Cannon's attorneys to stop by their office to sign the paperwork that would release them from the lawsuit, and to simultaneously pick up their signed paperwork that would hand him the rights to *The Corsican Brothers* script. "Jean-Claude kept anxiously asking me if we were really getting the rights. When

I finally convinced him that this was really moving forward, he set a meeting with Moshe at Moshe's house, later that evening on the same day. That afternoon I went to Cannon's offices on San Vicente Blvd. We exchanged the signed paperwork, with no sort of fan fare at all. They felt they were getting off easy, and cheaply. Little did they know that this piece of paperwork they were handing me would eventually have the potential to bring in millions of dollars in revenue, enough to save their company, had they only had the foresight and the patience." The ink was barely dried on Cannon's paperwork when Sheldon arrived at Moshe's house that evening. Jean Claude was there, and so was Moshe's attorney, who quickly scrutinized the paperwork and pronounced to Moshe that everything was kosher. Moshe and Sheldon both signed, and they were all in business on the movie that would soon be re-titled *Double Impact*.

Columbia Pictures was set to release the film theatrically in the U.S., while the production company was Stone Group, a merging of elements from Moshe Diamant's company (which was Vision International at the time), and Michael Douglas's company. The sole purpose was to produce movies together, the first of which was to be *Stone Cold* (1991), starring Brian Bosworth. The second movie was going to star Jean-Claude Van Damme, and was initially supposed to be the *Night of the Leopard* project. The producers had far more faith in the Brian Bosworth movie doing well at the box office, and lavished more money and greater resources towards that one. When *Double Impact* was released on home video, the distributor was initially RCA/Columbia Picture Home Video. Then Sony bought Columbia/TriStar, and Sony became the home video distributors. After further shuffling, somehow MGM ended up with the home video rights. It's all quite confusing, but when the movie was first released in the U.S. it opened with the well-known Columbia Pictures logo, of the Statue of Liberty holding up her glowing torch.

Double Impact would follow estranged twin brothers, Alex and Chad (both played by Van Damme), who reunite twenty five years after their parents' murder to avenge them. The cast included Geoffrey Lewis, Cory Everson, Alonna Shaw, Philip Chan, and Bolo Yeung. Chan and Yeung would be reunited with their *Bloodsport* co-star for the first time since that seminal picture. According to Sheldon, they weren't the only ones either. "Our Hong Kong producer, Charles Wang, played the Doctor in the Emergency Room, where Jackson is brought after being stomped by Chong Li. Charles ran a production services company in Hong Kong, Salon Films, which supplied cameras, lights, and other filming equipment for both movies. John Cheung was one of the fighters in *Bloodsport*, and was the local Stunt Coordinator in Hong Kong for *Double Impact*, and played one of Zhang's thugs as well. Kamel Krifa, one of Jean-Claude's old buddies from Brussels, was cast as the guy who runs Alex's Mahjong parlor, who gets his throat slashed by Peter Malota's character. Kamel also appeared in *Lionheart*, and played the rebel leader Abdel el-Krim in *Legionnaire*. This was the first movie for Peter Malota, who went on to work on a few more of Van Damme's movies, including *The Order* (2001) and *The Quest* (1996). It was also the first movie for Cory Everson, a world famous bodybuilder who Jean-Claude had introduced to Sheldon while he was re-working the script for shooting in Hong Kong. "After that meeting, Jean-Claude and I both said to each other, we gotta find a way to work her into the movie! Our Casting Director, James Tarzia, found Geoffrey Lewis for us, and Alan Scarfe as well. I liked working with Geoffrey so much that I used him again in my next movie, *Only the Strong* (1993)."

Sheldon's first choice for Alex's girlfriend, Danielle, was Tia Carrere. He felt that a guy like Alex, who had lived most of his life in Hong Kong, would have an Asian girlfriend. "We actually brought Tia in and did a screen test with her and Jean-Claude together, and she was terrific. So was Alonna Shaw, who eventually got the role, purely at Jean-Claude's insistence. We had some issues with Alonna down the road, because she did not want to do a nude scene, even though we had warned her well ahead of time that the role would require some nudity. She actually raised quite a fuss about it, until producer Moshe Diamant unequivocally told her she would either do the scene as written in the script or she would be promptly sent home and replaced. Fortunately she acquiesced, and that scene ended up being a favorite with adolescent boys all around the world."

One role they had trouble casting was Paul Wagner, the father of the twins. James Tarzia sent in lots of photos and videos of actors who were interested in playing the part, but they couldn't find anyone who had the right look and the suitable toughness required to play Van Damme's father, neither in Los Angeles nor in Hong Kong. "My buddy, Boaz Yakin, came to Hong Kong to help polish up some of the dialogue, and he made a great suggestion: Vic Armstrong, our British Stunt Coordinator. Vic had been a top stuntman for years, and had famously doubled Harrison Ford in all the Indiana Jones movies. Vic didn't consider himself an actor. Not to mention, he was also our Second Unit Director and our Stunt Coordinator, so it felt to him that he had more than enough on his plate already. Fortunately his brother, Andy Armstrong, was also there, serving as the director of our third unit. Andy said okay, so now we had that key role filled as well. Andy had also been a stuntman for many years, which came in real handy when we had to wire him up with bullet hits for the scene where the parents are ambushed and killed." Needless to say, no stunt double was needed for Andy Armstrong, and he probably would have taken offense had they even made the suggestion.

Sheldon has mentioned numerous times he never felt dialogue to be his strong suit so he reached out to Boaz Yakin. At a time when Boaz was ready to throw in the towel, his old friend brought him back in. "I was ready to quit the movie business when Sheldon came at me with an offer, to aid him and Jean Claude on *Double Impact* in Hong Kong. I was already in Paris, maybe for six months, and Sheldon had spent years trying to get his *The Corsican Brothers* script off the ground. He did several drafts of it and at one point it was going to be more of a mafia movie. Then he did a draft where the action shifted to Hong Kong. He invited me out to do some work on the script and I couldn't turn it down. Sheldon was deep into prep and didn't have time to punch it up so yeah, I did some work on it. One day I even had the opportunity to do a little bit of Second Unit directing."

At Sheldon's suggestion, the production hired Boaz and brought him and his brother (both huge Bruce Lee fans) over to Hong Kong for a couple of weeks to help punch up the dialogue. One of the memorable lines he contributed is "Take your fancy clothes and your black silk underwear and go back to Disneyland!" Boaz and his brother were fans of Hong Kong action movies in general and recommended to him the latest movie from a Hong Kong director named John Woo. The movie was *A Better Tomorrow* (1986). It wasn't readily available at video stores in the U.S., but there were multiple copies for rent at every video store in Hong Kong. "I rented it and was suitably impressed, so much that I urged both Jean-Claude and Vic Armstrong to check it out also. Everyone who saw Woo's movie was impressed with the way he handled the action, especially the gunfights, and his influence is noticeable in a few of our action scenes, especially the shootout in the drug lab where Jean-Claude battles the bad guys with a pistol in each hand, pistols that almost never run out of ammo, one of Woo's signature hallmarks." Ironically, Jean-Claude would end up being directed by John Woo a few years later in *Hard Target*, a movie written by Chuck Pfarrer and produced by Sam Raimi, both of whom Sheldon had introduced Jean-Claude to a few years prior.

For Boaz, he was in for a real treat. Being invited to work on the picture allowed him and his brother the opportunity of a lifetime, especially being such huge Bruce Lee fans. "I was a huge *Enter the Dragon* (1973) fan so meeting Bolo Yeung was a dream come true. My brother was with me and we totally geeked out over him and it was an honor to have dinner with him and his family." He confirms the John Woo influence as well. "At the time, only a handful of people were hip to John Woo, he hadn't broken through yet, and he was still this cultish figure. No one on the production had seen *A Better Tomorrow* except for me so I was able to introduce them to those films. After they saw it, yeah, that's exactly why you see Jean-Claude firing two guns. They were really influenced by it."

Another martial arts legend played a much smaller role on the production but made an impact nonetheless, James Lew. He was only a stunt player while shooting in Los Angeles. They used him as a stunt double for Bolo, because Bolo had a strong aversion to fire or electrical sparks anywhere near his body. The terrified look on his face when he's kicked into the electrical panel was a very real reaction. Bolo was used for only one of those shots, where there was no way to avoid seeing his face. There were other shots James Lew would be used for as well. They also substituted James when Bolo can be seen on the floor of the ship, unconscious, and the fire is rapidly igniting the spilled fuel.

Double Impact was a considerably larger film than *Lionheart* in so many ways. On *Lionheart*, Sheldon had set up and supervised every single shot, every set up. There was no Second Unit or even a smaller Splinter Unit. He did it all. *Double Impact* proved to be an entirely different beast altogether. It was more like one of the Marvel superhero movies, or a James Bond movie, where the Director is working with the principal talent on the First Unit, while other units are getting the action shots or the special effects shots. The difference on those huge franchise movies is that the producers are sometimes the ones who are calling most of the shots, while the Director is simply directing traffic with the principal actors. "On *Double Impact*, I was the one who was steering the ship creatively, because the project and the concept were mine and Jean-Claude's, it wasn't a pre-existing franchise. Nobody understood the concept and the characters better than Jean-Claude and myself. It turned out to be just as big and as complex as any huge franchise movie. Fortunately, I was surrounded and supported by people who had worked on huge movies before, and I relied on their help and advice in so many ways." Sheldon had a personal hero, Richard Kline, who had shot *Camelot* (1967) and *Star Trek: The Motion Picture* (1979), shooting it.

With Richard Kline, Sheldon is the first to gush over just how much his expertise added to the film. "I was such a big fan of Richard Kline. I originally wanted to be a Cinematographer myself, and Richard was one of my cinematography idols. One thing we had discussed ahead of time was using mixed light sources in the same shot, where you would have one half of a character lit by a cold blue light source, and other half lit by a warm amber light source, or a greenish fluorescent light source. Richard liked the idea, and even went so far as to put colored gels over some of our lights, to make the blues even colder and the ambers warmer. He was able to accomplish this with enough subtlety and finesse so that it looked stark but natural, and not like a colored lights carnival. The only time we went purposely overboard is the fantasy love-making scene, where I wanted to go totally Fellini-esque, to make sure the audience understood this was not really happening, that Chad was not actually having sex with his brother's girlfriend."

None of the producers had previously worked on anything of this size and scope before either, and initially there were some miscalculations. One correction they quickly had to make was adding a third unit. Fortunately, Vic had brought along his brother, Andy, and they quickly made him the Director of the Third Unit. An additional unit meant additional cameras and crew, additional assistant directors, additional script supervisors and camera assistants, etc., so the budget began creeping upwards very early on. One producer, Terry Carr, was in way over his head and had to be fired. Another producer, Rick Nathanson, who had worked with Moshe before, flew out from California to replace him.

Since this had grown into such a large production, Sheldon was entering a world he was very unfamiliar with and would have to adapt to the changes. "One thing I had to learn very early on was to just let go and let the Second and Third Units do what they had to do, once they understood my basic instructions, I could remain focused on the principal cast and on making sure the story was being told. The other units would get the shots I would later need in the editing room. With Vic Armstrong, I had little to worry about. In many of the scenes we had the two stars, Jean-Claude and Jean-Claude, performing their own stunts and interacting with other stuntmen. In those cases I would be working side by side with Vic, and many times I would step aside and let him run the set, once he understood what I wanted." Having worked with Second Units a number of times since then, Sheldon would grow to like this method of working, mainly because when utilized properly, it's possible to get twice as much accomplished in a fixed number of days. In effect, they're able to add days to the schedule without actually adding days.

Double Impact was shot in the pre-CGI days and since Jean-Claude played twins, there would have to be scenes where he appears onscreen with himself. The methods used to realistically achieve the effect had been in use for decades prior. "We used a very old technique for getting our shots with two Jean-Claude's in the same frame. It was the same split screen technique used in the Douglas Fairbanks, Jr. version of *The Corsican Brothers*, and on Disney's movie *The Parent Trap* (1961), and on *The Patty Duke Show* (1963-1966), where Patty Duke was portraying identical cousins. Basically you set up one side of the screen for one of the characters. We would have Jean-Claude with his hair, makeup, and wardrobe for Chad, on the left side of the screen. He would be trading lines with the actor who was the Alex double on the right side of the screen. The camera is rolling, and we play the entire scene. Then Jean-Claude rushes over to the hair & makeup trailer, takes a shower, gets his hair and makeup done for Alex, changes wardrobe, and then he gets back on the same set, but on the right side of the screen. We roll the camera, and we repeat the entire scene, but with Jean-Claude reading his lines to the Chad double. Now we've got the entire scene on two pieces of film. Later on, once I've chosen the takes I like, we meld those two pieces together in a film lab via an optical printer; the left side with Chad gets merged to the right side with Alex. There's a split somewhere down the middle where the two sides are joined together, but it's blurred to hide the line. We would also try to have some element that would help us disguise the line, like the vertical edge of a door or a wall. It's pretty simple and primitive, yet quite effective when it's done right. I would generally do one or two actual twinning shots per scene, and then cover the rest of it with close-ups, or with over the shoulder shots using one of the doubles. It worked so effectively that people have asked me whether Jean-Claude actually does have a twin brother."

"So what we did was sometimes we would put a pole there in front of me and I'd deliver the lines. Then I would have to do it all to the other side. I would have the timing of how much I talked here then how much I talked there. I'm good with timing, maybe the martial arts help, and also my director." Jean-Claude commenting on filming as two characters from "The Making of Double Impact" on the MVD Rewind Blu-ray release of *Double Impact*.

When Jean-Claude and Sheldon developed *Double Impact*, they consciously chose to take it in the exact opposite direction of *Lionheart*. In *Lionheart*, they tried to upend some unwritten rules of the action genre. There is no gunplay in the film at all. Lyon's brother is killed by drug dealers at the beginning of the movie, but he never goes after them. The guy he battles in the final fight had nothing to do with his brother's death; it's just a fight for money and honor, nothing personal. There's no revenge motive at all, but there's plenty of fights, all of them *mano a mano*. For *Double Impact*, they decided to go all-in for every action movie trope and cliché. This one would be all about revenge. The parents are killed in a hail of gunfire at the beginning of the story, and the twins spend nearly the rest of the movie exacting vengeance upon the murderers and their henchmen, every last one of them, using fists, feet, and gunfire, whatever is readily available to get the job done as quickly and as brutally as possible.

During the same interview on the *Double Impact* Blu-ray, Jean-Claude comments on working out the fight scenes with his co-stars. "The best way to describe the fight scenes is that everyone has a different style. Since I'm a real guy in terms of fighting, I started in martial arts then on to films, if not then I couldn't do what I do in *Bloodsport*. You can't do what I do if you don't train, okay? I know people; I spar with them and see their best stuff to see what the best they can offer is. With the best they can offer, we then choreograph a fight and have full confidence. Everyone has a different type of style. Cory was very powerful and flexible, Peter was all legs, and Bolo has … he's a legend."

The movie would prove to be a huge and unprecedented undertaking for Sheldon and the producers. No one had worked on a movie of this size and scale before. Even with the addition of a Third Unit, they were having a hard time trying to keep up with the shooting schedule they had concocted. Christmas and New Years were fast approaching, and they were running out of days before those holidays were upon them, and knew they'd have a mutiny if they tried to keep the American cast and crew in Hong Kong over the holidays. There was also a lot of bickering between Charles Wang, the Hong Kong producer, and the multitude of American producers. There were implications by some of the Americans that Charles was over-charging them and not coming through with some of his promises. Jean-Claude and Sheldon heartily disagreed with the accusations against Charlie (as they called him), and it only added another element of chaos, the fact the star and the Director were siding with Charlie Wang against Charles Layton and Moshe Diamant. Ashok Amritraj was always very careful to walk a fine line between the warring parties, which might be why nowadays he's a bigger and more successful producer than any of them.

The amount of producers on the picture proved to be far more stressful than imagined, especially for Sheldon. "Too many producers became one of our biggest headaches. The names of Michael Douglas and Paul Michael Glaser were never seen anywhere in the credits of the movie (although they appear on IMDB), and they never visited the set, or the editing room, nor did I ever meet either of them face to face. They were merely Executive Producers, who were involved with bringing Moshe some of the financing, and nothing more."

Finally, a very smart but painful decision had to be reached: the entire production would move back to Los Angeles over the Christmas and the New Year's holidays, and would resume shooting in Los Angeles in early January. They had pretty much completed filming on every location that needed to be filmed in Hong Kong. What would be left were mainly interiors, which they had been saving as cover sets, in case of rain. The cover sets would be built in Los Angeles, not in Hong Kong. They had filmed the exterior of a cargo ship in Hong Kong, and in Los Angeles they managed to find a great looking interior, inside an old World War Two Liberty Ship that was docked in San Pedro as a floating museum. The interior did not match the exterior of the contemporary cargo ship in Hong Kong, not even a little. Thankfully, it was never pointed out as a blooper, although it was a big one.

Once in Los Angeles, Sheldon and the rest of the crew would need to find a space in order to build the remaining sets. "We found studio space in Valencia, a quiet suburb just north of Los Angeles, and that's where we built our sets. One of them was the Mahjong Parlor where Chad first meets Danielle, the infamous black silk underwear scene. We see Chad step out of a van on the streets of Hong Kong, and into this dark, smoky place filled with chattering Chinese who are engaged in energetic games of Mahjong. It looked seamless, but the street was in the Mongkok district of Kowloon, and the interior of the Mahjong Parlor was in suburban Southern

California. The noisy crowd of Chinese players was all recruited by our Extras Casting people in Chinatown, near downtown Los Angeles. Every one of them spoke perfect Cantonese, and played Mahjong like pros.

The big final fight between Jean-Claude and Bolo was filmed mostly in the cargo hold of the old ship in San Pedro, and as far as Sheldon's memory goes, Jean-Claude himself designed the fight choreography. After the editor, Mark Conte, tried cutting that fight together, they would realize that it was not nearly as exciting as it needed to be. One of the reasons was that Jean-Claude wanted nearly every shot over-cranked; in other words, filmed in slow motion. "I warned him at the time that he was overdoing it on the slow-mo. Nowadays, you rarely see slow-mo at all in fight scenes, because faster motion and quick short cuts help disguise the fact that a lot of the fight moves are being performed by stunt players and not by the principal actors." Jean-Claude and Bolo were the real deal, and Jean-Claude wanted to clearly show that. The unfortunate effect with all the slow-mo was that it made it look like they were battling underwater.

Being pressed for time when filming on the ship, they didn't get all the coverage needed, so they decided to build a much smaller version of that cargo hold at the studio in Valencia, to pick up the shots still missing. Once again, Jean-Claude kept asking for slow-mo. Even with the additional shots inserted into the scene, it still lacked the excitement it needed for the final fight in the movie between Chad and Moon, and it still looked like they were battling underwater. Sheldon asked the film lab (the same one that was doing the split-screen work) if they could increase the speed of every slo-mo shot, simply by removing every other frame. This would in effect turn 48 frames per second into the normal 24 frames per second. In some cases they had over-cranked to 72 fps, which, by removing every other frame, would be brought down to a more reasonable 36 fps. The re-worked footage came back from the lab, they cut it into the scene, and the results were fantastic, one of Jean-Claude's most memorable fight scenes ever!

Double Impact was released into theaters on August 9, 1991. It did massive business on its opening weekend in the U.S., much bigger than any of Van Damme's previous movies. Columbia was so pleased with the numbers they ran a double page ad in both the Hollywood trade papers the following week. It went on to do huge business in every territory it opened in. The movie showcased all of Jean-Claude's talents and abilities, including his acting skills, playing the dual roles. Contrary to Menahem Golan's dire predictions, the movie proved that Van Damme indeed had the acting chops to perform two lead roles in one movie. He was able to make those two characters so distinct from one another that people were speculating whether there actually were two different actors in the movie, whether Jean-Claude actually did have a twin brother. *Lionheart* is the movie that boosted Van Damme into the ranks of movie stars who had their films released theatrically in the U.S. by a major studio like Universal or Columbia. *Double Impact* is the movie that truly turned him into an international movie star, an actor whose name was recognized and valued throughout the world.

A sequel had been discussed many times. If it was going to happen, it should have happened within a year or two of the original movie opening. There were many problems associated with the sequel rights, because Moshe had sold distribution rights for the movie all over the world, to different and sometimes competing distributors. Every one of these distributors would have had to have been included as part of the package in order for a sequel to be produced. They all had their fingers in the pie, and every one of them would have wanted at least their fair share of profits, as well as some say-so over the script, locations, co-stars, etc. Moshe and his partners may not have been expecting the movie to do quite as well as it did; instead they had expectations that *Stone Cold* would be the big hit that would generate sequels for years and years to come, and that American-born Brian Bosworth would be the one to become a huge worldwide action star, rather than the Belgian-born *Muscles From Brussels*. Jean-Claude and Sheldon came up with a story for a *Double Impact* sequel, which would have seen Chad getting into hot water with some local Chinese Triads in Los Angeles, and Alex having to cross the ocean to help his brother locally, but this time Alex would have been the "fish out of water" in unfamiliar territory. Sheldon wrote up a treatment, and then a partial screenplay, but put it aside when the complex legal issues became seemingly insurmountable. Van Damme would eventually go on to play dual roles two additional times for Hong Kong director Ringo Lam in *Maximum Risk* (1996) and *Replicant* (2001).

Only the Strong

During the promotion for *Lionheart* in Paris, Jean-Claude, Sheldon, and Sammy Hadida, went to Budo-Fest, a martial arts competition and exhibition in Paris. The three of them were in the audience when a Brazilian capoeira troupe put on a very memorable capoeira exhibition. It wasn't the first time he had witnessed capoeira, since Paco Prieto used a few capoeira moves against Van Damme in the pool fight in *Lionheart*. That show made a very big impression on Sammy, because he came to the realization that this exotic, non-Asian martial art discipline had never been showcased in an action movie before, and he became determined to make the first martial arts movie that was centered around it. A couple years later, when Sheldon was putting the finishing touches on *Double Impact*, Sammy dropped by to take a look at a few scenes from that still-unfinished movie. He must have liked what he saw, because he picked up that movie for distribution in France. Shortly after, he came to Sheldon with an offer: would he be interested in writing and directing a capoeira-based action movie? Of course he was interested, but he needed a few days to come up with a story. First chance he had, Sheldon called up his friend Luis Esteban and set things in motion.

Luis Esteban went to Cardinal Hayes High School and was neck deep in martial arts, studying different styles like Hapkido, Kendo, Praying Mantis Kung Fu, Fu Jow Pai, and several others. He spent time at Colgate University in Hamilton, New York, though he didn't graduate from there. After college, he served in the Marine Corps as the Amphibious Tractor Vehicle Crew Chief. He was honorably discharged as a corporal, never having seen actual combat. In the Marines, he would be able to study martial arts in Okinawa, Japan as well but it was nothing like what you would see in the movies.

What he would eventually take away from martial arts training would be how to use it to better himself. The love for the ideals of martial arts and how it can be used in a positive light would be the basis for what would become *Only the Strong*.

The story originated from Luis' own experiences in many ways, which he is happy to discuss. "After going through college, studying the martial arts, and serving in the Marine Corps, I came back to my old neighborhood and I wanted to do something. I knew I couldn't save everyone but I wanted to help a few people so I started teaching martial arts to a few 'at risk' students and hopefully give them the skills to lead them down a better path. This how *Only the Strong* originated, it's not a Frank Dux type story, and I never claim *Only the Strong* was true, this was just where the idea came from."

For a while back in the early 80s, Luis had been sharing an apartment with Lawrence Bender, well before Lawrence hooked up with Quentin Tarantino. They had some mutual friends back in New York City, including Louis Venosta, who scripted *Bird on a Wire* (1990), and the martial arts actor, Taimak, who had starred in *The Last Dragon* (1985). Lawrence introduced Luis to Sheldon as a budding screenwriter, who also happened to be another Marine Corps veteran. The two of them hit it off, and shortly after, they started batting around movie ideas, one of which eventually became *Only the Strong*.

One evening, Luis had dinner with Sheldon and his wife which Lawrence Bender had invited him to join. It wasn't meant to be a networking thing but he and Sheldon really hit it off. "We were just talking about some things and I told Sheldon about these kids, and I wasn't trying to turn them into model citizens, but they did show improvement, even getting better grades. Lawrence wasn't a big producer at that time, just roommates, and *Reservoir Dogs* wasn't on anyone's mind and certainly not a cult classic. It would eventually help create a career for Bender and of course Quentin Tarantino. They were just preparing to make the film and I would help Lawrence with the budgeting, reviewing things for him. That dinner really was a starting point for amazing things for all of us."

Shortly after that dinner when Sheldon had just finished the final sound mix of *Double Impact*, he invited Luis to visit him. "There was a screening of the film, Jean-Claude was there and that was the first time we met, I think Michael Douglas may have been in that little screening room as well, his company was part of the financing. What I'm trying to say is that Sheldon kept true to his word and helped me get some writing gigs which led to me starting a career in film which is what I always wanted to do."

Luis and Sheldon came up with the basic storyline well before they ever spoke to Sammy Hadida about it, and well before they introduced the capoeira element into the story. Since Luis had been a longtime martial arts practitioner in New York City, and at one time he was actually tasked to take a dozen of the most incorrigible students from a local high school, and instill some discipline by training them in martial arts. They drew from Luis' military career as well, to flesh out the lead character. His name would be Louis Stevens, which in Spanish would translate as Luis Esteban. Luis had a cool title which he had used on another project of his, and that was *Only the Strong*. Sheldon suggested they appropriate that title for the new idea, about the military veteran training this group of delinquent kids in martial arts.

Luis had already started work on a script dealing with a similar story but was still trying to figure it out. "It originally had a much darker twist, so when Sheldon took all that, he knew how to shape it into a much more commercial idea. He just knew how to keep from convoluting it with all the excess stuff and he was very clear on the beats. He laid out the beats and would guide me through, always making sure we were telling a compelling story. I would go write some stuff and come have Sheldon go over it. He would make some revisions based on his experience and I always appreciated his feedback."

It would be a very long circuitous path to 20th Century Fox. Sammy Hadida introduced Luis and Sheldon to a couple of investors named Stuart Shapiro and Steve Menkin, who owned a company named Freestone Pictures, which had not produced any movies yet. Combined with Sammy's production company, Davis Films, they put up the money to hire Luis and Sheldon to write a first draft screenplay of the story they had pitched to Sammy. Once the script was completed and turned in, Sammy next secured a foreign sales company named August Entertainment to make foreign pre-sales for the movie. Since they had no star at the time, the movie was pretty much sold as a Sheldon Lettich movie, and the fact that it would be directed by the same man who had directed *Lionheart* and *Double Impact*. There was no Van Damme this time, so the picture was sold on his name alone, and the fact that it would be featuring a unique martial art from Brazil known as capoeira. Another selling point was that Sammy Hadida would be one of the producers. Sammy had a reputation of having the ability to pick a winner, and a lot of foreign distributors would follow his lead. As mentioned before, when Menahem Golan had some hesitancy about releasing *Bloodsport* in theaters, Sammy stepped up and told Menahem he'd be happy take the movie off his hands and release it in theaters himself.

The first market they hit was the American Film Market (AFM), which was held in Santa Monica the first quarter of every year. They prepared promotional materials, posters and videos, touting Sheldon's recent credits and showing clips of Brazilians performing capoeira, which they were calling "the martial art for the 90s!" The CEO of August Entertainment, Gregory Cascante, made some pre-sales at the AFM, but it just wasn't nearly enough to shoot the movie with. They had projected the budget to be in the neighborhood of $6 million, and that's what the goal would be. The biggest, most lucrative territory in the world at that time was the United States, and it was absolutely essential that they get a pre-sale from an American distributor. The goal was to raise a commitment of $3 million from the U.S. and to get the rest of the budget from foreign territories.

The first U.S. distributor to show interest was Dimension Films, the genre division of Miramax, which was ostensibly headed by Bob Weinstein, Harvey's brother. It didn't take long before Sheldon found himself at a lunch meeting with Harvey Weinstein, at some upscale restaurant in Santa Monica, where he politely grilled him about the vision for the film, about who he had in mind for the lead roles, and what he thought the budget should be. "The lunch went very well, and we seemed to be on our way to getting our all-important U.S. deal. Later on I found out there was a slight hitch; Harvey felt the overall budget should be no higher than $5 million, and Dimension was willing to commit no more than $2.5 million for the U.S. rights. Sammy and Gregory thought this was all good news, but I held firm at the $6 million budget that we had so carefully crafted. With that $6 million budget, we would have roughly forty shooting days to film the entire movie. On *Lionheart* I had thirty nine days, with one unit, and there were times when we were scrambling to complete our days. I knew I needed at least that same amount of days for *Only the Strong*. *Double Impact* was a completely different story, with two and sometimes three units shooting for a total of 63 days. I held firm at not getting short-changed on this one, and unfortunately Harvey was not budging off his number either."

20th Century Fox soon entered the picture. No one really knows for sure who reached out to them, but very shortly they found themselves having a meeting with Peter Rice (Rupert Murdoch's nephew) and Jorge Saralegui, a Fox executive, both of whom would be overseeing the movie should they strike a deal with the studio. Fortunately, Fox were open to advancing them $3 million, for a $6 million overall budget. By this time, they had already been in discussions with Mark Dacascos to play the lead role, and had even shot a 35mm screen test with him to see if he had the chops to play the lead role in a feature film.

Sheldon and the producers found themselves to be in a some-what fortunate position with Fox, due to a very tragic set of circumstances which had occurred not long before. Fox had signed Bruce Lee's son, Brandon Lee, to a multi-picture deal, and he had starred in *Rapid Fire* (1992) for them, which performed quite well at the box office. His next movie was *The Crow* (1994); sadly, he tragically died in an on-set accident before he could finish shooting the movie. In order to complete the film without him, the production brought in an actor who looked very similar to Brandon, and who could also perform the martial arts moves which were required for the lead character. The actor they brought in was Mark Dacascos, who was also a mixed-race Eurasian, just like Brandon Lee. The executives at Fox saw Mark as a possible replacement who could fill Brandon Lee's shoes. His screen test convinced them. Supposedly, the story goes like this: Rupert Murdoch himself asked to see the screen test, and Sheldon heard that he told his nephew to sign this kid for a few movies, starting with *Only the Strong*. Now they had their $6 million budget, and 20th Century Fox, a genuine major studio, as the American distributor.

During the early 90s, Mark Dacascos was not a recognizable name. Aside from a few bit parts in film and television, his only significant film role was as Kenjiro Sango in Sam Firstenberg's *American Samurai* (1992). Right before that he was doing live shows at Universal Studios Hollywood where he played a young Conan, before he has the big muscles, then later in the show he would come back with a costume change and fight the big Conan. Nabbing the role of Louis Stevens would be a major stepping stone for the up and coming actor. Coming from a martial arts family, Mark began training at the age of four with his father, Al Dacascos. Over the years, Mark would win numerous competitions and tournaments during his early life, before entering the world of film.

No one really remembers exactly how Mark Dacascos found himself on the filmmaker's radar but Mark has a distinct recollection of those first meetings. "I don't know how Sheldon heard of me, maybe through my then manager, Katherine James, or my friend Luis Esteban. I was asked by my manager to meet with some producers but I just can't remember if Sheldon was there or not at that first meeting. Samuel Hadida was one of the producers who I would later go on to work with on *Crying Freeman* (1995), *Brotherhood of the Wolf* (2001), as well as *Only the Strong*. Steven Menkin and Stuart Shapiro were also there, but the thing I really remember is that once Sheldon decided I would be right for the role, he really fought for me to be there. I had never done a big studio movie, I had never been the lead, I had been the lead bad guy, done smaller parts, but not the lead good guy. I've always felt that it was Sheldon who really pushed for me, and I felt it was such a courageous move, only because there weren't a whole lot of minorities, or mixed races, as lead actors in studio films. I know it must have taken some big cojones for him to fight for me. It just wasn't the trend at the time to cast someone like me and Sheldon believed in me. I was twenty seven when he found me and twenty eight when we filmed. A few days after Fox watched my screen test, Sheldon called my manager and me, and said the studio approved his choice and the part was mine."

It may have taken a little bit for everyone else to see what Sheldon saw in Mark but they all would eventually come around. He was a unique talent and Sheldon was excited to introduce him to the world. "Mark was a very special trifecta of talents and abilities. He was a very good actor, he had amazing physical skills, and he looked like a movie star. He studied capoeira more intensely for this movie, and became a true *mestre* at it. The one thing extra I asked him to do was to build up his body, since this was the early 90s and the Schwarzenegger, Stallone, and Van Damme style bodies were still in vogue for action stars at that time. Mark took that request seriously and built himself up, not quite to the level of Van Damme at that time, but enough so that he fit the profile that audiences expected.

Mark was also an amazing gymnast, and didn't require a stunt double for any of those gymnastic feats in the movie. You could not have gotten Stallone, Schwarzenegger, or Van Damme to do any of those moves on their own, without a stunt double." In addition to all that, Mark was also great with martial arts weapons. Clearly, the director and star were not only on the same page, but completely in synch for the upcoming project.

As mentioned before, the film was very loosely based on experiences in Luis Esteban's life and the character Mark would be playing was very loosely based on himself. The casting of the role would be very personal for the writer who couldn't have been happier with the decision. "The conversation came up about who would play the lead in the movie and Sheldon was pretty clear that he wanted a fresh face. He wanted someone that could do more than just conventional martial arts. Mark is one of the most authentically nice persons I've met in this industry and in life. He hadn't studied much capoeira before the film but he did study gymnastics and because of his diverse martial arts background he was very flexible. He moved in ways no one else used to and that just became gold for the film. His casting in *Only the Strong* didn't happen overnight; he worked really hard to get the role. He had to prove himself to the producers and the studio even though Sheldon and I were both championing for him."

After *American Samurai*, Mark felt like he needed to shake up his world and try something new. He had experienced some capoeira when he was sixteen living in Europe with his family. They came back to the states that summer to compete in a martial arts tournament. "One of my father's students, Sifu Bill Owens from Oakland, California, let my family stay at his school while we were there for the tournament. Sifu Bill had just come back from one of his many trips to Brazil and he was there studying capoeira. He didn't teach us but he had showed us a bit of what he learned. That's when I saw it for the first time, at sixteen. Cut to the age of twenty seven, Sifu Earl White had been studying with Mestre Amen Santo in Santa Monica, California." For years, Sifu Earl kept telling Mark he needed to go check out Amen's classes and kept praising capoeira. He was very interested and curious but for whatever reason, he never made it there. Eventually, that would change. "After talking to Earl, I finally just up and went there one day. At the time, Amen was teaching out of a hangar at the little Santa Monica Airport. When I pulled into the parking lot I could already hear the berimbau (it's a single-stringed percussion instrument) and just walking up to the entrance of the school I was already smiling and maybe bouncing to the beat a little bit. When I walked in I was greeted by Amen and his big smile. I asked if I could just watch and he allowed me to do so. I sat there watching these people twirl, fly, and kick the whole time. Everyone was just smiling and having fun. I was just so enraptured by how these senses were being stimulated in such a positive way; I joined his school that day. I loved what I saw and I loved how I felt being around Amen and capoeira. This was in like October or November, then that January was when my manager called about the interview with the producers of the film."

Once Fox was on board with Mark, it would come time to fill out the rest of the crew and cast. As much as possible they tried to cast locally. Fortunately, Miami did have a cadre of film & TV professionals, most of who had worked on the TV show *Miami Vice* (1984-1989). There were locally based crew people, which saved a lot of money because they didn't need to fly them out from New York or L.A., and put them up in hotels. The Production Designer, Mark Harrington, was locally based, and he knew local set dressers, painters, and construction crews who he brought on board. One of his best contributions was to hook Sheldon up with another Miami local, Patricia Field, the woman who became the Costume Designer. "There's a very definite Miami-styled color palette in the movie, which was worked out between Patricia and Mark Harrington. The colors on the walls and in the costumes were not random, and they all blend very harmoniously. It's not something you'd generally notice in an action movie, but in *Only the Strong* it's there, and it was all very deliberate. Patricia Field went on to a certain amount of fame and notoriety a few years later when she became the Costume Designer on the TV series, *Sex and the City* (1998-2004). When the characters on that show famously wore and talked about *Manolo Blahnik* shoes, which was all Patricia's doing. She later went on to design the costumes for *The Devil Wears Prada* (2006)."

From Los Angeles, Sheldon brought along Jim Tarzia, the Casting Director from *Lionheart* and *Double Impact*, and he set up a local casting office with Ellen Jacoby, who had previously done the casting on *Miami Vice* and *Flipper* (1964-1967), and was familiar with all of the local talent in South Florida. Before Jim left for Miami, there was a casting session in Los Angeles, where they chose some of the key cast members, many of whom had long resumes from working on feature films and TV shows: Richard Coca, Ryan Bollman, Todd Susman, and the Jamaican gang leader, Jeffrey Anderson-Gunter. Most of the kids were found locally in Miami; few had ever been in a movie or on a TV set before. "Jim Tarzia had tossed a number of recognizable names at me for Kerrigan. I even had a meeting with Martin Sheen for the role, and he was interested, but too expensive. I then realized that Geoffrey Lewis would be not only be perfect for the role, he was affordable. I'd already worked with him and we had gotten along great. The executives at Fox tossed some bigger names at me for our female lead, but unless they coughed up some extra money (what's commonly referred to as "cast breakage") we had to go with an actress who'd played a few prominent roles, but was within our limited budget range." That actress turned out to be Stacey Travis, who instantly had a great chemistry with Mark Dacascos.

Paco Prieto had actually studied some capoeira before being cast as Silverio in *Only the Strong*, and even used a few capoeira moves in the pool fight with Jean-Claude in *Lionheart*, which is why he was being thought of for the film. He wasn't an actor, and had never really acted before; he didn't have any lines in *Lionheart*. His wife, Deborah, had aspired to be an actress at one time, and had studied acting. According to Sheldon, she knew just enough to begin coaching her husband, who actually had quite a few lines to deliver. "As I recall, we did a little bit of auditioning with him, just to make sure we wouldn't be embarrassing ourselves once the cameras began rolling. Paco convinced us he could handle the role and all the dialogue, so we went with him as the main villain. Quite honestly, it would have been difficult to find somebody who would have suited the character as well as he did, and who could perform in those fight scenes too, especially with the capoeira moves. The thing about Paco is that he truly is a bad-ass, and the audience can sense that, can see that. Unlike someone like Frank Dux, Paco doesn't talk about how much of a bad-ass he is, but other people who have known him for years (and I've met them) will tell you stories about him walking into a bar full of guys who had been harassing his wife, and just tearing the place apart single-handedly, walking out with just a few cuts and bruises, like something out of an old Charles Bronson or Clint Eastwood movie."

With Mark, being it was his first lead role, it would be important for him to jive with his fellow cast mates, and they could not have been more perfect for their roles. "Richard Coca, Ryan Bollman, and the rest of the kids were all fantastic. They were either the characters they played or they were just so darn good they just tapped into it. Before we started filming, these kids had already taken on the spirit of who they were playing and really embodied the characters. Stacey Travis was just a lovely human being. She's obviously attractive, super-talented, and a professional who was a dream to work with. Geoffrey Lewis was quirky and so smart. Those big eyes of his were so soulful. There were a few tough days for me where I didn't feel like I knew what I was doing but when I was working with him, I could just look into those eyes and then everything would just click and I'd be back in that moment. I didn't have much interaction with Paco, not in rehearsals or the make-up trailer; we just had different times going into everything. Almost all my interactions with him were on the set. He was very personable, professional, and he was so striking visually. He's tall, handsome, charismatic, powerful, and you could feel his energy. If you were ready to throw down, he was always ready to go, such ideal casting for that part."

Now that Sheldon had his cast and crew in place, it was time to make the trip to Miami. The only problem with that, Hurricane Andrew had just torn its way through and made a complete mess of the city. The start date was delayed for a couple of weeks because of the hurricane. "We had scheduled to film a number of scenes on Key Biscayne, and found it was devastated when we saw it afterwards. A lot of those opening helicopter shots are aerials that were filmed flying over that key (island) and you can see all the Australian pine trees knocked over, looking like rows of toothpicks." It didn't look anything like that when they were scouting. When the kids go on their overnight camping trip to the island, they could see some of the devastation, though they managed to shoot around all the downed trees, and made it look like a lush and tropical paradise nevertheless.

Mark had to work incredibly hard to meet all the physical requirements of the role. He was already in terrific shape but he would have to keep it up through the entirety of the production to meet what was asked of him. "Sheldon wanted me to put some weight on, some more muscle. Personally, I like to be as lean as possible; it's easier for me to move. I enjoy trail running, yoga, and surfing. They hired an old friend and colleague of mine to be my trainer so for pre-production I would train with weights six days a week for seventy five to ninety minutes in the morning. Then I would do capoeira three to five times a week and that included private lessons with Amen as well as the group classes. Then they hired an acting coach to go over the script with me and worked as much as we could to prepare. In addition to all that, I still did my own training so there was a lot of physicality but I also needed to get inside the character's mind. He was Special Forces, a military man, and I really needed to get into that mindset. I really feel that with all that training and everyone involved really prepared me for the three months of filming. I made it through without an injury. Capoeira is very physical and there were no strains, no pulls, and I just felt great every day. On a physical level, I was just very well prepared."

The production was about to get underway in Miami, people were flying in, Mark was training, so that leaves Luis Esteban. As Sheldon previously mentioned earlier, the screenwriter is the low man on a production and usually left behind. This would not be the case for Luis. "Thanks to Sheldon and Sammy Hadida, they allowed me to be a part of the production. They flew me out to Miami and I was really well taken care of. At the time, Peter Rice was the executive in charge at Fox. He was a really great guy and when the studio had notes, he would fly out, and we would discuss it. Sheldon never had a problem with me sitting down with him and discussing things. It's very rare, even today, to have a writer be that involved in the process. Sheldon recognized that I was prepared and wasn't going to waste his time."

"He was smart and knew we didn't have a whole lot of money and we needed all hands on deck. Sheldon is no idiot, if I hadn't been prepared the way I was, things would have been much different. I would not have been given the access and treatment that I was." Luis helped a bit with the choreography and was in the film. He would make up for the people hired who weren't prepared and not doing their jobs. "I stepped in when needed, when people weren't carrying their weight. Sheldon was very pragmatic and all these things came into play when the film was finished. He wasn't being altruistic in any way and had I messed up, he would have put me on the first plane out of there like he did with someone else."

The person Luis was referring to would be none other than Mr. Frank Dux. Frank's work on the film would be quite disappointing once they actually began rolling cameras. He and Paco scoured the city for martial artists, and found quite a few, most of who had never been on a movie set before. Miami is a very diverse, multicultural city, so they were able to find great choices in every shade and ethnicity, which came in handy because there was a Brazilian gang and a Jamaican gang, and in Miami there was no shortage of either Black or Hispanic martial artists, more like a surplus actually. Frank was also very helpful in training all these fighters, showing them how to do a movie fight, where kicks and punches are being exchanged but no one actually makes contact.

The important part of Frank's Fight Choreography job was figuring out the mechanics of the fights, and specifically how to incorporate capoeira moves into the fight scenes, something that had rarely been done before. Frank always seemed to be missing, especially when Sheldon (as well as the rest of the cast and crew) needed him most. "He had a cell phone, which was a fairly new and uncommon innovation at the time, and it seemed to have become his best friend. Whenever we needed him, we would just listen for the sound of his voice, and he'd inevitably be in the midst of some loud conversation with someone on his cell phone. Had he been talking to someone involved with our production, that might have been okay, but generally he was babbling away to someone who was not part of the production, someone who was not even in South Florida. One evening I was getting ready to call action on a shot – actors and cameras were in place, everything was ready to go – but the Assistant Director, Bob Simon, stopped me short because he spotted someone wandering through our set, off in the distance, completely oblivious, babbling on his cell phone. Of course, it was Frank."

Sheldon did his best to keep his cool but the issues continued. "One day, when he was supposed to be rehearsing a fight with Mark Dacascos and some of the fighters, Frank was nowhere to be found. Fortunately, we had the help of a very experienced (and local) Stunt

Coordinator named Artie Malesci, who had worked on *Miami Vice* and numerous other action shows that had filmed in South Florida over the years. Artie was able to step in, and with Paco and Amen Santo they were able to put their heads together and work out the fight sequence. Frank finally did show up, and rather proudly proclaimed to everyone within hearing distance that he had spent the afternoon wrestling alligators. Seriously!" Frank made it a point to show off the Polaroid photos of himself, posing with some rather pathetic-looking 3-foot long alligators.

To break up the monotony of the difficult days, Frank did provide one very good day, and that was when they filmed the big fight in the chop shop. "Frank and Artie worked out a number of gags, a few of which involved some very dangerous powered cutting tools. We also worked out a gag with a guy in a welding helmet threatening Mark's character with a lit acetylene torch. Frank wanted to be that guy, and I decided to go for it. Frank actually did a pretty decent job, and fortunately Mark was very quick and agile because that torch was lit – no special effects! – and Frank was seriously swinging it at him. You can clearly see it in the film; there were no camera tricks. Frank did his job that day, but there were hardly any capoeira moves in that scene." The fight scene had your typical action movie choreography, typical of the era, but when it was filmed, the entire team came together.

Unfortunately, they didn't have many days like that with Frank; soon Sheldon would begin to hear from others about his lack of work and professionalism. "Mark Dacascos is not a complainer, but he eventually came to me with a number of gripes about Frank. Apparently, when Frank had Mark and Amen's attention, he was supposed to be working out fight scenes with them, and instead he would regale them with tales about himself, about winning the Kumite and all of his other martial arts accomplishments and records, none of which had ever been witnessed or verified. Mark's parents, Al Dacascos and Malia Bernal, were well known martial artists themselves, and consequently Mark had grown up knowing many of his parents' equally famous martial arts friends, legends like Benny "The Jet" Urquidez, Ed Parker, and Don "The Dragon" Wilson, real champions with verified records. Mark pretty quickly figured out that Frank Dux was full of shit, and tolerated him only because Frank was my friend and I had personally chosen him to be the fight choreographer on this movie." Mark would reach a point where he couldn't handle it anymore, and had to speak up and say something.

Esteban chose not to discuss Frank Dux but Mark did air a couple of grievances. "Frank Dux was very nice and personable with me but I actually had to have a conversation with Sheldon about him. As far as I knew, and from what Frank had told me, he didn't know any capoeira. This was one of the reasons I had asked about having Mestre Amen to help with the choreography and technical advising. During preproduction, I had some nice conversations with Frank but it didn't have much to do with capoeira and that's what we were supposed to be discussing. Fortunately for us, Amen took over the position and guided us through."

Luis Esteban knew nothing about capoeira when they started the film. He wasn't sold on it in the beginning, since it's not a street fighters choice. "I trained a lot, I mean a lot, and I never once heard of capoeira. The trick was figuring out how to use it in a street fight. Even today, some people don't think capoeira stands a chance in a street fight. With Sheldon, Mark, and Amen Santos, we overcame all that when we put our heads together. We didn't want to deviate from the beauty of it knowing it's not the first thing to come to mind when getting into a fight on the streets."

Genuine Brazilian capoeira mestre – Joselito Amen Santos – was the teacher who Mark started training with back in Santa Monica; he would continue to do so for the movie. They brought him to Miami, and he would train all the kids there. After Frank, he helped with the choreography as well, finding ways to adapt capoeira moves into the fight scenes. He also found a genuine Brazilian capoeira troupe, headed by Cesar Carneiro, who were all living in Miami. They're the ones who perform some of the spectacular capoeira moves at the beginning of the movie, and also at the end, during the graduation scene.

It was important to everyone involved that the true spirit of capoeira would be captured in the film. It wasn't necessarily an easy task but according to Mark, having Mestre Amen on set to help guide them turned into a real blessing. "Mestre Amen came aboard to make sure everything looked as authentic as possible. Any day I was on set doing capoeira, he would be on set. As a technical advisor, in his opinion, we were doing it right. It's an art form and I think a lot of people look at it as being beautiful and dynamic but not real fighting. All the training and acrobatics is an expression but it also shows you that practitioners are very capable and if it comes down to a fight, they may just come out swinging with elbows or even knees. I was a beginner when we started the movie and I'm still very much a beginner all these years later. I didn't keep up with the intense training I did up to and during the movie. Amen was there with me and really guided me to help with understanding the philosophy of it." He would actually guide them all to make sure the moves, the music, all of it, was authentic and respectable to the art.

For a young actor getting his first big break, Mark was grateful to have someone willing to listen, or collaborate, with him. "Sheldon was the veteran filmmaker who gave me a huge opportunity and I trusted him completely. He was also very open to any ideas. He may not have agreed with everything or said yes but he always let me speak. Initially they weren't sure about having a capoeira technical advisor and didn't know who would play Louis Stevens' capoeira teacher in the movie. They came down to see Mestre Amen Santo at his school and liked him so I suggested that since he was my teacher in real life, why not have him be my teacher in the movie, he could teach all the other actors, and he could be the technical advisor on all this capoeira. Sheldon obviously approved that and Amen was hired. I have nothing but positive things to say about Sheldon and huge gratitude."

Luis' character just kept popping up in the film. Sheldon had fun just throwing him in front of the camera and he enjoyed every minute of it. "Remember the basketball court fight? I launched the whole thing by throwing a basketball at my buddy (Mark). I was not surprised at all about how great the film turned out. I was there every step of the way. All of the moving parts worked in tandem and everything from the colors, the overall composition; even the nature of the fights themselves, everything just worked and they set the tone." It wasn't an expensive film by today's standards but it certainly wasn't cheap either, they tried their best to get every cent on that screen.

Having the negative element removed from the production, everyone else would give their all to make the best film they possibly could. Once filming completed, the production would transition into post. Aside from the editing, the next most important element would be the soundtrack. Sheldon knew how important this next step would be and carefully guided it in the right direction, after a minor misstep. "The original score and the songs were completely separate entities for the movie. Gregory Cascante had met Harvey Mason at his son's school, where Harvey's son was also attending. Harvey was quite a well-known drummer for a jazz group called 4Play, but he had never scored a movie or TV show before. Gregory introduced him to one of our producers, Stuart Shapiro, who had an extensive background in the music business. Harvey has a bubbly and likeable personality, and mentioned to them that he was interested in branching out into film scoring. Stuart and Gregory felt strongly about giving him a shot, so while we were in post-production they introduced me to Harvey and suggested we use him to score our film. Trusting Stuart's musical experience and instincts, I went along with the suggestion, because I also knew that our budget was dwindling at this point, and we'd have a hard time coming up with enough money to hire a known composer, someone who had already scored a few films. Unfortunately, that turned out to be a bad call. Once I began hearing some of his temp tracks for the film, I started to have some serious misgivings about Harvey's ability to score this movie." Sheldon was ready to dump him but Stuart and Gregory begged him to wait until he began to record the actual tracks for the movie; these were only the temps that he had created using a synthesizer.

When the final tracks were done, Sheldon went to the studio where Harvey and an engineer were mixing them down, and again he felt most of them were not what he had envisioned as a score for the movie, and what he heard was simply not going to work. "I told the engineer to separate the various stems, the component parts of the tracks (brass, strings, keyboards, percussion, etc.), so if necessary I would have the option to re-mix and re-work them when we were integrating the score with the dialogue and sound effects. Other more experienced composers had, just as a matter of course, separated the stems, without having to be asked. That's just the way it was done. This engineer fought me, and wanted to mix the stems his way and lock them in stone, leaving no way to alter them later. I asked this guy if he had ever engineered a movie score before, and his resentful lack of a yes or no answer signaled to me that he hadn't. We were in his studio, which was costing us money, and the engineer was being paid by the hour as well. It was too late and would have been too costly to pull the plug on everything, so we just moved forward as best we could. At least the stems were being separated, so if worse came to worst I would have some options when we did the final mix." Thankfully Sheldon fought for that, because during the final mixing stage, he and the music mixer spent hours, even days shuffling and re-working stems to make Harvey's music integrate with what you were seeing on the screen. The only tracks they couldn't fix were the ones that covered the all-important final fight between Mark and Paco.

Eventually, after he showed the final fight with Harvey's music to Stuart and Sammy, everyone agreed that they needed a fresh take on the music, for this all-important final fight if nothing else. They brought on another composer to write and record, on a synthesizer, the music for the climactic battle. He wouldn't be completely pleased with that track either, especially when comparing it to the music for the final fights in *Lionheart* and *Double Impact*, but at least it was still able to hit the action beats and generate some excitement.

When people remember the music from *Only the Strong* they don't think about the score, it's the songs. The person who was most responsible for those great and memorable songs in the movie was their producer, Stuart Shapiro, who had been a concert promoter at one time in his life, and who produced a late night TV show called *Night Flight* (1981-1988). Stuart had a friend named Kao Rossman who lived in Brazil, and had close contacts with many local, indigenous Brazilian musicians and singers. Stuart sent Kao off on a mission to locate some indigenous capoeira-related songs that could be used in the movie. Kao brought a tape recorder along with him on these expeditions, and then sent Stuart a cassette tape filled with songs he'd recorded himself which Sheldon and Stuart would listen to. "We extracted a few that we felt would work in our movie. Among them were "Paranue" and "Zum-Zum-Zum". These were simple songs, with just the rough, non-professional vocals, accompanied by nothing more than a berimbau, a primitive Brazilian instrument that we featured in the movie. Stuart then put his music producer skills to work and added layers to the songs: percussion, horns, or strings, wherever they were needed. Kao re-recorded the vocals with a Brazilian singer named Serapis Bey, at a professional studio in Rio de Janeiro. Stuart mixed all the new tracks together, and he ended up with those spectacular and professional sounding Brazilian songs that we featured in our movie."

"There were non-Brazilian Hip-Hop songs in the movie as well, and those were produced via a Music Supervisor at Fox who went by the name, Mr. Wendell. I believe he's the one who hooked us up with a Miami-based Rapper named Mellow Man Ace, who actually appeared in our movie singing his song, "Babalu Bad Boy" at the high school during the student lunch break, right before Louis's first fight with the Jamaicans." There were so many songs in the movie that Fox actually put out a music CD on their own record label. The CD had none of Harvey Mason's score, but featured every song from the movie, and it did quite well. A few years later, Mazda wanted to use the song, "Zum-Zum-Zum" in their car commercials. The song was very aptly re-titled "Zoom-Zoom-Zoom", and became Mazda's theme song for the next few years, featured in all their radio and TV ads. Stuart Shapiro is credited by BMI as the producer and co-writer, and has made more money from royalties for that song than all the money he's made as a producer on the movie itself.

It was important for many involved to preserve the art of capoeira while still being an exciting film. Fox was hoping to turn Mark into the next action star. Esteban took a step back to reflect on what they wanted to accomplish. "In the late 80s and early 90s there was a barrage of martial artists in film. The action icon was very popular at the time. There were guys like Stallone, Snipes, and Seagal with everyone trying to break the next martial arts star. *Only the Strong* was more in the vein of *The Karate Kid* but nowhere near as successful. It was attempting to be about real people in this difficult circumstance and martial arts would be a natural extension of their lives. We didn't want to see our hero just destroy everyone, it was never about that, it was more about the love of life and art. Mark is just so well versed in what he does and he's such a nice guy you almost forget just how good he really is. I'm proud of the accomplishments he's had in his career and he's done very well for himself and his family. He's just very serious about the beauty of martial arts. Sheldon knew he was doing something very different and not everybody would be on board. We kept it pretty whole-

192 • Corey Danna

some, there's no nudity or swearing, there's one gunshot, and we did this all intentionally.

When the film was released on Aug 27, 1993, it had a very disappointing debut. Fox had done a test screening beforehand, and the audience scores went through the roof, one of the highest scores they had ever seen, something like 95% of the audience gave it a "Very Good" or "Excellent", Fox was very high on the movie, and they prepared a lavish promotional tour. It was something like twelve cities across the U.S. over fifteen days. Mark, Paco, and Sheldon would have gone to all these different cities and would have attended screenings, followed by interviews with the press and other promotional activities. Then they ran into a major roadblock, named *Double Dragon* (1994).

There were numerous possibilities why the film under-performed at the box office. One of them being Mark's commitment to *Double Dragon*, which Sheldon knew all too well. "While we were still in post production, Mark's manager, Catherine Jaymes, had booked him into a lead role in a movie that was ironically being produced by Imperial Entertainment, the same company that had produced *Lionheart*. That movie was titled *Double Dragon*, and it would be based on the video game of the same name. The director was James Yukich, a novice who had only directed music videos before. Plenty of other directors have successfully transitioned from music videos to feature films, but unfortunately he was not to be one of them. The movie was going to be filmed entirely in Cleveland, a city with no infrastructure for filmmaking, and for no other reason than it was the hometown of one of the producers, Alan Schechter, simply because he wanted to be lauded by people he grew up with as a hometown hero. I had warned Mark to hold off, to at least wait until *Only the Strong* debuted, but his manager was anxious to put some additional money in Mark's bank account. She was determined to move forward with *Double Dragon*, assuming all would go well (even with their untried director) and Mark would be wrapped on this movie before *Only the Strong* opened in theaters." Unfortunately, that would not be the case.

From the very first week, the production started running weeks behind schedule, and as a result, millions of dollars over-budget. Those weeks turned into months, and Sheldon knew it would be why Mark could not break away to start doing promotion for *Only the Strong.* "They barely wrapped production on *Double Dragon* in August, which gave Fox a very short window to do any kind of promotion at all. Fox had originally wanted to open our movie in mid-July, at the height of Summer Vacation. We had just barely managed to squeeze a PG-13 rating from the MPAA, for a movie that would be aimed at young audiences and their families, perfect summer fare. As the Fox executives saw that July opening date slipping further and further away, due to the overruns with *Double Dragon,* they began curtailing their big plans for the movie's release, and for their promotion of Mark Dacascos as an upcoming action star." What was originally a twelve-city tour was whittled down to a single city in the U.S., the city of Miami, where they had shot the movie and where locals still had fond memories of the shoot. Fox was left with no choice but to dump it into theaters at the end of August, with hardly any nationwide promotion.

From Mark's point of view, which is predominantly positive, there may have been another factor. "When we initially started the film, we had great support from the studio. By the time we finished, the studio heads had changed and they didn't really support the movie so when it was released to theaters, it was only there for a couple of weeks. The great thing is, capoeira is so dynamic, the music is catchy, and a lot of people like martial arts. So when word got out about this art, the movie kind of spread and grew. I also feel our audience grew was because the film is about more than fighting, it's about people trying to find their way and growing up."

With all the hard work everyone put into the film, it was disappointing to have the film fail at the box office. On a positive note, this would not be the end of it; the legacy of the film was just beginning. One big factor in the film getting a second life was HBO, which for a couple of years in the 90s ran the movie every weekend, in the afternoons, precisely when kids would be watching. This was an unexpected (but welcome) development for Sheldon. "It was a perfect PG-13 action movie for teenaged and pre-teen boys, and for teenage girls as well, who apparently swooned over Mark Dacascos and the other young guys in the movie. With its PG-13 rating it was a relatively safe action movie to screen over and over again on weekends, and it must have been showing some great numbers to the programmers at HBO, otherwise they would not have ran it as often as they did. The result was lots of fond memories in guys who were young teens back in the 90s, and who have maintained those fond memories as they transitioned into their twenties and thirties. Also, it's not one of those movies that you see as a kid, and then when you re-visit it a few years later you wonder why you were ever so enamored with it in the first place. I've watched the movie at special theatrical screenings over the last few years, with audiences that were predominately in their thirties and forties, and for the most part *Only the Strong* holds up quite well. Sure, there's a certain amount of cheesiness, but those action scenes and the genuine Brazilian capoeiristas are quite spectacular. Overall it's a fun experience, and those catchy Brazilian songs are as great as ever."

Only the Strong was the catalyst that launched Mark Dacascos' career and he couldn't be more grateful for the experiences the film has afforded him. "Sheldon had such a passion for the project, and without forcing it, he was very much pro-diversity by bringing different perspectives to the audience. He has such an immense respect for martial arts and different cultures. He really took a chance on myself and all the other young, new actors, and really gave us opportunities. He was a mentor and a supporter of the arts." It's truly amazing to see how this little film many people ignored while in theaters has become so huge. Mark encounters fans wherever he may be. "I was trekking many years ago in Nepal and people had seen *Only the Strong* on laserdisc over there, another time in Kazakhstan, it was brought up over there, everywhere I've gone there's been people who have seen that movie. They talk about the jinga, the music, and how it inspired them. That is such a wonderful tribute to Sheldon and everyone involved. I feel like we put out something so positive."

One goal that was very important to Mark was how the martial arts would be portrayed in the film. Everyone took such care to do just that and looking back now, he feels they accomplished exactly what he wanted to. "We know the martial arts has fantastic moves and all, but for me, martial arts should be holistic. If you're going to know how to fight or hurt people, you should also balance that with respect, humility, discipline, and empathy. I feel like our story really touched those elements. It wasn't about fighting, it was about using martial arts to help open up one's heart and mind so ultimately you can become a better person. To me, being a better person is what the martial arts are about. There's intense training and you can spar without hurting someone. It should be about helping you become a fuller, complete, and kinder person." There's no denying the fact *Only the Strong* has united and inspired people all over the world in exactly the way he hoped.

In a world where some of the most obscure (or even downright horrible) films are getting supreme editions on Blu-ray, *Only the Strong* has yet to be released on the format. It did receive a bare-bones release from Fox on DVD many years ago but this is one film begging to be preserved with extensive special features to be shared from parent to child. It's difficult to pinpoint why this has yet to happen but Luis Esteban can offer up a bit of insight. "The film had multiple people involved in the making of it and I think that's why it's not on Blu-ray but also why a sequel was never done. There were several companies involved and I don't think there was a clear-cut cooperation between the various entities. Mark and I have talked about doing a sequel and there's no shortage of ideas but we just couldn't get it together. My daughter was going to do a campaign for it on Facebook. Just gathering fans from all over the world to show just how much people love the film. It was so touching to me to see people in Spain, Iceland, and Romania who knew about the film. There are just so many hardcore fans of it. I've had people tell me how much the film inspired them and that's exactly what we were going for. I'm so grateful knowing that somehow this film has given so much to so many people and has taught positive values to kids who have carried those values with them and hopefully have helped them in certain aspects in their lives."

Sammy Hadida's French distribution company, Metropolitan Filmexport, put out a 2-disc Collector's Edition DVD a few years after the movie debuted in France. It had quite a few special featurettes, including an interview with Mark Dacascos and featurette about capoeira. Sammy unfortunately died a few years ago, but his brother, Victor, who was also a producer on the movie, may have taken the reins of Sammy's company in Paris. We can only hope someone will put all these featurettes together with the movie (and hopefully some new ones) and release a Blu-ray Collector's Edition sometime in the near future.

After *Only the Strong*, Sheldon found himself in an interesting dilemma, two projects to choose from. First, he was offered a project titled *Heart of Stone*, which was to star Brian Bosworth. Around the same time Sam Raimi and Rob Tapert asked him if he would direct the pilot episode of their *Hercules: The Legendary Journeys* (1995-1999) TV series, which was going to film in New Zealand. He decided that he would rather take the feature film, which was going to shoot in Miami. That turned out to be the wrong choice, because the Bosworth movie got cancelled after he had done a few months' worth of pre-production on it, while *Hercules* and its spinoff, *Xena: Warrior Princess* (1995-2001), went on to become long-running worldwide success stories. "I probably did a big favor to Sam and

Rob by turning down their project, because I didn't like the script, didn't like or even understand the humor, and I probably would have tried to emphasize the action over the silliness. Apparently the silly, tongue-in-cheek humor had a lot to do with that show's success, none of it ever seemed even remotely funny to me. I've never been able to sit through an entire episode of either *Hercules* or *Xena*, but those two shows have millions of fans all over the world."

The Quest

In 1996, Jean-Claude Van Damme released a film he hoped would be the perfect companion piece to his mega-hit debut, *Bloodsport*. *The Quest* (1996) was meant to take the same basic concept and turn it into a lavish, mega-budgeted, action/adventure. Not only would the film be difficult to complete, it would eventually lead to betrayal, the breaking down of friendships, and a lawsuit which was broadcast on television across America. It became a messy situation between Van Damme and Frank Dux, a situation Sheldon would find himself right in the middle of.

Sheldon first had conversations with Jean-Claude about the project in the early 90s, shortly after *Only the Strong* had been released. Jean-Claude and Moshe Diamant were both impressed with the film, and the fact that it had received a theatrical release via 20th Century Fox. The project that would eventually become *The Quest* was initially titled *Enter the New Dragon*, and it was quite obvious they both wanted to produce a bigger, better version of *Bloodsport*, without having to get permission to use the title, and to avoid having to include partners (like Mark DiSalle) to share the profits. Jean-Claude's first offer to Sheldon was to co-write the script and co-direct the movie, which Sheldon politely rejected. "I had a number of reasons for turning that offer down. First of all, I had other producers pursuing my services as well, among them Warner Bothers for *G.I. Joe*. Secondly, I was aware of rumors circulating that Jean-Claude had actually co-directed both *Lionheart* and *Double Impact*, so to be co-directing this movie with him would have only solidified those rumors."

While Sheldon wasn't available to commit to the project as a writer or director, he did help when he could and made a few suggestions. The script had quite a few writers involved, Sheldon included. "Steven Klein is a pseudonym for Gene Quintano, who did not want his name associated with the final film. I'm the one who suggested Frank Dux as a co-writer, since Jean-Claude and I had agreed over the years that Frank had a great imagination, knew a lot about martial arts, and had the potential to be a really good screenwriter, especially for a project of this nature." Frank ended up being hired by Moshe's company, Signature Films, for what would be his first ever gig as a screenwriter. He was paid a fee, and became eligible to join the Writers Guild of America. Since there was no proof, no writing sample, to showcase his writing abilities, Frank was initially paired with a proven screenwriter named Ed Khmara, who had writing credits on a number of movies including *Enemy Mine* (1985), *Ladyhawke* (1985), and *Dragon: The Bruce Lee Story* (1993). After all was said and done, Ed declined to have his name appear on the credits of the finished movie.

Frank would be the co-writer of the very first draft, with Ed. The two of them pretty much created the template for the film. Sheldon would be the one who first suggested the film take place in the past, that way it wouldn't seem too much like a *Bloodsport* clone. It was actually a very dramatic change in concept, because the fighters couldn't just hop on a plane and arrive at the location on the same day. Every one of them had to go on a journey, over land or over water, in order to compete in the tournament. The journey itself became a very important part of every fighter's story.

Sheldon's actual participation on *The Quest*, with the production or otherwise, was basically nothing. After he had turned down the offer, aside from the few suggestions mentioned before, he had very little to do with it. The only other involvement was to suggest a few fighters for the cast. The first would be Takis Trigellis, a Greek martial artist, who ended up also having small roles in *Legionnaire* (1998) and *The Order* (2001). The other one was Brazilian fighter, Cesar Carneiro, who he had worked with on *Only the Strong*. The film went into production and suffered through many difficulties, including going over budget. There would be reports of an unhappy crew, Roger Moore publicly speaking out negatively about the film, about Van Damme, producer Diamant, and so on. It would eventually be completed and released into cinemas on April 26, 1996. With an estimated budget of $30 million dollars, it would have a rather successful run with a worldwide gross of over $57 million dollars. *The Quest* would be Jean-Claude's directorial debut and his final starring role under his five movie contract with Universal Studios. While it seems on the surface the film was a success, the trouble was just about to begin, with a lawsuit filed by Frank Dux against Van Damme.

Frank contended that in the early stages of setting a deal with Jean-Claude and Moshe Diamant that he was to be hired as a writer on the film. Frank contended in his lawsuit that Jean-Claude had verbally promised Frank he would receive some profit participation from the proceeds of the film. The amount promised was either one percent, or one and a half percent. What this means is if the film ends up being $10 million in profit (not an unheard of amount); Frank would be owed $100,000 as his participation. There were no witnesses to this conversation, which took place very informally in Jean-Claude's kitchen. There would later be paperwork and written contracts hammered out by lawyers. These contracts were signed by Moshe, Jean-Claude and by Frank. None of these contracts ever made mention of profit participation. Frank contended that he secretly had a small tape recorder hidden in his pocket, upon which he recorded this promise that Jean-Claude had verbally made to him. It would prove to be a lie; Frank had no tape recorder in his pocket. Even if it had been true, it would have been irrelevant, because a written contract always supersedes an oral promise. Nevertheless, Frank hooked up with a hungry young attorney named Steven Kramer, and they formally sued Jean-Claude for this allegedly overdue profit participation. They were seeking at least $1 million dollars in damages.

Once the trial began, certain things which on the surface should have no relevance were brought up and used in the courtroom. One such incident was the fact Frank Dux briefly dated Van Damme's sister-in-law. Sheldon tried to stay out of it all except he was slowly being pulled into the middle. "Dux had a very brief romance with Denise Portugues, and it was over well before *The Quest* went into production. This later became a major point of contention between Frank and myself, because during the trial, Frank blurted out in court, in front of the judge and jury, that Jean-Claude had betrayed him as a friend because he was lusting after Denise himself. I not only thought this was complete nonsense, but more importantly, it was something that was not provable, and was absolutely irrelevant to the case that was being tried. It was an unforgivably stupid thing for Frank to say, in a court of Law, during a trial that was being broadcast on television, and was fodder for tabloids more than anything else. When I brought this up to Frank afterwards, in private, he vehemently disagreed with me, and this turned into a shouting match between the two of us. On top of all the other lies that Frank had been presenting during the trial, this was the final straw for me. I decided then and there that I could no longer call this guy my friend, and I flat out told him so. That was the end of my friendship with Frank Dux."

Legionnaire was filmed long before the trial. Frank actually felt the fact Sheldon did not direct the movie could be used to get him on his side against Jean-Claude. "I truly was caught in the middle, between two men who had both been my friends, and who had also been business associates. Jean-Claude's attorneys tried to use me as a go-between, and asked me to convey to Steven Kramer that they were offering a $50,000 settlement to Frank to get him to walk away from the lawsuit, an offer which was rejected without a second thought. I also let both parties know that I did not want to be put up on the witness stand, that I wanted nothing to do with this trial, and that I would not be a friendly witness to whichever side served me with papers and forced me to testify. Eventually I was served with papers, by Jean-Claude's attorney, Martin Singer. I reported to the court, as ordered, and took my place on the witness stand, so I was an actual eyewitness to part of the trial. The rest of it I watched on Court TV."

One of Jean-Claude's contentions was the fact he was not a producer on the movie, so he could not have made a valid promise of future compensation to Frank Dux. Steven Kramer countered by holding up a poster of the movie, and asking Sheldon if he could identify one of the Executive Producers listed on the poster, whose name was Eugene Van Varenberg. Of course he would know who that was, Eugene was Jean-Claude's father, and Sheldon stated so for the court. This pretty much blew away Jean-Claude's contention that he had no ties to the film as a producer, but Sheldon was under oath. "He was pissed off at me for years afterwards for answering that question truthfully. This is why I didn't want to be called in to testify, because I knew there would be traps like this waiting for me. Fortunately for me, Jean-Claude won the case, and we were able to eventually reconcile. How could I possibly testify, under oath, that I didn't know who Eugene Van Varenberg was, when I had been friends with Jean-Claude and his entire family for many years?"

Frank's lies were so much more egregious and more transparent as well. The first Big Lie has already been mentioned, which was the falsehood about the concealed tape recorder. Now Frank was in a court of Law, where proof was required rather than just hearsay. He was asked to produce the telltale tape and play it for the judge and jury. Frank didn't have the tape, and he had a very convoluted explanation as to why he couldn't present and play this recording as evidence. According to Frank, he had this tape locked inside a safe, which was securely tucked away inside his San Fernando Valley apartment. When the Northridge Earthquake struck in January of 1994, Frank said his apartment building was so badly damaged that it was condemned by the city. Because of the dangerous conditions, neither he nor any of the tenants were allowed access to their own apartments, for months. When Frank was finally able to gain access to his apartment, he immediately went to his safe to retrieve that important piece of evidence which would prove Jean-Claude had made the profit participation promise to him. Frank would open the safe only to find out it was empty. Someone had cleaned it out during the period of time that Frank was denied entry to his own apartment. The one piece of evidence that Frank needed to make his case had been stolen! Fortunately for Jean-Claude, however, his attorneys managed to track down the woman who had been the apartment manager of Frank's building, both before and after the earthquake. They put her up on the witness stand, and she contradicted everything Frank had been saying about the building being condemned, and about Frank being denied access to his apartment. That would turn out to be the second Big Lie, and it pretty much blew Frank's already-flimsy case out of the water. Not long afterwards, the jury rendered their verdict in favor of Jean-Claude. Case closed. Frank appealed, but lost the appeal as well. Then, to add insult on top of injury, he was ordered to pay Jean-Claude's court costs.

Afterwards, Frank left town with his tail tucked between his legs. He headed up to Seattle, and lived there for a while. Sheldon had moved on, and Frank would be out of his life for good, or so he thought. "I didn't hear from him again for quite some time. Then, in the spring of 2016, there was a screening of *Bloodsport* at the Laemmle NoHo Theater in North Hollywood, and the theater invited me to do an audience Q&A before and after the movie. I accepted the invitation, and I asked Jean-Claude if he wanted to tag along as a surprise guest. Jean-Claude said yes, but we were going to keep it a secret until the actual screening had concluded. Then I received my own big surprise: Frank Dux had contacted the theater, saying to them he wanted to be up on the stage with me for the Q&A, so he could answer questions about the "real Kumite". I immediately backed off, not wanting to be up there in front of an audience with Frank." To this day, Frank has not backed away from his wild tales about winning the Kumite, knocking out fifty two fighters in a row, etc.

Had Sheldon been up there with Frank he would have to make a choice; either agree with everything Frank was saying about himself and his accomplishments, or flat-out say to his face, in front of the audience, "Frank, you're full of shit, none of this is true." Either way, it would have been an awkward situation. "I told the theater management that either I'm up there on the stage, solo, or Frank's up there, but I was not going to be up there standing next to him, nodding agreement with all of his bullshit; either that or getting into an ugly and embarrassing name-calling altercation with him. The theater acceded to my wishes. They could not bar Frank from entering their auditorium, but they had no obligation to invite him up on the stage either." The unfortunate downside of all this was that Jean-Claude quietly bowed out, not wanting to be in the same room with Frank subsequent to their contentious trial.

What's truly unfortunate is that fans of the movie would have had the thrill of their lives had Jean-Claude actually made an appearance that night. Instead they won a lackluster consolation prize in the form of the real Frank Dux, regaling them with tales of how he actually defeated the formidable Chong Li. "I was feeling generous, and allowed Frank to freely speak his mind from his seat in the audience. Not once did I call him out for the bullshit he was spewing about winning the Kumite. Afterwards, he posed for photos with the fans. He even posed for a photo with me and a few of my buddies. That was the last time I saw Frank Dux, in the flesh. Since then he's been spouting various fictions about my contributions to the screenplay of *Bloodsport*, claiming that I had plagiarized the script from an earlier screenplay he had written, which was oddly titled *Return of the Ninja*, and which he has never shown to me or to anyone else, most likely because it doesn't exist. If it somehow does, that title certainly does not seem to promise a story about a martial arts tournament."

One of the most important casualties of the trial would be the deterioration of the friendship between Sheldon and Jean-Claude. Together, they launched their careers and created some historic and beloved cinema, only to have the bond torn apart by someone possibly motivated by greed and fame. As time passed, the dissension between them lessened and Sheldon would finally receive a phone call from an old friend. "A few years after the trial, I unexpectedly received a phone call from Jean-Claude. He told me he had hooked up with producer Brad Krevoy, who had the financing to produce a series of moderately-budgeted movies for Sony, and they were looking for scripts. I pitched him the story for *The Hard Corps*, which I was having no luck in trying to set up with Don Wilson and Leon Isaac Kennedy in the lead roles. Jean-Claude instantly liked the story, about a boxer and his bodyguard, and he told me to get in touch with Brad Krevoy. I emailed the script to Brad, who read it right away, and was very quickly interested in purchasing it and putting it into production. It was that simple." Within days, Sheldon had a deal with Brad, who was also open to letting him direct the movie.

Perfect Target

After the release of *Only the Strong*, Sheldon would be as busy as he had ever been with projects being brought to him. With the way things work in Hollywood, an immediate payoff just wasn't in the cards. "I had been hired by Warner Brothers to write and direct a *G.I. Joe* movie. The studio flew me to Pawtucket, Rhode Island, for a tour of the facilities where Hasbro designed and manufactured all their *G.I. Joe* toys. A few months later, I turned in a first draft screenplay, and then later a revised screenplay which I worked on with my friend, Courtney Joyner. I believe Warner Brothers was under the gun to put the movie into production before a certain deadline had passed. They decided not to move forward with my script." The project eventually fell out of their hands and into limbo for several years, until Paramount acquired the property and finally made their movie, *G.I. Joe: The Rise of Cobra* (2009).

Courtney and Sheldon ended up working together on another screenplay afterwards, a spec titled *Cop War*, which was about a literal shooting war that develops between two rival police precincts. It was a bit of a departure, mainly because it was about cops and had nothing to do with the military. Nonetheless, there was a lot of interest in the script at the time, and there has been interest and options over the years from various producers and studios, among them Albert Ruddy, who produced *The Godfather* films. It was optioned a few years later by Bob Yari's company, and was headed towards pre-production when, like with too many of his other projects, Yari's company abruptly went belly-up.

Another project during this period (early to mid-1990s) was *Hell on Wheels*, which was basically an updated version of the old TV show *The Rat Patrol*, which would have taken place in Iraq during the First Gulf War. Instead of old-fashioned World War Two era Jeeps with center-mounted machine guns, it focused on Fast Attack Vehicles (FAV), which were specialized three-man dune buggies with machine guns or grenade launchers mounted front and rear. They looked like bad-ass G.I. Joe toys, but they were very real, and were actually used by Marines and Navy SEALs to infiltrate into Iraq during the initial war against Saddam Hussein. The script was co-written by Bob Underwood, who had been a writer and producer on many TV shows, but had not yet had a feature film produced.

The script was optioned by Largo Entertainment, producer Larry Gordon's company and they were focused on producing the movie, with Sheldon directing, in Israel, which had the perfect look to double for Iraq, and had plenty of leftover Soviet military vehicles lying around from various wars with their Soviet-supplied Arab neighbors. "I was introduced to an Israeli producer named Jacob Kotzky, who was intended to be the line producer and to set up the production services in Israel. Jacob had already produced a few movies in Israel, including *Iron Eagle II* (1988), and also *Cover-Up* (1991) which starred Dolph Lundgren. We didn't manage to get *Hell on Wheels* off the ground, but a couple years later I would direct *The Last Patrol* (2000) for Jacob, which would star Dolph Lundgren."

It was during this busy period that Jean-Claude approached Sheldon about co-writing and co-directing with him what would turn out to be *The Quest* (1996). The project was initially called *Enter the New Dragon*, and it was intended to be a tournament movie very much in the vein of *Bloodsport*. The producers would be Jean-Claude and Moshe Diamant, and the movie would film somewhere in Asia. "I balked at making a commitment, but not only because I was engaged with a number of other projects at the time. These other producers also wanted me to direct the scripts I had written, but Jean-Claude and Moshe wanted me to co-direct with Jean-Claude. There had been some whispers floating around that Jean-Claude had already co-directed with me, on *Lionheart* and on *Double Impact*. If I agreed to co-direct this new project, it would be confirmation to some of my detractors that I had not been the sole director on those other films, unlike on *Only the Strong* where there was no doubt." He felt it would be best for him and his career if he did not officially engage with this project. However, he assured Jean-Claude that he would not just walk away from him completely and would make himself available to offer advice whenever needed.

One piece of advice Sheldon gave him right away was to have the movie take place in the past, in an earlier era when the various fighters could not just hop on a jet and arrive at the tournament within a day or so, like they did in *Bloodsport*. This would further distance it from *Bloodsport* and not make it seem like such an obvious sequel, especially to a movie that neither he nor Moshe had any sequel rights to. Also, it would be a fresh approach to a tournament movie, especially since so many clones and rip-offs of *Bloodsport* had already been produced. Jean-Claude and Moshe both liked this idea, but since he was too busy with the other projects, they still needed a co-writer to work on a screenplay with Jean-Claude. Sheldon suggested giving Frank Dux a shot.

Jean-Claude and Sheldon had both known Frank for quite a few years, and had worked side by side with him on a few movies. Neither of them gave any credence to his Kumite stories or war stories or CIA stories anymore, but they both agreed he had a vivid imagination, and also possessed a certain amount of knowledge about martial arts. They had both said to one another that if Frank would just write these fantasies down as what they were, fiction, he could do well as a book author, much like Ian Fleming or Tom Clancy. Jean-Claude and Moshe decided to give Frank Dux a shot at being a bona fide screenwriter. Frank had one more factor going in his favor: he didn't as yet have any produced screenwriting credits to his name, so the price to hire him would be cheap.

Just as insurance, Moshe also hired an experienced screenwriter, Ed Khmara who wrote *Dragon: The Bruce Lee Story* (1993), to work with Frank as his writing partner on the project as well as a mentor to guide him along, ensuring that Moshe and Jean-Claude would have a shootable screenplay at the end of this effort. A few other writers were brought in later, Sheldon included, to punch up the script. Ed Khmara could have received a Story credit along with Frank, but he declined. Ed had enough credits already and *The Quest* wasn't a movie that he necessarily wanted to include on his IMDB page.

Sheldon watched as many of the projects he had been working so hard to develop become Hollywood casualties. It was a weird time for action films, right at the beginning of the shift when those big action stars were starting to lose their box office clout. *Perfect Target* (1997) came along right around this time. Starring Daniel Bernhardt, the story follows a mercenary who is hired to head up a security team protecting a foreign president. Unbeknownst to him, the president has been set up for assassination, and the mercenary becomes the fall guy in a race against time to clear his name. It wasn't a script Sheldon had written though it was certainly in his wheelhouse. "I wasn't there at the very beginning; I was brought on sometime later when the producers reached out to agents looking for a director. As far as I know, the project originated when producer Alex Tabrizi hooked up with Daniel Bernhardt, who had already starred in a couple of the very low budget *Bloodsport* sequels for FM Entertainment. Alex found a screenplay called *American Knight*, written by Peter Brosnan & Michael Lanahan, which he felt could serve as a vehicle for Daniel to star in. Alex brought this package to a new company called Quadra Entertainment, which was headed by Christian Halsey Solomon. I had a great initial meeting with them, and also with Daniel Bernhardt. Nobody seemed too enamored by the script, which had some great elements but desperately needed a re-write. The budget was going to be quite low, just a little over $1 million, but they were planning to shoot the entire movie in Puerto Vallarta, a resort town in Mexico, and they assured me that $1 million would go a long way down there. There was a lot of action throughout the story, a chaotic assassination while the president is giving a speech to a crowd, and a big action finale." Action takes time to shoot properly, and time costs money. Sheldon had many misgivings about the project but he hadn't shot a movie in a while, and was tiring of deals falling through, over and over again. He was itching to get back on a set and call "Action!" With nothing else looking remotely promising, he made a deal and signed on.

Shortly after signing on, Sheldon found himself meeting potential crew and casting for actors in Mexico City, then scouting for locations in Puerto Vallarta. This project actually seemed to be moving forward! Although the budget was lower than anything he had ever worked with before, on the positive side, Puerto Vallarta was a beautiful seaside resort town, and he enjoyed all the potential crew people he was meeting with. "I happened to speak a little bit of Spanish, which came in very handy down there. I wasn't unfamiliar with Mexico either. When I was in my 20s, I had a taken a train trip down there with a buddy, to visit another friend who was studying Art at the somewhat famous Instituto Allende in a quaint little Colonial town named San Miguel de Allende, a place where a lot of expatriate Americans have been relocating for the past few decades. I spent quite a bit of time exploring Mexico, seeing the good, the bad, and the ugly, traveling around via buses and trains, and made it as far south as Oaxaca. When I finally got back to the States I found myself coming down with a case of hepatitis (Type "A"), most likely from eating food made and sold by indigenous street vendors. I'd come down with something that felt similar during my year in Vietnam, and foolishly thought I'd somehow developed an immunity to foodborne microbes, whether in Southeast Asia or Latin America. I learned the hard way that I'm no Anthony Bourdain, and haven't made that sort of mistake since."

The script wasn't quite where it needed to be right before filming started. There needed to be another pass before things really started getting under way. Though Sheldon did contribute quite a bit to the shooting script, he didn't have a writing credit on the film. The problem was that the producers did not want to go signatory with the Writers Guild, although they agreed to be signatory to the Directors Guild, as Sheldon explains it. "I was introduced by the producers to George Saunders, a non-WGA writer who did most of the re-writing on the script, and is credited as a Screenwriter on the film. George and I ended up becoming good friends, and we wrote a number of spec screenplays together, one of which, *The Hard Corps* (2006), I ended up directing a few years afterwards, with Jean-Claude and Vivica Fox in the lead roles."

George Saunders began his career as a professional ballet dancer, having appeared on Broadway in South and North American dance companies. While attending Juilliard, he trained to be an actor. After moving out to Los Angeles, he fell in love with film and screenwriting, a move that would quickly earn him a lifelong friend. "Sheldon was already attached to direct *Perfect Target* and the script wasn't usable. They needed someone to come in and re-write it quickly. With Sheldon's direction and input, I came up with a new draft in about ten days. This was the draft they used to shoot the film in Puerto Vallarta. Our first meeting was very professional at first but over the years has grown into a great friendship."

There was an instant connection between the two collaborators which found its footing on this particular film. George explains the situation a bit more and outlines how their collaborations work. "I'm not sure why Sheldon chose not to do the re-write; it may have just been suggested that way by the production company. I had submitted a script which the director of development had passed to Sheldon. He must of saw something in it, noticed that I could write action and he may have been too busy figuring out the logistical issues of the film. Since then we've worked on numerous projects together. For this film, I would go in first then pass it to him; he would take a crack, and then pass it to me. It seems to work best for us when we went back and forth. It was a bilateral kind of relationship in terms of writing scripts. I want it known that it really was a collaborative effort between Sheldon and I."

Daniel Bernhardt was already attached to the film before Sheldon came on board and the producers wanted full control over the casting. Sheldon had developed the role of Miguel Rodriguez specifically for his friend, Paco Prieto, who had done an amazing job as the main villain in *Only the Strong*. The producers did not feel Paco was a strong enough actor. "Daniel Bernhardt had met him before, probably at my house, and seemed to have developed some kind of personal issues with him. Eventually I acquiesced to casting Jim Pirri in the role, and he did a terrific job in the movie, but did not have the same kind of magnetic screen presence that Paco had. I also did not cast Dara Tomanovich. There were a couple other actresses that I had auditioned in Los Angeles, who were my choices, but the producers nixed those, and Dara just showed up in Mexico one day, unaware that I had not even seen an audition tape from her. Nowadays there would be an uproar over casting a Serbian in a role designed for a Hispanic actress. You'd think one could find an appropriate Hispanic actress in either Los Angeles or Mexico, right? Dara wasn't my choice, but she did a pretty decent job, after all."

The Casting Director in Los Angeles was Jim Tarzia, who had also cast Sheldon's previous movies. He had already cast Brian Thompson, as Major Oxnard. In their defense, however, they did send Robert Englund to play Shackwell, and that worked out just great. Most of the smaller roles were cast in Mexico City by Claudia Becker, who had been a long-time fixture in the Mexican film industry. She's the one who brought in Julieta Rossen, who was a very popular TV star in Mexico. When Julieta arrived for her audition, she actually had a couple of bodyguards alongside her, proof of her popularity throughout Latin America. For the role of Presidente Cassilas, Claudia brought Mario Ivan Martinez, who played the Doctor in *Like Water for Chocolate* (1992). Every time they had a casting session, Claudia would have lunch brought in to her office, and during one of these lunches she introduced Sheldon to Herradura 100% blue agave Mexican tequila. He would never touch Jose Cuervo again.

While the producers held control over Sheldon in regards to casting, he was still able to bring in Brian Thompson, who was excited to be back working with his pal. "*Perfect Target* was a marvelous coming together of a team. Robert Englund is such an excellent actor and he was always about doing the best job possible. It was great just being in Mexico together, partying together, collaborating on the set together, so I think on this set more than the others Sheldon and I did together, there was a real sense of team work and effort. When you're a supporting actor, you get quite a few days off so I hope Sheldon was able to enjoy some of that as much as I did. Being a supporting actor is the best job on the planet. Especially if you're shooting on location and in great weather, you'll shoot a day or two, and then you'll get like three or four to memorize lines. This has been my experience on almost every film I've worked on. The lead actors get their asses handed to them, people may think they're being selfish when they say they're too busy or don't have time to socialize but their batteries get drained so quickly. Some of those performers will work so hard and never get a day off because that's who the audience wants to see. They're putting in twelve to fourteen hours a day all while trying to memorize their lines for the next day. It's all they have time for and it's really exhausting. Daniel really put in all that work on *Perfect Target*."

Daniel and Sheldon would become pretty good friends during and after the shoot. He and Sheldon came up with another project titled *The Tough Guy*, about an action star (like Daniel or Van Damme) who's working on an action movie that's so low budget that the producers can't afford a stunt double for the star. On location they happen upon a real tough guy who just so happens to be a ringer for the star, and they recruit him to be the star's action double. The double gets mistaken for the real actor when some criminals kidnap him in order to demand a ransom from the producers. Now the movie star has to step up and become a genuine tough guy in order to rescue his double from the bad guys. Daniel and Sheldon liked this idea so much; they actually sat down together and wrote it up as a screenplay.

Daniel had some contacts in his home country of Switzerland who were interested in turning *The Tough Guy* into a movie, with Daniel both directing and starring. Sheldon had the opportunity to spend a couple of weeks in Zurich with Daniel, meeting with these folks who were interested in turning this script into a movie. They even went so far as to actually purchase (not just option) the screenplay from them. Around the same time there was a very wealthy European businessman named Alberto Lensi who had purchased the rights and the title to *Bloodsport*, and who wanted to make a reboot of the original movie which would have been titled *Bloodsport: A New Beginning*. Alberto and his wife, Heidi, had a magnificent chalet in the Swiss ski resort town of Stadt, in addition to homes in Paris, New York, and Miami; these folks were loaded. Sheldon seems quite sure they could have bankrolled the movie without having to get bank loans or find outside financing. After they visited with them in Stadt, Alberto hired Sheldon to write the screenplay. Daniel would have directed and starred in the movie.

Then complications began to set in (as they nearly always do). Realizing he was going to be on the hook for quite a bit of money if he financed this movie out of his own pocket, Alberto told Daniel and Sheldon that he would only move forward with the production of the movie if he had some assurance that it would open theatrically, and not just go straight to video. Sheldon told him that the only way to assure a theatrical release for a movie with *Bloodsport* in its title was to have Van Damme star in the movie. Daniel Bernhardt's name was not enough to guarantee a theatrical release, and they all knew that. "Alberto wanted me to call Van Damme. I explained to him that I hadn't spoken to Jean-Claude in a while, and besides that, Jean-Claude had reached such a pinnacle in his career, that I didn't think he would want to go backwards and star in a re-boot of the first movie that had put him on the map, many years ago. Nevertheless, without Van Damme, I didn't see how this movie could open theatrically. We pretty much left it there, with Daniel still pushing to get this movie made with him both starring and directing. Despite the fact there had already been a few *Bloodsport* sequels, with Daniel starring in them, and they had all gone straight to video."

A few months later, Sheldon was back in Los Angeles. Coincidentally, Alberto was in Los Angeles as well. They spoke on the phone, and discussed getting together for a drink, just to reconnect and maybe toss around some other options for the *Bloodsport* project. Daniel was out of town. He had been hired by Nu Image to star in a low budget tornado movie for them, which was currently filming in Bulgaria. It was just going to be Sheldon and Alberto, or so he thought. "Then, out of the blue, Jean-Claude called me! He was in Los Angeles too, staying at his condo in Santa Monica, and wondered if I might have some time to get together with him that same evening. I was nearly speechless, but after catching my breath I managed to ask Jean-Claude if he might possibly have any interest in a re-boot of *Bloodsport*. Now it was Jean-Claude's turn to catch his breath, and his response to me was something like "Hell yes!" I was very wrong when I speculated that Jean-Claude wouldn't be interested in re-visiting *Bloodsport*. I explained to him what the situation was with Alberto Lensi. Jean-Claude's first question to me was "Are you sure this guy has the rights?" I suggested that Jean-Claude could ask the man himself, because he was in town, and had even planned to have a drink with me that very evening. I was sitting in a small café in Santa Monica, talking with my cell phone when all this transpired. Within minutes I was back on the phone with Alberto, and we agreed to meet at Madeo, an upscale Italian restaurant on the edge of Beverly Hills that was very popular with agents and actors, mainly because it was on the ground floor of the building that housed the very powerful ICM agency. I had been to Madeo before with Jean-Claude, and knew he would feel comfortable having a meeting there. I tried to call Daniel in Bulgaria, but was unable to reach him on his local cell phone. I figured it might also make more sense to try and call him again, after the meeting, when I might know if Jean-Claude was actually on board with Alberto and with this project."

Jean-Claude, Alberto, and Sheldon met for their meeting at Madeo, and after exchanging a few pleasantries, Jean-Claude got down to business and politely asked Alberto for proof that he actually owned the rights. Alberto assured him that he did. He was represented by the very prestigious law firm of Loeb & Loeb, which was nearby in Century City, and suggested that Jean-Claude could have his own attorneys call Alberto's people in the morning to get all the necessary proof in the form of signed documents. Jean-Claude had met plenty of bullshitters and pretenders in the movie business, and could sense that this guy was not of that species. The two of them quickly began feeling comfortable with one another.

Jean –Claude had another very important question. "Who is going to direct the film?"

Alberto seemed to intuit that Jean-Claude was not going to like his answer, but he had to tell him what deal had been struck with Daniel. The deal, Alberto explained, was that Daniel would both star and direct, but of course that would have to be modified if Van Damme was going to be the star of the movie. This would still leave Daniel as the director.

There was a long pensive moment, Jean-Claude asked the next obvious question, "Why isn't Sheldon directing?"

This left Sheldon in a very awkward quandary. Daniel wasn't there at the meeting; he was on the other side of the world, not currently reachable by phone. He wasn't able to make an appeal on his own behalf. Even if he had been there, Jean-Claude was being asked to star in a movie with an unproven director. More than just the lack of experience, Daniel was also an actor who had stepped into Jean-Claude's shoes for those sequels to his own movie; the whole situation wasn't exactly how Sheldon imagined it would go. Jean-Claude and Daniel had never met before. Sitting there in Madeo, face to face with Alberto, how could Jean-Claude have been expected to say yes? "Everything about the situation was awkward. On the other hand, I had directed two of Van Damme's most successful and popular movies, and the two of us were still good friends, as evidenced by the fact that I was one of the first people he phoned when he got into town. Eventually, Jean-Claude point-blank told Alberto that if he agreed to star in the movie, Daniel would not be directing it. He made no demands that I should direct the movie, but pretty much signaled that he would be comfortable with that arrangement."

With all that business out of the way, and Jean-Claude having made his decision, Sheldon asked the guys, "Who's going to call Daniel and tell him?"

Alberto gave that unpleasant task to Sheldon. "After our meeting, I tried calling Daniel in Bulgaria again, and this time I got through to him. Needless to say, Daniel did not take the news very well. To him it all sounded like a set-up, that I had moved all the chess pieces into place while he was conveniently out of the country. I tried to explain the circumstances that led to our meeting, but he wasn't buying it; it all sounded too coincidental and convenient. Daniel had introduced me to Alberto and had brought me on board to write the script, a job that I was being paid for. From Daniel's point of view, it looked like I was re-paying him by stabbing him in the back. Our friendship was never quite the same after that."

Alberto's attorneys did send all the pertinent paperwork to Jean-Claude's attorneys, who were able to verify that he did indeed own the rights to *Bloodsport*. Jean-Claude and Alberto then had contracts drawn up which solidified their business relationship, and the fact that Van Damme would be the star of the movie. Sheldon was ostensibly on board as the director, though there were never any contracts drawn up or signed; Alberto was keeping his options open, but it seemed very unlikely that Daniel would again be given the opportunity to direct. Alberto and Jean-Claude then tried to raise financing from various sources, but were not able to come up with a sufficient budget to insure a theatrical release. Van Damme was no longer quite the box office draw that he used to be, though they could have raised enough money to make the movie, just not quite as much as Jean-Claude was hoping for.

Then a new problem cropped up. Daniel wanted Sheldon to give him a co-writing credit on the script. "It's true that Daniel worked somewhat closely with me while I was writing the script, but putting his name on a script that was under the jurisdiction of the Writers Guild, after the fact, would not have been a simple matter. There were signed contracts which stated that I was being hired to write the screenplay, without any co-writers. There had been checks issued to me, and only me, for these writing services. The Writers Guild is very protective of their members, and they simply would not have gone along with this, not without thinking that the producer was unfairly twisting my arm. I explained to Daniel that this simply would not have been possible at this late stage in the game, he just wasn't buying that. It seemed to me that he wanted some form of compensation for being pushed out as director. We had all promised him a prominent co-starring role in the movie, but that wasn't quite enough for him. He started telling Alberto that the script was not very good, even though he had been praising it before. He finally convinced Alberto that another writer needed to be brought on board, to do a complete re-write of the screenplay.

Alberto did eventually bring on another writer, who did a complete top-to-bottom re-write, and also re-titled the script *Bloodsport: Death for Life*." Things just kept going steadily downhill from there. Eventually Alberto was introduced to Edward R. Pressman, who also came on board as a producer. Sheldon was no longer the director, and Jean-Claude was no longer guaranteed to be the star of the movie. The project took even more twists and turns. Robert Mark Kamen, who wrote *The Karate Kid* (1984) and *Taken* (2008), was hired to do a completely new draft of the screenplay. The story now took place in South America, and the protagonist was a veteran of the war in Afghanistan. A new director was brought on board, and then another one. Alberto and Ed were spending lots of money, but eventually the project went nowhere and simply appears to be in limbo, although it is still listed on IMDB, with Alberto Lensi and Ed Pressman as producers.

Getting back to *Perfect Target*, Sheldon would have a certain amount of free reign, as long he stayed within the budgetary parameters. The producers went along with the biggest request, which was to have a full Second Unit shooting simultaneously alongside the First Unit, much in the same way he did on *Double Impact*. "As I recall, our shooting schedule was a paltry twenty days, which I was able to stretch to forty days by having a Second Unit shooting for those same twenty days as well. Our schedule seemed so impossible that the Bond company insisted that they have a representative with us, on set, for the entire schedule. Amazingly, because of good and precise planning, and because I had some very talented people like Chad Stahelski as Fight Choreographer and Philip Tan as Second Unit Director, we managed to pull it off." Chad would go on to direct the *John Wick* (2014) and it's sequels. Our Second Assistant Director, Patricia Riggen, went on to direct *The 33* (2015), a feature film starring Antonio Banderas, and many TV series after that.

Sheldon has nothing but praise for the stuntman turned director. "Chad Stahelski is beyond a doubt the best Fight Choreographer

I've ever worked with. He would work out actual shot lists for a fight on small pieces of paper, keep those in his pocket, then pull them out and refer to them. The fights were worked out ahead of time, in his head, and then he would stick to his vision, shot by shot. He's also one hell of a stuntman, and did all the doubling for Jim Pirri. There was a lot of doubling for Jim, because he was not a fighter. When we did a fight scene, I would shoot the dialogue that leads up to the fight, and then shoot the aftermath when the fight is over. Once the punches and kicks started flying, I would pretty much just stay out of Chad's way. During the water fight in the stream, I operated a third hand-held camera just to get a few wide shots to pull back from the more detailed fight moves. I rarely, if ever, butted in to say something about the camera angles."

Chad was introduced to Sheldon by Daniel Bernhardt, who had worked with him on two of the *Bloodsport* sequels. He brought along a young protégé named David Leitch, who wanted to learn the stunt trade. This was one of David's first movies, but he would later go on to double Van Damme in *Replicant* (2001), and then in *The Order* (2001). David and Chad are now a couple of the most sought-after directors in the film business." It's no wonder the action scenes look so awesome in this movie, there was some amazing talent on that crew.

Brian Thompson remembers his time working with the duo quite fondly, as well as a few interesting little details about their relationship. "David Leitch doubled Jean-Claude and Chad Stahelski did stunts and choreography. David had just stopped teaching school; he was a school teacher before getting into film. He and Chad had just started working together in some capacity, I don't remember the whole story, but those guys are great."

Chad Stahelski is an absolute genius when putting fight scenes together. For the big action scenes, the entire action team would escort Sheldon to scout the locations. This team consisted of Chad, Philip Tan (Second Unit director), Julian Bucio (local Mexican Stunt Coordinator), and Tim Rigby (Bernhardt's stunt double). They walked the locations and figured out where the various stunt gags were going to take place. Many of these gags were in the script already, but some were improvised on the spot because they had found something cool, something that was just calling out for a stunt. Sheldon would do a re-write afterwards and incorporate those new gags into the script, so by the time they got to the set with cameras and cast, most of it was actually written down in the script pages.

As an interesting side note, the Second Unit Director on the film, Phillip Tan, his son, Lewis Tan, played Cole Young in *Mortal Combat* (2021). Lewis and his mom were on location the entire time they were in Puerto Vallarta. Lewis would hang out with Sheldon's daughters every day at the hotel swimming pool, especially bonding with his youngest daughter, Angelique, who was the same age as him. Angelique went on to be the youngest co-star in *The Last Patrol*, and had a couple of dialogue scenes with Dolph Lundgren in that movie.

As mentioned before in the book, screenwriters usually get the short end of the stick and once their job is done, their involvement in the production is usually limited. George Saunders was given the opportunity many screenwriters never get. "Sheldon was busy in the jungles with the actors but I was there on set for most of the shoot. The movie was masterfully done, with some intense action and the opening sequence, as cruel as it was, the cock fight was really a nice touch. I was fairly new to screenwriting at that time and under Sheldon's auspices, it was structured very well. I had only been in the business five or six years so it was a really important film for me."

Overall, everyone had a very positive experience shooting in Mexico. One thing that really stood out to Sheldon was the actors union, Asociación Nacional de **Actores** (ANDA). They have a union representative on-set every day, not just to make sure the actors are being treated well, but also to make sure the actors themselves are behaving and doing their job. Apparently, if an actor is late to the set, that actor gets fined by the union.

As promised up front, there was an amazing amount of production value and the team was able to complete principal photography on schedule, in twenty days, days which were filled with fights and big action scenes. They filmed in the very center of Puerto Vallarta, in the town square and all over their historic cathedral, and never had any issues getting the sets cleared of locals for the big action moments. Compared to filming in cities like Hong Kong and Jerusalem, Puerto Vallarta was a dream come true for the filmmaker. This was ostensibly a tourist town which is dependent on keeping foreign tourists happy. Never was there a single issue, never had to pay a bribe to police, or to shopkeepers for cooperation.

They also had some amazing local cast and crew. The Second Assistant Director, Patricia Riggin, went on to become a respected director herself. The Steadicam Operator and Second Unit Director of Photography (DOP), Checco Varese, went on to be Patricia's DOP. on *The 33*, then moved on to be the DOP on a number of American TV shows, and most recently was the DOP on *It: Chapter Two* (2019).

Unfortunately, Daniel Bernhardt was not enough of a name to get a theatrical release, so the movie went straight to video, everywhere. It's quite possible that there were never any theatrical prints struck. The movie was not any kind of success, and even though it was DGA signatory, Sheldon doesn't recall receiving any more than a single Director's residual from ancillary after-markets. Which is a shame, *Perfect Target* is an excellent action picture, one that deserves to be seen and appreciated.

Legionnaire

The French Foreign Legion has much in common with the U.S. Marines. Both are relatively small, elite units, made up of an eclectic collection of misfits, iconoclasts, and non-conformists. The Marines are often the shock troops of the American military, and the Legion serves a similar role for France. They've both been given the dirty jobs, the dangerous, potentially high-casualty missions that the regular Army would prefer to keep their distance from. Being a former U.S. Marine himself, the French Legionnaires would feel like cousins wearing a different uniform to him.

The French Foreign Legion script Sheldon wrote for Sylvester Stallone took place in the present day, and was about a couple of American guys who join the French Legion on a lark. It was an idea Stallone had come up with on his own. The script Sheldon would really want to write took place during the "classic" period of the Legion – late 19th and early 20th Century – famous for inspiring novels like *Beau Geste* and the movies that were subsequently based on those. That's the movie that Van Damme and Sheldon would make with *Legionnaire* (1998).

They actually began discussing a French Foreign Legion movie for Van Damme around the time they first met, which was right around the time Sheldon was working on the script for Stallone. Ironically, he and Jean-Claude did end up making a contemporary Foreign Legion story with *Lionheart*, which had him playing a Legionnaire who deserts in order to help his family in America. That was a very different type of a role for him, when compared to the more simplistic roles he was given at that time, like in *Bloodsport*, and *Kickboxer*. Even after they made *Lionheart*, Sheldon would keep after him with the notion he had about a classic French

Foreign Legion story, which they both agreed would be a perfect role for him. Perfect, but different than anything else that was being offered to him.

Around 1992, Jean-Claude was hired to star in *Street Fighter* (1995), which was being financed by Capcom, the Japanese company that owned the *Street Fighter* arcade game franchise. Ed Pressman was hired by Capcom to produce the film, and Universal Pictures was hired by Capcom to distribute the movie worldwide. After meeting Jean-Claude, and realizing just how popular he was all over the world, Ed began pressing Jean-Claude for another movie to do after *Street Fighter*, one that Ed would be producing on his own. He asked Jean-Claude if there were any scripts he was interested in pursuing. Jean-Claude would go to Sheldon and mention that Ed Pressman was looking for another project. It doesn't matter who spoke up first, but they quickly realized that now might be the time to finally get their Foreign Legion project off the ground.

They quickly came up with a basic storyline, which would take place in the 1920's. Jean-Claude's character, Alain LeFevre, would be a playboy bon-vivant, who inadvertently hits on the girlfriend of a ruthless Mafioso in 1920's Marseilles. The Mafioso and his henchman come after Alain, intending to kill him. He ends up joining the Foreign Legion, in order to adopt a new identity and flee the country. Jean-Claude and Sheldon came up with the three multinational characters who he befriends once he's in the Legion and safely in North Africa. The Mafioso then orders a couple of his thugs to join the Legion, and to use that cover to track down Alain wherever he might be. There's a big battle near the end, similar to the battles in *Beau Geste* (1966) and other Foreign Legion movies. After the battle is over, Alain and one of his new buddies travel back to Marseilles to rescue the girl.

They pitched this story to Ed Pressman and his production associate, Allesandro Camon, and very quickly a deal was in place. Sheldon was hired to co-write the screenplay with Jean-Claude, and was also hired to direct the movie. Within a few weeks, he began reading every book he could get his hands on about the French Foreign Legion. Much later on, he brought on his pal Boaz Yakin, to do a re-write. The project was set to be epic, until things went south. "I always felt really bad about what happened on that film with Sheldon. He was set to direct it, and I did this epic re-write on it that both he and Jean-Claude loved. It was set to be a real movie-movie and could have been one of Jean-Claude's best films. There were some cheesy filmmakers that really shafted Sheldon on the budget then went behind his back and brought on Peter MacDonald to direct. It was just a shady deal that was all about budget and only wanting something that was purely a genre film, nothing more." The movie sits very uncomfortably between wanting to be an old school adventure film and a more fast-paced 80s actioner. "Sheldon deserved to be able to make that film the way he had envisioned it and the way we wrote it. It's always made me sad."

Another screenwriter, Rebecca Morrison, was brought in by the producers to do yet another re-write. For Sheldon, things were beginning to unravel and this would be the first nail. "Rebecca Morrison added this "tragic love story" element; a somewhat hackneyed plot device about a woman whose fiancé leaves her abandoned at the altar. I had wanted the movie to be more of a straight forward action story, with the character of Katrina basically being the catalyst for the plot to kick into gear, and later the damsel in distress who has to be rescued from Galgani, the powerful mafia boss who has taken her captive and forced her into sexual servitude. My version of the movie had Alain returning to Marseilles to rescue Katrina, which would have entailed a big gun battle with Galgani and his minions. Peter never wanted that ending, and preferred a much more peaceful resolution, with Alain just walking into the nightclub, taking Katrina by the hand, and simply walking out with her, with no opposition from Galgani or his henchmen. Obviously, this ending was about as wrong as it could be for a 90s action movie with an action star like Van Damme. That would be the ending Peter shot after he pushed me off the movie. Of course it didn't work, which is why the editors had to concoct a way to abruptly end the story in Morocco after the big battle at the fort." More than any other factor, this is why the movie had a very limited theatrical release; it didn't have an ending. The entire story sets up Alain's eventual rescue of Katrina. In the released version of the movie, Alain never even sees Katrina again after he's left France, except in flashbacks. There's absolutely no payoff for the audience, especially for a mid-90's audience that's expecting a big action finale.

There was no real collaboration between Sheldon and Rebecca. She had previously worked as a Story Consultant with producer Christian Halsey Solomon at Quadra Entertainment, the same company that produced *Perfect Target*. "*Legionnaire* was in the works before I had ever met either Christian or Rebecca. I'm the one who first told Christian about the *Legionnaire* project, and introduced him to Ed Pressman. Christian talked his way into becoming a producer on *Legionnaire*, and brought Rebecca along with him. She was basically a wannabe screenwriter, and saw this as an opportunity to be hired as a bona fide writer, with WGA residuals on the back end. The real, genuine screenwriter who was brought on was my friend Boaz Yakin, who didn't need to come to location, and did all his work on the script from his home in Los Angeles." Rebecca's career went nowhere afterwards. She was hired to do some work on a straight-to-video Mark Dacascos movie, and that was pretty much the last anybody heard of her in the business.

The big question then is why did Van Damme allow Peter and Rebecca to get away with destroying their story the way they did? Sheldon is one of the only people close enough to Van Damme at the time to have an answer. "It was drugs, specifically cocaine, which Van Damme was seriously addicted to at the time. It's no secret; it was all over the tabloids and movie fan sites at the time. Everybody knew about it. He's admitted it many times, most famously in his movie *JCVD* (2008), where he confesses at length, on-camera, about drug addiction derailing his career. Sadly, I witnessed it first-hand, how he couldn't focus on anything beyond his next hit of coke. Of course, Peter saw that quite clearly as well, but he used the addiction to manipulate Jean-Claude to his own selfish ends."

Peter apparently used the same maneuvers on Russell Mulcahy, and had Russell pushed off of *Rambo III* after just a couple weeks of shooting. The big difference between the *Rambo* movie and *Legionnaire* was that Sylvester Stallone was not on drugs (and never had been) and was able to maintain firm control over the script (which he co-wrote with Sheldon) and over Peter. The Israeli crew who worked on the film would later collaborate with Sheldon on *The Last Patrol* (2000) and *The Order* (2001), and would confirm what happened. "From what they told me, Stallone was the de facto director of the movie, and Peter was basically functioning as a glorified 2nd Unit Director. They also told me how Peter was constantly undermining and back-biting Russell in every way he could, same as he did to me during the pre-production of *Legionnaire* in Morocco. Ironically, Russell and I have both gone on to direct other feature films, while Peter has simply defaulted back to being a 2nd Unit and TV director."

"Peter MacDonald was coerced upon us as a 2nd Unit Director and additional producer, mostly because he was represented by the same agents as Jean-Claude at the time. Peter and his agents viewed this project as an opportunity to get himself bumped from 2nd Unit to the actual director of the movie, same as with *Rambo III*. That intention was quite obvious from the moment Peter came on board. He would not allow me to hire any crew people I had worked with in the past. I wanted my friend, Edward Pei, who shot *Only the Strong*, to be my cinematographer on this one too. Ed was both available and affordable. Instead, I was forced to use Peter's buddy, Doug Milsome. In nearly every case I was forced to use former associates and friends of Peter MacDonald, who was very methodically stacking the deck against me and setting himself up to take over. One choice I was able to make on my own was Lee Cleary, for 1st Assistant Director. I had never worked with Lee before, but I interviewed him in London, and the two us hit it off. He was very supportive of me the entire time we were scouting in Morocco, and pushed back on Peter's interference many times." When Sheldon was finally dismissed from the production, Lee quit the very next day, which left the production in turmoil until they could find a suitable replacement. Lee has since gone on to be the 1st A.D. on some of the big Marvel movies like *X-men* (2000) and *Fantastic Four* (2005).

Sheldon had been far more involved with this particular project since he had originally been hired to direct as well as write the script. He spent a good year working on this project, both researching and writing the script, and then going on scouting expeditions all throughout Morocco and France. "I selected the costumes at a costume house in England, and also all the weapons that would be used in the movie. I was also involved with casting the supporting actors, most of whom I interviewed in England with Casting Director Irene Lamb (who was famous for casting the first two *Star Wars* movies). I chose all the locations that were used in Morocco, and even made shot-lists and set up shots during pre-production scouts, which Peter tagged along on. What was especially galling to me was that Peter then used all these set ups, after surreptitiously disparaging my directing abilities to Ed Pressman and the other producers. The ambush at the water hole was basically laid out by me, and then Peter simply followed my plan, almost verbatim, as a 2nd Unit Director would be expected to do."

The film opened theatrically in a number of European countries: France, Germany, Spain, Hungary, Romania, and a few others. Sheldon did receive writers' residuals over the years which brought in decent after-market money. Not nearly as much as something like *Bloodsport* or *Double Impact* but respectable. It actually brought in more residuals than *Lionheart*. One can only speculate what could have been had Sheldon's original vision been brought to the screen. "I would have given it the big action-filled ending that it so desperately needed. I wrote different versions of the ending, based upon which of the guys would have gone back with Alain. I had a version where Mackintosh goes back with him, another version where one of Galgani's henchmen has a change of heart and goes back with Alain to rescue his girl. I reverted to my old *Rambo* paradigm where my protagonist, now "battle-hardened," returns to the civilian world after serving as a soldier in a war zone, and brings his military skills with him to take care of an unresolved issue. I'm quite sure that the audience would have found that much more satisfying than the lukewarm non-ending that Peter MacDonald gave them."

In the early 90s, sometime after *Only the Strong*, 20th Century Fox sent Sheldon a script to consider as a director, which was titled *Speed*. "I had a meeting with a couple of executives there to discuss my take on the project, which I liked very much. I asked who they were considering to star in the movie, and was surprised when they answered that they were considering Keanau Reeves. The guy who co-starred in *Bill and Ted's Excellent Adventure* (1989), a goofy comedy, was being considered as the star of a big action movie? I was taken aback by this response, as we were still in the era of big muscled, hyper-macho action stars like Stallone, Schwarzenegger, and Van Damme. Apparently the studios were shifting their paradigm for action heroes. Rather than going with guys who had big muscles and karate skills, but no previous acting experience, they decided they would go with real actors to star in their movies, and teach them the necessary karate and action skills, whatever they couldn't be taught, the studios would fill in with stuntmen and action doubles."

This quickly became the new standard. The studios would cast an actor like Matt Damon to play an action hero like Jason Bourne, and then teach him enough martial arts and fighting skills to play a believable CIA super-agent. Much of the action, however, would be filled in by stuntmen and action doubles. There would be lots of fast cuts to disguise the fact that they were using doubles. There would be no more of those long drawn out, slow-motion action moves like the ones that Van Damme was famous for. If slow-motion was needed, like the "Bullet Time" sequence in *The Matrix* (1999), then special effects trickery and computer graphics would take over and create something unique that would surpass all of Van Damme's real-world karate skills. This new standard was made even more convenient for the studios when they began churning out super-hero movies, because now nearly all the characters were wearing masks and costumes. The actors portraying Batman or Captain America don't even need to take karate lessons anymore, no need to fake it if stuntmen disguised by masks and costumes are doing all the on-screen fighting.

Around this time would mark the shift to when actors were transformed into action stars. The days of seeing guys like Van Damme or Lundgren on the big screen were replaced with actors like Keanu Reeves or Nicholas Cage. Sheldon's long-time friend and collaborator George Saunders has his own idea of how the change came about. "When the new millennium came in with Keanu Reeves doing *The Matrix*, we started looking for and appreciating a different kind of action hero. The action stars of today are more genteel and not quite so in your face and bloodied. They think more, they're more sensitive, and they're guys like Chris Pratt or Chris Evans. They're a more sensitive type of hero. It's said that things go in cycles. That's what producer Mark DiSalle told Sheldon when he conjectured that Martial Arts movies would be making a comeback. So maybe someone will come along and play a roll where he's just a muscular killing machine who doesn't put much thought into the consequences. The closest thing we have to one of those traditional heroes is John Wick. Keanu Reeves executes these movies expertly. The other guys are sort of stuck in the Marvel universe and with these other costumed superhero epics."

Boaz Yakin knows action just as well as Sheldon. He's been involved in projects with Van Damme and Lundgren, he also wrote and directed *Safe* (2012) starring Jason Statham, who may be the closest thing we have to an action hero in the 80s sense, and he's still having his films released theatrically. Boaz takes things a little further: "I think the transition away from the traditional action films started with Jerry Bruckheimer and movies like *The Rock* (1996) with Nicholas Cage. He would take these cool, quirky indie actors and put them in these massive budgeted action films. That shift happened, and then along comes these superhero movies which are essentially an extension of that. The action guys had their moment in the mid-80s through the early 90s then guys like Cage or Bruce Willis had their successes and that sort of put the shift into motion."

In 1999, a year after *Legionnaire's* release, Van Damme would star in *Universal Solder: The Return* (1999). While the actor has a massive resume of films (many of which contain some of his best work), it wouldn't be until Stallone recruited him to portray the main villain in his highly successful film *The Expendables 2* (2012) that he would once again achieve box office success. For a director like Sheldon Lettich who specialized in those types of films, he would have to learn to adapt to the new reality as well.

The Last Patrol

After the release of *Perfect Target* in 1997, Sheldon would spend several years developing a project with producer Jakob Kotzky that picked up major steam before slowing down to a standstill. This particular project was titled *Hell on Wheels*, an updated and super-charged version of the old *The Rat Patrol* (1966) TV show, which took place during the First Gulf War with fast moving, militarized dune buggies. The script had been optioned by Largo Entertainment, with the intention of filming in Israel. The folks at Largo introduced him to an Israeli producer, who they had in mind to be the Line Producer of the movie. The two men would eventually become good friends while they were putting together a shooting schedule and a budget for the movie, but the project itself never got off the ground. A few years earlier Jacob had co-produced a few movies in Israel with financing from American companies and with American stars in the lead roles. The first of these was *Iron Eagle II* (1988), which starred Louis Gossett, Jr., and next was *Cover Up* (1991), which starred Dolph Lundgren.

The option eventually lapsed, but Jacob loved the project and was determined to produce it in Israel. The problem was that *Hell on Wheels* was a relatively expensive project. It would have been packed with big battle scenes involving numerous vehicles, all racing with and shooting at one another, plus helicopters, explosions, etc. Think *The Fast and the Furious* (2001) meets *American Sniper* (2014) and the movie needed a big budget. In order to get that, they needed a star, someone who was in their mid to late 20s or even early 30s. There was no place in it for someone like Van Damme, or Stallone, or Dolph. Bottom line, they just were never able to attach a suitable actor whose name could help get this movie off the ground.

They grew close with a few actors, like Christian Slater and Dean Cain, but their names weren't quite enough to attract the kind of money they needed. Jacob had his production infrastructure placed in Israel and crew members who were chomping at the bit to work on a movie. After a while, the waiting around became very frustrating for both he and Sheldon, they were itching to make a movie.

While waiting for something to pop on the dune buggy project, Jacob happened upon another opportunity that came together quite quickly. There was an international distribution company called Silverline Entertainment, they had hooked up with a couple of TV writers, Steve Brackley and Pam Long, a married couple who had written a post-apocalyptic screenplay titled *The Last Patrol* (2000), which Jacob felt he could produce for a reasonable budget in Israel. There was a lead role in it which was perfect for Dolph Lundgren, who had worked in Israel with Jacob on *Cover Up*. Jacob and Sheldon had spent months working together to try and get *Hell on Wheels* off the ground, there was a certain comfort level between the two of them, plus his previous work with Van Damme gave Sheldon the perfect credentials to direct a Dolph Lundgren movie. Jacob approached Dolph to star, and then he approached Sheldon to direct. With the two of them onboard, they now had a pretty decent package for Silverline to begin making some foreign pre-sales.

From the very first moment they met in Los Angeles, Dolph and Sheldon both agreed that the script needed a complete top to bottom re-write. Sheldon told him that once he was firmly onboard, he would begin re-working the entire screenplay. It wasn't what attracted either of them to the project, simply put; they both wanted to work together, and were looking forward to making a movie in Israel. Jacob had promised both of them that he had more than sufficient funds to make the movie, he also promised that Sheldon would have free rein to re-work the screenplay into something that both he and Dolph would be satisfied with. Neither of those promises turned out to be anywhere close to the truth.

Once Sheldon and Dolph were committed, the rest of the film needed to be cast, he wasted no time beginning the process. "We did some preliminary casting of lead characters in Beverly Hills, which is where we found Sherri Alexander, Brooke Parker, Rebecca Cross, Joe Michael Burke, and Terry Big Charles. Steve Brackley and Pam Long were very pushy about their choices for the lead characters. There was another actor who was a good friend of both Jacob and myself, who we wanted for the part of Lucky Simcoe, but Steve and Pam were adamant about using their choice. Jacob and I decided not to rock the boat, even though we much preferred our actor." This was the first of many skirmishes to come with Steve and Pam, who up until then had never had any involvement with an action movie before. In fact, this would have been their first feature film ever. The rest of the actors were cast in Israel, and they were all Israeli's who spoke American-accented English.

Once in Israel, the casting would continue, this time searching for performers native to the country. For the main villain, Jesus Carerra, Jacob suggested to Sheldon an outstanding local actor named Juliano Mer-Khamis. Juliano was from mixed parentage; his mother was a Jewish Israeli and his father was a Muslim Palestinian. He's a very well respected performer among the acting community throughout Israel and the Palestinian Territories, and famously taught acting classes to young Palestinians as the Artistic Director of the Freedom Theater in the West Bank town of Jenin. Unfortunately, he would face conflict with some of the Islamic extremists in the area, who felt young Muslims should not be encouraged to aspire to an acting career. Apparently, there had been warnings from the extremists to permanently close the theater. A few years after they completed the movie, Juliano was viciously ambushed and killed by a masked gunman. Hundreds of mourners, Jews and Muslims, attended his funeral.

The film involves, quite extensively the use of child actors. While many have heard the rumors about how difficult it can be to work with kids, Sheldon's approach worked out perfect for himself as well as the rest of his family. He began taking his family along with him on location since the *Only the Strong* shoot in Miami. His family was there for a number of months for both pre-production and production, and they even enrolled the kids in local schools while they were there. It was a great experience for all of them. Sheldon also brought them along during the time he filmed *Perfect Target* in Puerto Vallarta, Mexico. Israel was an exceptional case because he had relatives living there, so on *The Last Patrol* it worked out great because his wife and kids were able to meet members of the family who had not been to the United States yet.

One of the plot elements in the story involves a group of kids from a Black Evangelical church who get stranded in the desert when their bus breaks down. That seemed to create a problem for production because at the time there were hardly any Black people at all living in Israel, especially Black kids who could speak English with an American accent. One of these kids, a girl named Tamara, even had a number of dialogue scenes with Dolph's character. The solution ended up being very simple for Sheldon and the film. In fact, the answer was right before him in his own home. "Jacob had met my family and had been to my home many times, and he felt that my youngest daughter, Angelique, might be able to play that part. Turns out he was correct, and she performed amazingly well in a couple of one-on-one dialogue scenes opposite Dolph. For the other Black kids, we lucked out because there happened to be a group living in nearby Beersheba who called themselves the Black Hebrews. They were originally from Chicago, so their accents were perfect. They practiced the Jewish religion and had some kind of belief that they were one of the Lost Tribes of Israel that had somehow ended up in Chicago. The entire group had immigrated to Israel a few years earlier, and had no plans to return to America, which worked out very well for us."

The Last Patrol aka *The Last Warrior* tells the story of Army Officer Nick Preston (Dolph Lundgren) as he and a small group of survivors who are trying to live their lives in a post-apocalyptic wasteland. After a massive Earthquake rips California in half, Preston and his group fight every day to stay alive, try to avoid a plague that's thinning out the already shrinking population, as well as protect each other from a vicious group of prisoners with the intention of trying to control those they think are powerless.

When the film entered pre-production, Sheldon was ready to give the script the re-write he was promised. Certain things he wanted to keep, but there was much more to be improved upon. "There was just so much I disliked about the script, that I hardly knew where to begin. What was good about it, however, was the dialogue. Dialogue is what soap operas are all about; no action, not much in the way of plot, but lots of talking." Pam Long was great at writing soap opera dialogue, something she had been doing for years on Daytime Soap Operas like *The Guiding Light* (1952-2009), and *One Life to Live* (1968-2013). Her husband, co-writer Steve Brackley, worked with her on a couple of short-lived TV shows, but pretty much did nothing else of note either before or after. Following *The Last Patrol*, Pam went on to write and produce a couple of well-regarded TV movies that starred Dolly Parton, *Coat of Many Colors* (2015) and *Christmas of Many Colors: Circle of Love* (2016). Looking at Pam's career history, it's easy to deduce that it was Steve and not Pam who guided the concept and plot of *The Last Patrol* and Pam was along to help him write the dialogue.

With Sheldon Lettich at the helm and Dolph Lundgren in the lead, one would think *The Last Patrol* would have been a non-stop, action extravaganza, which it sadly was not. With the entire situation out of his hands, Sheldon had to make do with the resources available to him. In this particular situation, two key elements were missing from the equation, a good script and an adequate budget. The writers had spent most of their careers working on soap operas and TV shows, and not on action movies, so it was light on action. Those two writers were also producers on the movie, and according to Sheldon they felt their script was precious, perfect, and untouchable. "As I'd mentioned, I promised Dolph that I would re-write the script and make it more suitable for him and myself, but Steve and Pam were adamant that a re-write was not going to happen unless they were the ones doing the writing. Since this was being sold as a Dolph Lundgren action movie, you'd think they might welcome some input from the writer of *Double Impact, Bloodsport, Rambo III*, and other successful action films, but their oversized egos would not allow that."

Jacob actually had his secretary create a Word document that Sheldon could work with on his computer to do the re-write but as soon as Steve and Pam got wind of this, they ordered Jacob to fire him, send him back home, and bring another director on board. He refused to do that and came to Sheldon with a sincere plea to just do his best to film the script that Steve and Pam had written. Otherwise, Jacob would have no choice but to send him and his family back home. So he acquiesced and resolved to simply make the best of the situation. Had his family not been there with him, the outcome could have turned out much differently.

As mentioned before, there was a severe lack of money to film big action sequences. There were a couple of other action scenes in the original script, including a car chase across the desert, at night, but was discarded because there simply was not enough funds in the budget. Sheldon had some very formidable help with the action sequences they did have. Dolph's stunt double was a South African named Wade Eastwood. Wade had done quite a bit of stunt work on low budget Nu Image movies in South Africa and Romania, including *Bridge Of Dragons* (1999) where he doubled for Dolph. He has since gone on to a very rewarding career as a Stunt Coordinator and Second Unit Director several *Mission: Impossible* films and a few other Tom Cruise flicks as well. He also had help with stunts and 2nd Unit from Greg Powell, an esteemed British Stunt Coordinator who had worked on *James Bond* films, *Harry Potter* films, and a list too long to name. Sheldon had met Greg on *Legionnaire*, and they were looking forward to working together on that one until his unfortunate firing due to the whole Peter MacDonald debacle. Greg was not pleased with that outcome, and had come onboard *The Last Patrol* for a couple of weeks as a favor to help him out.

The main advantage of filming in Israel for any picture is the fact they have a production infrastructure that's been in place for many years, with great technicians and equipment. Nearly everybody there can speak some English, which is especially advantageous when hiring local actors. For Sheldon, the only real disadvantage was that the Israelis are an extremely talkative people, who never shut up, not even when cameras are rolling and actors are speaking dialogue. Even though the crew may have been chatty, he was still able to enlist a terrific Director of Photography from Israel who, given the budget, really made the most out of their locations. If you don't recognize the man's name, you should be ashamed of yourself. If you grew up in the 80s and paid attention to the movies released by Cannon, then you've seen a film shot by David Gurfinkle. He worked on such classics as *Enter the Ninja* (1981), *The Delta Force* (1986), *Over the Top* (1987), and many more.

Sheldon had never worked with David before, but they subsequently ended up collaborating again on the follow-up movie, *The Order* (2001), which they shot in Israel as well. After working with Sylvester Stallone on *Over the Top*, he was later hired to shoot *Rambo III*. If you remember the drama previously discussed about that particular film then Sheldon's revelations will come as no surprise. "Ironically, Peter MacDonald got David fired also, the same time he got Russell Mulcahy fired. Actually, Peter got most of the Israeli crew fired from that movie as well. That's how I ended up hearing the dirt behind Russell's termination on *Rambo III*, because I was working with that same crew on *The Last Patrol*, and would end up working with them again on *The Order*.

As someone who has followed Dolph Lundgren's career, essentially from day one to present, it's hard not to notice his talent as an actor tends to get overlooked. There are only a handful of filmmakers who have really given him an opportunity to flex his acting muscles and Sheldon was one of them. In fact, he felt comfortable enough with Dolph's acting abilities to give him a couple of long dialogue scenes that were filmed without a cut. One of them is with the character, Cookie (Ze'ev Revach), where the two of them carry on an uninterrupted 2-page dialogue scene. The other scene was with actress Sherri Alexander, who played Sarah McBride. The 2-page scene between them was even trickier because they were on their feet and moving, with the camera following them, but neither Dolph nor Sherri missed a line of dialogue. They finally had to cut when the two of them go down on the ground and tussle with one another. An interesting bit of trivia, Sherri married author Michael Crichton (*Jurassic Park*) a few years afterwards, and was pregnant with their child when Michael unexpectedly passed away. Sherri is nowadays a very wealthy single mom.

The Last Patrol was not a particularly well received film. It's not bad by any means and there's plenty to enjoy, particularly Dolph Lundgren's performance as well as the exciting and climatic action scene. It's difficult to gauge the films' financial success for various reasons nor does Sheldon have the information. He really could not ascertain how well the movie did because it was not a Directors Guild signatory film, so he would get no residuals from home video or TV. The reason that Jacob was not obligated to sign with the DGA was because his was a foreign production company and the movie itself was being filmed on foreign soil. Since Sheldon was not one of the writers, he didn't qualify for WGA residuals either, so he has no way of telling how well the film did through that route. Looking back on the film, Sheldon only has one thing to say summing up the experience, "It's the least favorite of all my movies and we will leave it at that."

The Order

After the unfortunate events surrounding *Legionnaire* and the lawsuit between Van Damme and Dux, Sheldon's relationship with Van Damme had been damaged. In addition, Van Damme's cocaine habit had only helped to further the rift between them. After separating himself from this whole mess, he had taken the job to direct *The Last Patrol* in Israel, the same country he would later use to film *The Order* (2001).

While in Israel working on *The Last Patrol*, Sheldon ran into an obscure Israeli producer who knew both Van Damme and himself, and also knew his current producer, Jacob Kotzky. His name was David Dadon, and he was trying to ingratiate himself with all three of them at the time. Knowing about the recent bad blood between Jean-Claude and Sheldon, David apparently decided to insert himself between them as a peacemaker. "I was on a beach in Tel Aviv one night, with my family and Kotzky, when David walked up to me with a mobile phone in hand and told me he had someone on the phone who wanted to say hello. I took the phone, and to my surprise it was Jean-Claude! This was very unexpected and awkward for both Jean-Claude and myself, but we did manage to break the ice and have a few cordial words with one another. Maybe one of us, or both of us, suggested getting together when we were both back in Los Angeles. Despite the discomfort and the awkwardness of the phone call, when I was finally back in Los Angeles we did connect with one another. The real catalyst for the two of us reconnecting was probably producer Avi Lerner."

Avi's distribution company, Millennium Films, had picked up *The Last Patrol* for distribution in the United States. Avi and Jacob Kotzky were both Israelis and had known each other for years, going way back. Jacob had some positive things to say about his experience working with Sheldon on that film, and Avi just happened to be looking for someone to direct *The Order*, a project he was planning to shoot in Israel with Van Damme in the lead role. Even though Sheldon had not worked with Jean-Claude for several years at that point, in Avi's eyes he had still directed two of Van Damme's biggest hits, *Lionheart* and *Double Impact*. Sheldon had just directed a movie in Israel, with Dolph Lundgren in the lead role, so that was another big plus in his favor, the fact he was comfortable working in Israel with an Israeli crew.

Jean-Claude and Sheldon ended up getting together in Los Angeles though he can't remember the particulars of that first meeting. "I'm quite sure he mentioned to me that Avi Lerner had offered him a movie. Shortly afterwards, I was invited to have dinner with both Jean-Claude and Avi, at some restaurant in the upscale Sunset Plaza neighborhood along the Sunset Strip. Avi's girlfriend, Heidi Jo Markel, was also with us. I'm not sure if the movie was discussed at all. Avi just wanted to observe how well Jean-Claude and I were getting along together, knowing that there had been some bad blood due to the situations with *Legionnaire* and with the Dux lawsuit." They had a couple more dinners together, and a few meetings at Avi's house high above the Sunset Strip. Somewhere along the way *The Order* was mentioned, and Sheldon would eventually be sent the screenplay.

The original notion for the movie was to do an Israeli-based version of the movie, *Black Rain* (1989), which was about an American detective (played by Michael Douglas) who travels to Japan to investigate a crime that was committed by Japanese Yakuza in New York City. Once in Japan, he teams up with a Japanese cop to further investigate, and they both become targets of the local Yakuza. Les Weldon, who had worked on many projects for Nu Image, co-wrote the original script with Danny Lerner, Avi's brother. The lead character was a tough New York City cop named Mike Moran, in a role that seemed to be tailored for Steven Seagal. "I believe the script was actually sent to Seagal, and he apparently turned it down. All this transpired during a period when Nu Image had spun off a division that was called Millennium Films, which was intended to be a more prestigious version of Nu Image, and would produce films with bigger budgets and bigger movie stars. Avi's goal was to move on from B-movie actors like Frank Zagarino, David Bradley, and Bryan Genesee, to eventually begin working with major action stars like Van Damme, Stallone, and Schwarzenegger." He would succeed beyond his wildest dreams with *The Expendables* (2010), but his first steps were to make movies with Seagal and Van Damme, both of whom had starred in feature films that had been released by major studios. *The Order* became Avi's first step upwards to begin competing with the likes of Carolco.

Though the script had already been written, Sheldon would contribute quite heavily to the shooting draft. The reason he has no screenwriting credit on the film is because Avi would not make a deal with him to direct the film if it had be under the jurisdiction of both the Director's Guild of America (DGA) and the Writer's Guild of America (WGA). He was instructed to pick one, and he chose the DGA. Whatever work he did on the screenplay had to be done under the table, and Jean-Claude (who was not signatory to the WGA at the time) took the credit for any writing input that Sheldon made. To be fair to Jean-Claude, any changes Sheldon made to the script were discussed in detail with him and he contributed quite a few ideas to those revisions.

By this point, Sheldon had worked on a number of Van Damme projects, and had grown tired of having to come up with unique and different French names for his characters. "How many times can we name him Luc or Jacques or Alain or Pierre? Jean-Claude was from Belgium, not France, and his real last name was Van Varenberg, which certainly sounds more Germanic than French. Belgium itself is divided into two distinct linguistic regions, French-speaking Wallonia and Flemish-speaking Flanders. Not one of Jean-Claude's previous movies had ever hinted at a Flemish rather than a French heritage, and he wanted to break the paradigm with this one by giving him a Flemish-sounding name. So he started by making his first name Rudy. At the suggestion of Jean-Claude's mother, he made his last name Cafmeyer. They made his dad's name Oscar, and the actor who played him, Vernon Dobtcheff, gave a very authentic-sounding Flemish accent. They also felt that making him a cop or a former soldier was beginning to sound over-done after starring in so many movies playing similar characters, so they went in a completely different direction with his profession too." Israel is a land filled with antiquities from various eras and cultures, and the filmmakers decided they would go with a profession that was based in antiquities. Rather than aping the Indiana Jones character, they decided to make Rudy someone who dealt in antiquities, but not a straight-laced archeologist; rather, a thief, someone who traffics in stolen antiquities, not for the appreciation of their beauty or historical significance but for their dollar value. In other words, he's more of a rogue and a bad boy rather than your typical movie hero, breaking the mold to try something new and different for Van Damme.

The Order is such a unique film on the resumes of both, director and star. It's not a traditional action film which they both had been associated with for most of their careers. It was more of a grand adventure, more in line with Jackie Chan's *Armour of God* (1986) than what was expected of Van Damme. This was orchestrated purposely by Sheldon and the star. "I tried to model the tone after movies like Hitchcock's *North by Northwest* (1959) or *The Man Who Knew Too Much* (1956). They were thrillers, with their protagonists in life threatening situations, but they never took themselves too seriously." One of Sheldon's favorite sequences in *The Order* is the chase through Jerusalem, with Rudy disguised as an Orthodox Jew, which has aspects lifted from a couple of French action-comedies from the 1960s, the Jean-Paul Belmondo film, *That Man from Rio*

(1964), and also *The Mad Adventures of Rabbi Jacob* (1973). Sheldon felt the movie would have worked better overall had they maintained that comedic tone throughout, "in the third act we went a little too serious with the story, which I believe left the audience disappointed after we took them on such a fun ride." What would end up making *The Order* an old school Van Damme movie would be the numerous fight scenes and in particular the martial arts fights, which had been noticeably absent from a few of his previous films from that era.

German-based company Koch Films recently released a Special Edition Mediabook for *The Order* which features an exclusive interview with Jean-Claude. He offers up an anecdote about filming the fight scenes in Jeruselum. "We have a fight on a roof in the city of Jeruselum; today if you put your foot there you get shot. What a privilege to be able to fight on those. Of course, I was disguised as a Hasidic Jew so people watching this didn't know it was me, all they see is a Hasidic Jew fighting an Arab. On one side of the wall you have the Arabs, the other is the Jews, and they're rooting for the Jewish guy or the Arabic guy to win like a boxing match. It's a movie! It was such an amazing experience."

Since Sheldon had recently finished *The Last Patrol* in Israel, he already had a leg up on the production which would prove to be a major asset to the film. "We weren't starting from zero; I knew some of the crew and they knew me. There were a few new people who had worked with Avi Lerner and Danny Lerner in the past, who I wasn't familiar with. One of them was Yossi Wein, who had directed a few movies for Nu Image in the past, and who had also been a cinematographer on some of their low budget movies. Yossi wasn't particularly talented, but I felt they were pushing him upon me simply because he was an old buddy and they wanted to give him a gig. At first they wanted Yossi to be my director of photography, but I saw some of his cinematography work and wasn't impressed. David Gurfinkle was far superior in every way, and fortunately the Lerner brothers knew David and had worked with him before as well. David really knew his business, especially with regard to lighting, and he had been the director of photography on a few big feature films like *Over the Top* (1987). He was also the original director of photography on *Rambo III*, until he was pushed out once Peter MacDonald took over as director. We both had that in common: getting screwed over by Peter Mac. Plus David was my director of photography on *The Last Patrol*, so there was a certain comfort level between us, and we looked forward to working with one another again."

Sheldon and the producers finally settled on making Yossi the Second Unit Director. Sheldon wanted the Stunt Coordinator to be Wade Eastwood. Wade had been Dolph's stunt double on *The Last Patrol*. He has since moved on to be a top Hollywood Second Unit Director and Stunt Coordinator, who has held that position on every one of the *Mission: Impossible* movies and a few other Tom Cruise films as well. Wade had crossed paths with Danny Lerner on a few early Nu Image movies which had filmed in South Africa. Somehow Wade had rubbed Danny the wrong way; to the extent Danny simply would not consider Wade at all, not even as a stunt player. "Danny would literally shudder with revulsion when Wade's name was even mentioned. I was stuck with Yossi, who not only was barely qualified to direct the Second Unit on a stunt heavy movie like this one, but who I later realized was a serious alcoholic as well. I could literally smell the vodka on his breath while we were on-set and working. Luckily, we did not have any serious accidents or mishaps while filming the many stunt sequences in the movie, which I mostly attribute to our Stunt Coordinator, Scott Ateah, who had worked on *Replicant* (2001) with Jean-Claude in Vancouver, and who we brought over to work on this movie." The duo ended up using Scott again on their next movie, *The Hard Corps*, which was filmed in Scott's hometown.

David Leitch is quickly becoming one of Hollywood's go to action directors having helmed mega-hits such as *Atomic Blonde*

(2017), *Deadpool 2* (2018), and *Fast & Furious Presents: Hobbs & Shaw* (2019). Before his big break as a director, he would be Jean Claude's stunt double. Sheldon was quick to hire him for *The Order*. "I also attribute the lack of accidents or serious mishaps partly to David Leitch, who had also been Jean Claude's stunt double on *Replicant*, the movie which was his previous film for Avi Lerner and Millennium. David was quite sharp and helpful to us in many ways and is now a major Hollywood player."

Sheldon would work with many major players in Hollywood, both in front of and behind the scenes. One particular legendary actor would make one of his final film appearances in *The Order*: Charlton Heston. "What impressed me most about Charlton Heston was his humble and accommodating attitude. This man had won an Oscar and starred in iconic films like *Ben Hur* (1959) and *Planet of the Apes* (1968), and he wanted me to address him as Chuck, and not Mr. Heston. I had scheduled rehearsals on the weekends, to rehearse the scenes that were coming up for the following week. There would be a stunt rehearsal, for Jean-Claude, Peter Malota, and all the fighters and stunt players. Then there would be a separate actor's rehearsal, where the actors and I would rehearse the scenes that were slated to be filmed the following week. Heston would show up for these rehearsals with his script in hand, bound inside a leather binder, all his lines marked with a highlighter." To Sheldon's delight, Heston was totally prepared, with the attitude of a young actor who had a part in his first feature film, eager to impress the director and other actors.

It was no surprise that when casting for *The Order* began; Sheldon and Jean-Claude would jump at the opportunity to bring in friends and past collaborators like Abdel Qissi and Brian Thompson. It was another opportunity to travel the world for Thompson and the chance to spend some time with his long-time friend. "I'm a fan of the whole *Indiana Jones* adventure genre so when I read the script for *The Order*, I was really excited by it. I really enjoyed the action/adventure twist to it, especially being able to play this outrageous religious leader. I found that character to be really challenging and fun. I did play him pretty close to the script, whatever was written, I said. There were some good monologues that really built nicely and made sense within the context of the character. When you have a religious order trying to do nefarious things it can end up on shaky ground and this was all really solid."

In addition to Thompson and Qissi, there's another performer who everyone may have missed, named Takis Trigellis. Even though he's Greek by birth, Takis played the French Fighter in *The Quest*. Sheldon met him in Los Angeles during a lunch with his manager. This was while Jean-Claude was casting fighters for that particular film. "Just impulsively, I called up Jean-Claude and told him I was having lunch with a guy who might be perfect to play one of the fighters in the movie, and Jean-Claude replied, "Send him over!" Takis rushed over to a casting session in Sherman Oaks, met with Jean-Claude, and within a short while he was cast in the movie. It was as quick and as simple as that! Afterwards, Takis would get in touch with me whenever he saw I was involved with a new movie. He called me about *Legionnaire*, and I told him I couldn't guarantee anything, but I was going to be doing casting sessions for the movie in London, and if he just happened to be in London around the same time, I might find a way to squeeze him in. To my everlasting surprise, when I arrived in London and stepped into the lobby of my hotel, there was Takis, patiently waiting for me in the lobby! I didn't even know which hotel I would be staying at, but somehow Takis managed to track me down! He was living in Germany at the time, but got himself on a plane, at his own expense, and flew to London just to get an opportunity to be in the movie! Of course, I couldn't say no, and he was actually perfect to play one of the Legionnaires, even if he would just be a glorified extra and didn't have any lines. I did manage to get Takis officially cast as Corporal Metz, and he stayed in the movie despite the fact that I eventually departed." A few years later, the same scenario would be repeated when Takis found out Sheldon was directing *The Order*. He called Sheldon and asked if there was a role for him, and pretty much repeated the same offer from before: if Takis happened to be in Israel while they were casting, he would find a way to get him into the movie. Sure enough, when Sheldon reached the hotel in Tel Aviv, there was Takis, waiting for him in the lobby. He ended up being part of the cadre of red beret security guys for Cyrus, Brian Thompson's cult leader, and this time he actually had the opportunity to get into a brief, on-camera physical scuffle with Jean-Claude.

Another repeat actor in the movie was Sasson Gabbai, who played Yuri, Rudy's sidekick and partner-in-crime. Unlike the others mentioned, Sasson was not part of the Van Damme & Lettich stock company, so to speak. He played Moussa in *Rambo III*, in a very similar sidekick role, as the Afghan guide who leads Rambo into Afghanistan. Sasson was perfect for the role, but one of the reasons he was chosen for *The Order* is because Sheldon actually did want to have a repeat with an actor who had been in one of his previous movies, same as he did with Voyo Goric, who was in both *Russkies* and *Lionheart*. Sasson went on to garner quite a bit of acclaim for his leading role in an Israeli film titled *The Band's Visit* (2007), in which he played the leader of an Egyptian Police Band that gets stranded overnight during a visit to Israel. The movie garnered quite a few nominations and awards worldwide, and was even adapted into an award-winning Broadway musical. Apparently, Sasson will be reprising his role as Colonel Tawfiq in this musical adaptation.

Ben Cross was a great addition to the cast; he was brought in by one of the producers, John Thompson, who had previously worked with him on a couple of other films. Ben was an Oscar nominee for his leading role in the movie *Chariots of Fire* (1981). Coincidentally, one of the lead actors for *Legionnaire*, Nicholas Farrell (who played Mackintosh) was his co-star in that one, playing one of the young athletes competing against Ben's character.

One major issue the film battled from the beginning would be the animosity between Jean-Claude and his co-star, actress Sofia Milos. Sheldon believed her and Jean-Claude to be like oil and water, and very quickly the level of dislike between the two escalated rapidly. "Honestly, I did not pick Sofia, and never had an opportunity to audition her. She was chosen by producer John Thompson while I was busy scouting locations in Israel and Bulgaria. On *Double Impact*, I made sure do a reading with Jean-Claude and the two actresses who were up for the female lead, one of whom was Tia Carrere. Had we been able to do something similar with Sofia, Jean-Claude and I could have looked for signs that she might become a problem. At least she would have realized that she was auditioning for the part, and that we weren't just pursuing her like she was Meryl Streep or Barbra Streisand."

The problem with Sofia was not just the animosity with Jean-Claude; she became quite the prima donna for the rest of the crew as well. She had been in very few films prior to *The Order*, playing minor parts, but insisted to everyone that she was the co-star of the movie, equal in stature to Jean-Claude. Sheldon, along with John Thompson, would very politely and patiently try to explain to her on more than one occasion that the movie was being financed solely upon Jean-Claude's name, not hers, and no one else's. "I'm quite sure that her big ego was what set Jean-Claude off, because he has quite a big ego himself, but at least he's earned it, unlike Sofia. On the next movie I made with Jean-Claude, *The Hard Corps*, we had as our female lead Vivica Fox, who had certainly earned a certain amount of diva credentials, yet we had no problems with her whatsoever. She and Jean-Claude got along great, there were never any issues between them at all. Bear in mind, we also had Oscar-winner Charlton Heston on the set of *The Order* and there was never any display of movie star egomania out of him, not at all."

Sofia wasn't the only actor to be cast by the producers without any input from either Jean-Claude or Sheldon. The casting of

Oscar Cafmeyer was very important to Jean-Claude especially, and they had a few well-known actors in mind to play the role. Jean-Claude had even spoken to Alain Delon about playing the role, and Mr. Delon had told Jean-Claude that he would be very interested, if an offer were made to him by the producers. The others they had in mind were Klaus Maria Brandauer and Jurgen Prochnow, both of whom could be seen as realistic choices to play the father of Van Damme, plus their names would have added further prestige to the film. Unfortunately, no offers were made to any of them. One morning Sheldon went into the café at their hotel in Bulgaria, he was surprised to see an elderly Franco-British gentleman who he had not seen before, sitting at a table, sipping a cup of tea. The man was Vernon Dobtcheff, and to his great surprise, Vernon had been cast by the producers to play Oscar Cafmeyer. Vernon certainly had the correct look to play a professor of antiquities, but otherwise, there really wasn't anything about him that would make one believe he was the father of Jean-Claude Van Damme. Jean-Claude was severely disappointed, but the guy was already in Bulgaria, had been booked and paid, and his first scene in front of the cameras was only days away. At this late stage in the game, there was no way to get the producers to change their minds and cast a completely different actor. Fortunately for them, Vernon would be a total sweetheart to work with, and an excellent actor as well. This was not the first time that producers had made a unilateral casting choice without Sheldon's input (see *Perfect Target*), nor would it be the last.

Also during the interview for *The Order* Mediabook from Koch, Jean-Claude discusses the casting for the role of his father. "One thing I regret, but that's what they (the producers) wanted, was with my father. He didn't look like my father, like Alain Delon did for example. I have friends that would be happy to, and I would be honored, to do a movie with me. Can you imagine Alain Delon as my father? The person who played my father was a great actor, he was maybe a better actor than me but the face didn't go with it. I didn't feel like he was my father. I felt more like I was adopted in a sense."

While Brian Thompson enjoyed much of his time on set and on location, his experience working with Jean-Claude wasn't a particularly pleasant. "At that time, Jean-Claude's drug use was really taking a toll on him. He was erratic, irrational, and extremely unprofessional. Sadly, you really couldn't rely on him to remember things either. David Leitch and I had worked out an elaborate sword fight and Jean-Claude just wouldn't learn the choreography. What choreography he did learn, you really weren't sure if it was going to happen. I was honestly scared on set when we had those swords in our hands. He was showing up to set late, it made filming extremely tense, difficult, and I felt so sorry for the producers and Sheldon. He had put so much into the film and just couldn't get Jean-Claude to take anything seriously."

About forty percent of the movie was filmed in Israel while the rest would be shot in Bulgaria, especially most of the interiors, which were constructed on makeshift sound stages at an old sports complex in Sofia. They had two Olympic size swimming pools, one that was outdoors and one that was inside a warehouse structure to use. They built a Jerusalem set inside the outdoor swimming pool. Much of the chase scene through Jerusalem was filmed on that set. Choosing to do it that particular way allowed them the luxury of not having to deal with the huge crowds of onlookers and movie fans in the real Jerusalem. One thing Sheldon realized very quickly once Van Damme arrived in Israel: despite all the other differences between Arabs and Jews, they were all Jean-Claude Van Damme fans. No disagreements there. "That made it hell to film a movie in such a tightly packed city, with nothing but narrow winding streets and alleyways, and thousands of fans wanting a photo with Van Damme, or an autograph, or just a glimpse of him. He had a phalanx of bodyguards surrounding him everywhere he went in the city, but that wasn't helpful when we had to shoot a two-person dialogue scene, because we had to clear those crowds (and bodyguards) out of our shots. Those crowds were generally noisy as hell, which is not great when you're trying to record dialogue."

Eventually, maybe once the novelty wore off, or out of respect to Van Damme, the crowds actually began cutting the production some slack. When they were filming the fight scenes on the rooftops, for example, the Assistant Director would politely ask (in Hebrew and Arabic, via bullhorns) for the crowds to duck their heads until they called "Cut!" Thankfully, they would comply. As soon as Sheldon would yell "Cut!" he would see literally hundreds (if not thousands) of heads suddenly pop up. "There was no way to compel them to duck out of the way for our shots, but I think that they began feeling privileged to be witnessing Jean-Claude Van Damme filming a fight scene, right in the middle of their own neighborhood! It may have dawned on them that this might be a once in a lifetime occurrence, never to be repeated. The same was true for us." Here Sheldon was, filming a movie in the very heart of Old Jerusalem, a city tied to three major religions for centuries, and they pretty much had the run of the place. Much was owed to Avi Lerner, who happened to be a friend and supporter of Ehud Olmert, the Mayor of Jerusalem at the time they were filming (and who would later be elected Prime Minister of Israel).

The courtyard where Rudy encounters the hostile crowd of Muslims was constructed within the confines of a swimming pool in Sofia, Bulgaria. After the chase commences, and he runs up the steps, then shooting commenced up on the real rooftops of the Old City of Jerusalem, right above the famous Damascus Gate. That's where Rudy gets into the long fight with Abdel Qissi's character. When the two of them go tumbling off the roof, they're back to the set in Sofia. The set in Sofia is also where they shot the Crusader battle, horses and all. It would have been far too difficult for the production to pull that off in the real Jerusalem.

With Brian Thompson being only in a portion of the movie, he was able to take short trips to Turkey, see the Bulgarian countryside in the winter, taking some time to refresh himself during the rigors of filming. Even with all the time he was able to relax and explore, nothing had prepared him for the awkward first night in the hotel where the cast and crew were staying. "The first night we arrived I found out that our hotel had a brothel in it. I hadn't even unpacked my suitcase when there was a knock on my door. When I opened it, there was this beautiful girl standing there in this full-length mink coat. There were two hulking bodyguards standing on either side of her and she just seemed nervous, her nose was sweating, and not wearing much else under that coat. They were offering her to me but I politely declined, gave her a tip, and wished her well. I was shocked, I'm still not sure if that was real or someone from the production playing a trick on me. That was the only time anything like that ever happened to me." Whatever the circumstance may have been, it was certainly a memorable production for all involved.

Post-production was a relatively smooth process, made even more eventful, especially for Sheldon, by the hiring of legendary Italian film composer, Pino Donaggio. "Producer John Thompson is the one who brought us Pino. I had one initial meeting with Mr. Donaggio in Los Angeles, where we sat down in an editing room and spotted the entire film for music cues. There were temp tracks from other films mixed in, which gave Pino some idea of what I was looking for before heading home to Venice, Italy. We were supposed to get together in Venice when he had temp versions of his music cues, so that I could listen to them and give him my notes. This was supposed to occur when I was back in Israel to record ADR with the Israeli actors. Danny Lerner did not want to pay for my flight from Tel Aviv to Venice. Pino even said I could stay at his home in Venice, so there wouldn't have been the additional cost of a hotel room. Danny still nixed it feeling that I could just as easily listen to the cues on a computer and then give Pino my notes over the phone. At this point I could have and should have just purchased my own plane ticket. That may have been one of the biggest mistakes of my life. I was being invited by Pino Donaggio to stay in his home, in Venice, Italy, to review the music cues for my own movie and I missed the opportunity. Pino was also surprised they were not sending me to Venice, which wasn't a huge distance from Tel Aviv. I had relatives living in Israel, who I hadn't seen in a while, so I decided that I would just visit with them for a few days, and go along with Danny's suggestion to have a phone conversation with Pino after he sent me the temp tracks." To date, Sheldon still has never visited Venice. The music score for *The Order* was terrific, especially the opening theme, which is among some of the best ever composed for any of Sheldon's films.

Prior to *The Order*, Jean-Claude had done *Replicant*, which had many of the same players. It was produced by Millennium, and among the producers were Avi Lerner, Danny Lerner, and John Thompson. Les Weldon had done a re-write on the screenplay. The movie was slated to be released in theaters by Artisan Entertainment, which was a subsidiary of Lionsgate, but somehow the deal was derailed, and Artisan released it Direct-to-Video (DTV), which was a great disappointment to everyone involved. There had been talk about *The Order* being released theatrically, although the distributor this time would be Columbia-Tri-Star, which eventually became Sony. Many believe the fact that *Replicant* was released DTV hurt their chances of a theatrical release. Jean-Claude's previous film before that, *Inferno* (1999), also went straight to video. The studios began to see a pattern with Van Damme's movies, which would lead to *The Order* being released DTV.

The Order may not have been the huge success everyone was hoping it would but the film still stands out for fans, including co-star Thompson. "Despite everything, when the film was finished, Sheldon really had pulled off some shining moments. I particularly enjoyed the relationship between Jean-Claude's character and his father played by Vernon Dobtcheff. I was also impressed with the production value of the finale, the temple ruin full of gold, it really looked amazing. The Bulgarians are exquisite with their hand-made work, the wardrobe, and the artistry of the sets they make. That country is just filled with remarkable craftsman."

It's a lot more difficult to track films on the DGA website than on the WGA site, and since he was not listed as a writer on *The Order*, Sheldon can't track the residuals for it. There's really no way to track the films actual success. Sheldon wasn't listed as a writer, so the WGA site doesn't offer up many answers. The German distributor, Koch Films, did release a Special Edition Blu-ray for the movie a few years ago, which had a plethora of special features, including new interviews with Sheldon and Jean-Claude. They also created a new cover, which was exponentially better than the DVD cover initially released in the U.S. Most companies would not have gone through the trouble and expense to release a new Blu-ray if the film hadn't done well for them. If anything, maybe audiences are appreciating the movie far more nowadays than when it was first released.

The Hard Corps

There was a five year gap in between *The Order* and *The Hard Corps* when Sheldon spent most of the time working on spec scripts. A spec script is an unsolicited screenplay, or a script written with the hope of being able to option it to a production company, a studio, or even a producer. There was a script he wrote which has been mentioned before, *Stryker's Force*, which he did with Leon Isaac Kennedy. During this time, there was some hope it might end up being optioned. "There was a very obscure low-budget producer (whose name I can't remember) who Leon Isaac Kennedy introduced me to. According to Leon, this guy wanted to produce the *Stryker's Force* script which we had co-written many years ago. It was originally intended to be a possible sequel to *Lone Wolf McQuade*. This was the same script that Leon had submitted to Menahem Golan many years earlier, which Cannon Films was interested in producing with Leon and Michael Dudikoff in the starring roles. This was the project that Leon and I had tried to sell, with Van Damme playing the co-lead character. As I'd mentioned, Menahem did not want Van Damme in the movie, and Dudikoff turned it down. Leon and I still owned the script." Even though they owned the script, getting these things made is never easy and not all producers deliver on their promises, to which Sheldon can attest. "Leon had somehow hooked up with this producer, and both of them wanted to make *Stryker's Force*, at a very low budget, with Don Wilson playing the co-lead. One of the first questions I asked this producer was if he was prepared to either option or purchase the screenplay. He was willing to do neither, most likely because he barely had a penny in his pocket."

Sheldon had a couple of meetings with Leon, Don Wilson, and this producer to discuss the possibility of doing the project. Everyone seemed to be interested, but only verbally; there were never any contracts or even deal memos drawn up, nor was there ever any money placed on the table. In other words, it just wasn't happening. "We had a meeting where Don introduced me to Art Camacho, who apparently was being considered to either direct the movie or serve as the fight choreographer. I told everyone that I wasn't interested in selling the screenplay unless I was also directing the movie. Everything was simply all talk at this point. This producer never so much as even took any of us out to lunch, a sure sign that he had no money."

After re-reading the screenplay, which was written in the early 1980s, Sheldon realized that it was hopelessly out of date. Plus it would not be an inexpensive movie to produce, and so far he had not seen any signs that this producer had any cash, he had only seen the tiny office on Sunset Blvd. He suggested to Leon the idea of writing a completely new screenplay, something that could accommodate both Leon and Don Wilson, though it would have nothing whatsoever to do with *Stryker's Force*. Leon didn't agree with the idea, he was banking on a new starring role in a movie, and an easy payday since he would have shared the screenplay money with Sheldon.

Sheldon still wanted to try his hand at something new instead of updating the script. He turned to his friend George Saunders to help develop it. "I got in touch with my buddy, George Saunders. After *Perfect Target*, we had worked on a couple of spec scripts together since then. I explained the parameters to him, basically what in those days would have been called a "Salt & Pepper" buddy movie, with the lead characters being played by one White guy and one Black guy. I told him about my experiences with the two European bodyguards in Germany when I was over there promoting *Lionheart*, and brought up the notion I'd originally had of Van Damme playing a bodyguard. We ran with that idea for the White guy, then decided to make the Black guy a boxer who had crossed swords with a notorious and dangerous Rap Music producer, someone modeled after Suge Knight. Then we threw in a sister to the boxer, someone who could serve as a romantic interest for the bodyguard, which would result in igniting a dangerous friction with her brother." George and Sheldon liked the idea, and gave it a title that Sheldon had previously used on a couple of other projects. He and Leon had even tried using *The Hard Corps* as an alternate title to *Stryker's Force*.

Sheldon pitched the idea to the producer, as well as Leon and Don, and everyone seemed to like it. The biggest stumbling block was that there was no script at the time, not even a treatment. Naturally, he tried to get these guys to cough up a little money to pay them to write a treatment. No one was willing to do that. Everyone liked the idea, but no one was willing to stick their neck out for any kind of a commitment; no money, no deal memo, no contract. There was nothing to tie any of them to this new idea. There was nothing that would protect George and Sheldon, other than a Writers Guild registration, and conversely there was nothing that would protect this would-be producer either, something that would tie him to this idea or to any future screenplay or movie that might result from it. George and Sheldon were the only ones with a stake in this idea, so they decided to just press forward on their own with a detailed treatment. The one major upside to the lack of paperwork or money meant they would own whatever was put down on paper, free and clear, unless someone decided to either option or purchase it. The treatment was finished in a very short period of time, and Sheldon presented it to the producer. "He was very pleased with what we had written, and urged us to write the full screenplay, but was again unwilling to draw up paperwork or to even pay us a small pittance to move forward. I started to get the feeling he didn't have a pot to piss in. George and I were undeterred, because we liked this idea so much, so we simply pressed forward and wrote the full screenplay." Sheldon registered the finished draft with the Writers Guild, which clearly established that he and George were the sole owners of this literary property, free and clear, with no attachments or encumbrances.

George Saunders was excited for the chance to work with his friend again. Even though they had the spec scripts they had worked on, nothing had been produced since *Perfect Target* had been released in 1997. Something felt different about this project and he was excited for the collaboration. "The story was completely Sheldon's and he had brought it to me. When we eventually started to write *The Hard Corps*, we wrote it fairly quickly. He would take a pass at it then I would take a pass at it until we made it to the third or fourth draft."

Don Wilson liked the project quite a bit, and after everyone realized the producer would not be able to come up with the money to make this movie, Don wanted to try and produce it on his own. Sheldon told him they needed a budget of at least $5 million, which would have cost more than many of Don's past movies. He promised Sheldon he would come up with the $5 million, and he did make a number of sincere attempts, but he just wasn't able to raise that amount on his own.

There was another producer, a friend of Sheldon's, who read the script, and thought it would be perfect for Steven Seagal (which it would have been). The producer pitched it to Steven, who was interested enough that he set up a meeting with Sheldon at his house in Mandeville Canyon. "This wasn't the first time I had met with Seagal. Back in the early 90s, Seagal, Van Damme and I all had the same attorney, named Andy Rigrod. Andy introduced me to Steven back then, and I had met with him at the same house before, when he was still married to Kelly LeBrock. Steven and I even came up with a movie idea, which we both pitched to producer Bruce Berman at Warner Brothers. The problem Steven had with me at the time I discussed *The Hard Corps* with him was that there was a perception in town that I was Van Damme's director, that most of my produced movies had starred Van Damme, and that the two of us would regularly hang out together." There was an intense rivalry between Seagal and Van Damme around that time, with the two of them openly insulting one another on *The Arsenio Hall Show* (1989-1994). "Apparently, the perception in Steven's mind seemed to be that I would always be in Van Damme's corner rather than his. Even though he liked the project, Steven felt it might be risky to allow one of Van Damme's best buddies to direct him in a movie. "

A few months later, Jean-Claude called Sheldon. He had been approached by producer Brad Krevoy about starring in a few movies, which Brad and his partners, Donald Kushner and Pierre Spengler, would produce for Sony. Jean-Claude had already committed to one movie, titled *Second in Command* (2006), and he was looking for a couple of other scripts. Sheldon pitched *The Hard Corps*, and he was instantly sold. He put Sheldon in touch with Brad Krevoy, who also liked what he was hearing, and who (unlike the last producer) was ready to make a deal on paper and to pay for a short option on the script. It was that simple. Reading the script was almost a formality for Brad; all that he cared about was that the story had action, and that Van Damme wanted to do it. Very quickly they were in business.

There was quite a gap in time from when George and Sheldon first wrote the script until the thing started to get some traction. According to George, "It took another five or six years before we actually got it produced. Once Jean-Claude took a look at it, things started to move rather quickly."

Brad and his partners had some kind of a deal with Castel Studios in Romania, and they told Sheldon the entire movie would have to be filmed in Romania. They would even fly him to the Romanian capital of Bucharest, where Jean-Claude was in the midst of filming *Second in Command*. He did some scouting there, looking for locations that would work for *The Hard Corps*, which was an Urban story with a predominately Black cast. "I very quickly realized that we couldn't successfully shoot this movie in Romania, not simply because it didn't look quite like an American city, but because there were no Black people anywhere to be seen. We had a very important scene, in a nightclub that was supposed to be packed with Black people, where Van Damme's character was supposed to stick out like a sore thumb. Where would we find all those Black extras? Brad suggested that we could bus down a number of Africans from Germany or France, but that sounded like an empty promise to me. One of the Romanian producers had one of the worst ideas of all, which was to put dark makeup on some of the Romanian extras to make them look Black, an idea which would have made Vivica Fox walk off the set and call the National Association for the Advancement of Colored People (NAACP)."

The entire project was at an impasse, because Brad and his partners wanted to make the movie, but insisted they shoot in Romania. Jean-Claude and Sheldon left Romania, and they flew to the city he had been currently living in, which was Vancouver, British Columbia, Canada. Jean-Claude had starred in a number of movies shot in Vancouver, starting with *Timecop* (1994). He had recently starred in *Replicant* (2001), which had also filmed there. During that time he owned an entire floor in a luxury condominium building in the downtown area, and enjoyed the people, the climate, and the amenities of this very cosmopolitan North American city. While driving through the city streets on the way to his home, they noticed Black people, on the sidewalks, driving cars, eating in cafes, etc. They had to ask themselves: why not film *The Hard Corps* in Vancouver, which had the right look and had everything else they needed, including plenty of Black folks? Plus, Van Damme had his home there, with his wife, his kids, and his dogs. Brad wouldn't have to fly him to the other side of the world and put him up in a fancy hotel suite. There were experienced film crews, with all the necessary infrastructure in place. "Everything about it just made sense. We got on the phone with Brad, and learned that there were a few financial details which had to be addressed, mostly relating to Brads partners. Donald

Kushner had some kind of financial interest to Castel Studios, and it was absolutely necessary that he had to film at least part of the movie in Romania. We compromised: most of the movie would be filmed in Vancouver, but we had to commit to filming at least a couple of weeks at Castel Studios in Bucharest. That's how it went down. Vivica didn't want to go to Bucharest (I can't remember the reasons why) so we juggled the schedule to film all her scenes in Vancouver."

Once all the minor details had been hammered out, the filmmakers would begin to stack the film with actors, newcomers as well as seasoned veterans, to bring this thing to life. Lettich always has a way of bringing in performers who, on the surface, sound out of place but in actuality are perfect for the film. "Vivica Fox had previously worked with producer Brad Krevoy on a movie titled *Boat Trip* (2002), which also starred Cuba Gooding, Jr. Brad had promised Jean-Claude and myself that he would get both Cuba and Vivica to co-star in the movie. When push came to shove, Brad didn't want to cough up the money to get Cuba on board. Another suggestion was Wesley Snipes, who also would have been terrific as Wayne. Brad didn't want to pay extra for another expensive star. The problem was that Brad was paying Van Damme $3 million dollars to star in the movie. Cuba and Wesley would have wanted to go favored nations with their salaries, which meant they would have to be paid the commensurate amount that Van Damme was being paid. That would have been an extra $3 million out of the budget. Brad preferred to save money by going with a much cheaper actor. I honestly believe this was a huge mistake. I'm quite certain Sony would have opened this movie theatrically if we had two well-known action stars playing the lead roles. Vivica Fox was a known quantity, but she was not a name-above-the-title box office star like Snipes or Gooding."

Sheldon kept Saunders in the loop when filling out the roles and George was very excited by one of the cast members in particular. "We were so very lucky with Sony Pictures and I knew Sheldon would do a wonderful job directing it. When they cast Vivica Fox,

I just knew. She's always wonderful no matter what the project and this was no different." The real surprise for him would go to the films' star. "Van Damme does some of his best work as an actor in this film. After a certain age, he knew there were things he couldn't do anymore so he wisely changed his focus to the acting side of his personality and is terrific."

Everyone wanted DMX to play the villain, even Brad Krevoy, who was willing to pay extra to get him into the movie. He wouldn't have been nearly as expensive as Wesley Snipes or Cuba Gooding, because they only needed him for a couple of weeks rather than the run of the show. Having DMX's name on the poster alongside Van Damme definitely could have helped them get a theatrical release. He was actually interested in playing the role. Sheldon even flew down to Los Angeles to have a face to face meeting with him and his agents. The problem (and this was not disclosed to them ahead of time) was that DMX was scheduled to begin a somewhat lengthy prison sentence around the same time the movie would be filming. The producers were willing to work with him in juggling the schedule, but neither the bond company nor the insurance company would sign off on him.

There were quite a few restrictions placed upon production, mostly so the producers could use various tax shelters and other incentives to save money. All the actors and crew had to either be citizens of the United Kingdom, or else residents of British Columbia. They were only allowed two actors who were American citizens, and Vivica Fox was one of them. The other one would have been DMX. Most of the supporting cast were Canadian citizens who resided and paid taxes in British Columbia. Although Doug Milsome wasn't Sheldon's first choice to be the cinematographer, he had a British passport and same with the editor, Matthew Booth.

Raz Adoti, who played the role of Wayne Barclay, was a British Nigerian from London. "Raz did an amazing and flawless job portraying an African-American, although in actuality he had a rather pronounced London accent. British actors have been perfecting flawless American accents for decades. Idris Elba is a shining example. The reverse has certainly not been true, one of the worst examples being Kevin Costner attempting a British accent in *Robin Hood* (1991)." There's not a movie-going soul on this planet who would disagree with Sheldon on these points. Now that the leads had all been placed, it would be time to roll the cameras.

Once filming was underway, things moved forward at a satisfactory pace. Sheldon was satisfied with the progress, though there were still some hurdles in the way. "Unfortunately, we did not have a competent fight choreographer on the movie, simply because the producers did not want to pay for one. We had our local stunt coordinator, Scott Ateah, who was good with the stunt work but was not a fight choreographer. A local stuntman, Steve McMichael was hired to be the fight choreographer, but he really didn't know much about actually choreographing a fight scene for a movie. Jean-Claude and I pretty much ended up choreographing the fights ourselves. The producers most likely figured that they really didn't need to hire and pay a fight choreographer, because Jean-Claude and I would figure out a way to do it on our own. I'm glad to hear that there's been some praise for that fight scene between Jean-Claude and Raz, but it could have been so much better. Especially if we'd had someone like Chad Stahelski or David Leitch to figure out the actual fight moves." This was before either of them launched into super stardom, so both would have been available and affordable at the time.

The Hard Corps may have been light on the action scenes which made Van Damme a household name, but Saunders explains this idea best. "It was never meant to be a straight up action picture, it was more of a drama, with some action, in the same way as the Harrison Ford film, *Witness* (1985). We really wanted to concentrate on fully developed three-dimensional characters so it worked much better on that level. Sheldon has always been a kickass action guy and *The Hard Corps* was very much a departure for him. We were very careful to try and use the actions scenes as a means to move the story along and the action to help build the characters instead of just being action for actions sake." In the pantheon of Lettich/Van Damme pictures, this one definitely stands apart from the others.

The Hard Corps would be a modest success for Sony and a very pivotal film for Sheldon. The film was firmly sitting in the era of DTV product when the action stars of yester-year were now used to being in these smaller pictures and the big red carpet premiers were no longer expected. It was the end of an era, not only for the stars, but filmmakers as well. "It's the last film I actually directed. Since then I've been hired for a few movies, and even did months of pre-production work on a couple of them, but for various reasons those movies never made it in front of the cameras. One of those movies was titled *Metro Dog*, a family film that I co-wrote, about a dog that gets separated from his family in Moscow, and winds up in the vast Metro system beneath the city. I actually spent months scouting for that one in Moscow, Prague, and Budapest. We eventually decided to shoot most of the movie in Belgrade, Serbia, where I did many months of scouting, casting, and other pre-production activities. Quite a bit of money was spent by the producer, who eventually got cold feet when he realized just how costly this production was going to be."

"I have a strong association with the kinds of action movies that were being made in the 80s and 90s. Movies like those are not being made any more. Same with the actors who starred in my movies; Van Damme is not getting the kinds of offers he was getting twenty years ago. Also, there are plenty of other directors out there; lots to choose from, and new ones are graduating from film schools every day. I haven't been nominated for any prestigious awards, like Oscars, Golden Globes, or Palm d'Or, and while a few of my films have been successful, none of them has ever done blockbuster business at the box office. You put all those factors together, and you can understand why there's very little incentive for producers to hire me nowadays rather than to try somebody new."

Max

Sheldon has collaborated with Boaz Yakin on and off during their thirty five year friendship but it wouldn't be until the film, *Max* (2015), they would formally make a film together. Shortly after meeting through a mutual friend, they both would spend time working for Sylvester Stallone and White Eagle Productions. Sheldon was working on *Rambo III* and the French Foreign Legion project while Boaz had been brought in to develop a script based around the idea of Stallone playing a tough New York City priest.

It was 1986 when Sheldon would meet Boaz Yakin. Boaz had moved out to L.A. after having optioned his first screenplay, *Cold Fire*. He was only nineteen and a sophomore in college but the trek out west would prove to be an exciting one. "I met Sheldon through my friend Pascal Folbare who I went to NYU with. Because of Pascal, I met Sheldon's wife Toni and she felt we would get along because we were both writing the same types of things, and were both working for Sylvester Stallone at the time. She suggested I get in touch with him and I did, we quickly became friends."

Boaz had a couple of thing going with White Eagle but nothing ever came to fruition. "I optioned the *Cold Fire* script and it was the first time I was ever paid for something. I pitched the idea to United Artists about a cop who is sent to prison in order to get revenge for his wife or partner's murder against the leader of the Mexican mafia who is currently in the prison. They paid me to write it and showed it to Stallone who was excited about it. He didn't make that movie but he did use my ending for a different prison movie he made, *Lock Up*. They didn't use anything from my script but did steal the ending. I pitched the tough priest idea to his production company, which was basically an updated version of *Angels with*

Dirty Faces (1938) or *Boys Town* (1938) with Spencer Tracey and Mickey Rooney. Stallone optioned the idea and I wrote it for them, a couple of versions, then I bailed on it because it wasn't looking like it would happen."

Sheldon was impressed with the young Boaz and the two men quickly formed a friendship. "Shortly after White Eagle Productions, Boaz was hired to write *The Punisher* (1989), the one starring Dolph Lundgren as the title character. We were both fans of comic books and genre movies, especially Sci-Fi and Horror, and Boaz was dying to meet Sam Raimi, whom he knew was a friend of mine. I did end up introducing Boaz to Sam, and they became good buddies as well. Sam in turn introduced Boaz to the co-writer of *Evil Dead II* (1987), Scott Spiegel, and the two of them became very close friends for years and even ended up co-writing *The Rookie* (1990), which became a feature film starring Charlie Sheen and Clint Eastwood (who also directed). Boaz, in turn, introduced both Scotty and myself to an old friend and ex-roommate of his from New York, a budding producer named Lawrence Bender."

This part of the story is pretty interesting and a perfect example of how Hollywood can work. The best person to tell the story is Boaz since he was there, smack dab in the middle of it all. "Sheldon is a focal point of many things that people just don't know about. As Sheldon mentioned, he introduced me to Sam Raimi and we became friendly. Sam introduced me to Scott who became my best friend for like thirty years. Sheldon was the crux of all that. When I was in my early 20s, I decided that I'd had it with the film business. I was ready to move to Paris and become a novelist, which I did do for a year and a half before being dragged back into the movie business. Sheldon called me up about this assistant who was working in the room next to him while he was prepping *Lionheart*. The guy ended up being Quentin Tarantino, who I was told was a big fan of *The Punisher* and wanted to meet me. I came in and met Quentin, who was this hyper ball of energy, but I was moving to Paris and didn't know what I was supposed to do with this guy. Coincidently, Sheldon introduced Quentin to Scott Spiegel as well. Scottie got Quentin his first gigs doing some script stuff. Scottie had worked with Lawrence Bender, who was also a close friend of Sheldon and myself, and of course those two hit it off immediately. Lawrence and Quentin would go on to make *Reservoir Dogs* (1992) and that might never have happened if it hadn't been for Sheldon."

It's amazing to think of all the creative people in this small circle of friends who have gone on to create films that have changed the face of cinema. At the center of it all: Sheldon Lettich. He's so humble and matter of fact while discussing, it's almost as if he has marginalized his role, no matter how impactful it truly was. "After I met Quentin and introduced him to both Scotty and Lawrence, they soon went on to make their own films. Lawrence ended up producing the low budget cult classic *Intruder* (1989) which Scotty wrote and directed, and had cameos by both Sam Raimi and Bruce Campbell. A couple years later, Lawrence would produce Quentin's *Reservoir Dogs*, followed by *Pulp Fiction* (1994), which won Oscars for both Quentin and Lawrence. The associations and friendships continued with Scotty writing and directing *From Dusk Till Dawn 2* (1999) for Lawrence and Quentin, a movie that Boaz also had a story credit on. A few years later, Boaz and Scotty would form a production company, Raw Nerve, with director Eli Roth, which was responsible for the creation of all three *Hostel* (2005, 2007, and 2011) movies, one of which Scotty directed. Scotty also shared writing credits with me and Josh Becker on *Thou Shalt Not Kill... Except*. Quentin gushed over the fact I had a story credit on that movie, which in some ways may have been an inspiration for *Once Upon a Time in Hollywood* (2019). Both films featured a bloody climactic massacre of the Manson family." Would there have been a *Reservoir Dogs* if Sheldon had never introduced Quentin to Lawrence? No one knows for sure but it's definitely something worth pondering about.

Boaz has no problem confirming the connections and the fact these connections don't happen much anymore in Hollywood. "In the 80s and 90s there was this little network of friends who would try to help and support each other and I don't think it's quite the same way anymore. Now it's really competitive and not always pretty, so I really just don't feel that happens much now. Sure, there were rivalries but also camaraderie's and Sheldon was at the center." The group grew to include writer/directors like Courtney Joyner (*Class Of 1999, Prison*), Darin Scott (*Tales from the Hood*), and Larry Brand (*Halloween: Resurrection*). Many would go on to work for Cannon Films, Roger Corman, and Charles Band's Full Moon Entertainment. All were personally invited to the very first screening of *Reservoir Dogs* by their close friend and fellow *genre-meister*, Quentin Tarantino, who would very shortly move onward and upward to become the toast of Hollywood. This was a time in Hollywood like no other and one which may never be repeated, though it did lay the groundwork for a collaboration that would result in a very unexpected type of action film.

The use of dogs in the military goes all the way back to the days of the Roman Empire. Dogs were also used in World War One, mainly by the British, but mostly to carry first aid equipment to wounded soldiers on the battlefield, and also as mascots. In World War Two, Americans began using dogs more extensively, especially in the Pacific islands, where they were used as sentries to alert soldiers that enemy troops were nearby, and also to track enemy soldiers through the jungles. The dogs (mostly German Shepherds) pretty much had the same duties in the Vietnam conflict. Sheldon had actually met a few of the Sentry Dogs and their handlers in Vietnam. Sadly, nearly all of these dogs were left behind in Vietnam because the United States military was fearful of them bringing back some exotic canine diseases to the U.S. homeland.

Dogs would become far more essential to the U.S. military after the September 11th attacks, with much of the fighting now taking place in deserts and in mountains, with an enemy that was constantly laying Improvised Explosive Devices in the paths of American soldiers. The dogs that were used in Vietnam and in World War Two had hardly any training at all. In 1974, after the Vietnam War, the U.S. military began training dogs in earnest to become what are now called Military Working Dogs (MWD). The training was done at Lackland Air Force Base, outside of San Antonio, Texas. The dog handlers themselves received extensive specialized training as well, also at Lackland. The Army dog handlers were given a new Military Occupational Specialty (MOS) of 31K, as a Working Dog Handler. This was no longer an improvised or haphazard occupation. It was now a highly trained position, for both the dogs and their handlers.

German Shepherds had been the dog of choice for the military and for police, and for action movies as well, from *The Adventures of Rin Tin Tin* (1954-1959) onwards. There was a new player on the team now: the Belgian Malinois. Mals had originally come from the Belgian town of Malines, and they were like a slightly smaller, more compact and agile version of the German Shepherd, even more aggressive and focused on whatever task they were given. Mals are very eager and energetic dogs that love to be given tasks by their handlers. Most armies and police forces around the world have switched to the Belgian Malinois as well. Sheldon had witnessed them in action in Israel and Serbia, generally with elite Special Forces units. "I've seen them jump through open car windows and I've seen them dash up the front of a truck to get at a bad guy on the roof. They're amazing athletes, and since they weigh less than a typical German Shepherd, it's easier to parachute or rappel out of an aircraft with them. Since they're lighter, they can more easily be lifted up and shoved through open windows, or carried across a soldier's back like a piece of equipment. I've seen all of this done with Mals. Also, they are less prone to hip dysplasia and other ailments that affect elderly German Shepherds. They have an amazing sense of smell, almost as good as a Bloodhound's, and can be trained to sniff out hidden explosives, which is why they were so useful against an enemy that was constantly burying IED's on roads and footpaths." If you're a soldier or a cop, you couldn't ask for a better canine companion.

The seed for *Max* had been planted a number of years earlier, when one of Sheldon's beloved dogs died of cancer. "I've found that the only surefire way to console myself when one of my dogs passes away is to get a new dog, a replacement, as soon as possible. My wife and I went to our local animal shelter to see what rescue dogs were available. Amazingly, we found something that you almost never see at a municipal animal shelter: an intact litter of four puppies, males and females, all of them about eight weeks old. The sign on the cage said they were German Shepherds, which sounded good to me because I had had Shepherd mixes in the past, and I wanted a breed of dog that was big and energetic, that would make a good watchdog in addition to being a family dog. We had a house with a large backyard, so there was plenty of room for a couple of big hardy dogs to run around and play, and almost never have to be brought inside the house. What was unusual about this litter was that they all had fawn-colored bodies but black faces; it almost looked like they were wearing black masks." Those black masks would be a dead giveaway they were Malinois and not Shepherds, but at this point in time, he had never even heard of a Belgian Malinois. They picked out one male and one female and brought them home; sadly, they just didn't have room for the other two.

Within months, the dogs had grown bigger, and they were changing. They looked less and less like a typical German Shepherd, mostly due to those black faces. One morning Sheldon was reading an article in the local newspaper about dogs that had been deployed as bomb sniffers at the Los Angeles airport. "They had a photograph of one of those dogs, and it looked surprisingly similar to our female, Tina. The photo's caption said the breed was a Belgian Malinois. I got on my computer and put that into the search engine, and within moments I was learning all about the Belgian Malinois, and how they were being utilized by police and military forces all around the world." Bottom line: Sheldon and Toni had scored a couple of amazing and valuable dogs at the local animal shelter, without even realizing it.

Sheldon uncovered some amazing stories about military dogs. In particular, there were three different accounts of military dog handlers who had been killed in either Iraq or Afghanistan, and in each case the families of the handler had asked if they could take possession of the dog who had been their son's best friend in the months before he died. To Sheldon, this sounded like a movie. "Boaz and I had watched *The River Wild* (1994) together, and we were both bemoaning the fact the family in the film had a dog with them on their river rafting excursion, a Labrador Retriever I believe, and the dog did absolutely nothing to help the family when they were taken hostage by bad guys. We contrasted this with *The Hills Have Eyes* (1977), where the family has a couple of German Shepherds with them on a camping trip, and the dogs come to the family's rescue by chewing up the bad guys. That's what *The River Wild* needed! When I read the accounts of these families requesting possession of these highly trained military dogs, I felt this might be our antidote to the letdown we felt with dogs that were merely window dressing when their family was in trouble."

Boaz was very much on the same page as Sheldon when watching these films. "*The River Wild* always stuck in my head as a reminder of how the dogs were never used properly in an action capacity in film. In the original *The Hills Have Eyes*, audiences went insane when the dog got revenge on the bad guys. It always stuck in my head that someone should do a straight up cool action movie with a German Shepard or a Rin Tin Tin kind of dog. I was telling Sheldon that and it stuck in his head too, so he really pushed me to push for it. Sheldon loves dogs and he loves the military which is a huge part of his background. I had this idea of wanting to do something with a dog and I told that to Sheldon. He was in as soon as I mentioned dogs. At the time, we had no clue what we were going to do except that we wanted it to be a throwback to something like a more adventurous *Old Yeller* (1957). A year after we originally talked about it, he showed me an article about these military working dogs so things progressed from there."

Sheldon would pitch his idea to Boaz, who liked what he was hearing. The next step was to do some research, and Sheldon would jump right in. "I had a couple of Belgian Malinois in my backyard, but these were not trained Military Working Dogs. I decided to contact the Marine Corps Public Affairs Office in Los Angeles, to see what kind of assistance they could provide. I mentioned the fact that I was a former Marine myself, which scored me a few points with them. What really made the difference to them, however, was the fact that I had written *Bloodsport* and *Rambo III*. Suddenly I was given V.I.P. access. The Marines arranged for me to visit with actual Marine Corps Dog Handlers at Camp Pendleton, which was about a hundred miles south of Los Angeles, and was also the place where I had actually served for a couple of years while I was in the Marines."

Shortly afterwards, Sheldon would drive down to the Military Police K-9 Unit at Camp Pendleton. There were at least a hundred dogs there, mostly Belgian Malinois and German Shepherds, all in various stages of training. "I spent most of the day talking to a Staff Sergeant who had spent a couple of tours as a Dog Handler in Iraq and Afghanistan. Then I met a number of other Marine Dog Handlers, and their dogs, and I observed them training together. The potential for this story to work as a movie was just getting better and better. A couple weeks later I arranged for another visit, but this time I brought Boaz along. Just like me, he saw this story taking shape as we met with the dogs and their handlers, and observed them training together in the field. Later that evening, we had dinner in the nearby town of Oceanside, and started laying out the story. We created our main characters, who were three teenagers, somewhat similar to the teens in *Russkies*, with the addition of a girl. Justin and Chuy would be similar to the characters, Fresh and Chuckie, from Boaz's film *Fresh* (1994)."

Now that the groundwork had been laid for the story, work would begin on the script. Boaz and Sheldon would collaborate together and according to Boaz, they developed a system of writing. "Every duo develops their own way of writing and Sheldon would write a couple of things, then I would go in and write over them then add my own scenes. Sheldon would come back write over mine and we would just trade off, back and forth. After we optioned the script, nothing happened for at least a year and a half."

Sheldon's recollection of the process parallels Boaz's memory. "We used a system I have used with other co-writers before, where I "plow the road," and then Boaz follows behind me to "lay down the pavement." I laid down most of the major story beats and developed scenes in some detail, and then I emailed those pages to Boaz, who was on the other side of the country in New York. Boaz is much better with character and dialogue, so he would flesh out the characters more deeply and he also re-wrote most of my initial dialogue. Then we would trade the material back and forth until we were both satisfied."

The producers who were interested brought in some other writers to do a re-write and they just didn't get what Sheldon and Boaz were going for. They eventually came back to Boaz and he gave them an ultimatum, he would agree to direct but only if they would go back to the original draft he wrote with Sheldon. The executives at MGM thought Boaz would be good fit to helm the project and things moved forward shortly after.

While Sheldon wasn't directly involved in the actual production, he would accompany Boaz and the producer on the initial scouts to North Carolina and Georgia. He would also visit the set in North Carolina for about a week while they were filming. As personal as the project may have been to Sheldon, he never had any intention of directing it. "Boaz had some very good agents at Creative Artists Agency (CAA), and they're the ones who got this project set up. There was never any talk of me directing the film. Boaz had more recent credits than I did, and he had directed *Remember the Titans* (2000) for Jerry Bruckheimer, which starred Denzel Washington and was a huge box office success, a much bigger success than any film I had directed in the past."

On May 12, 2014, *Max* would go into production with Boaz behind the camera. The cast would include veterans like Thomas Haden Church, Lauren Graham, and Jay Hernandez as well as rising stars Robbie Amell, Josh Wiggins, and Mia Xitlali. Sheldon's job was essentially done but he was certainly happy with how things were heading, especially with the actors. "I think everyone in the film did a terrific job. It was Mia Xitali's first movie. Josh Wiggins was a relative newcomer, but his career has been climbing upwards since the film was released, same with Robbie Amell and Luke Kleintank."

The action in *Max* predominantly involved the dogs. As exciting and well put together the scenes were, it certainly was not an easy task and would require a fair amount of time, cooperation, and planning to pull them off the way they were intended. Boaz brought on some terrific handlers to bring the vision to life. "We would storyboard out what we thought we would want the dogs to do. The handlers would then come in to look them over and tell us what they thought the dogs could actually accomplish. They were always very clear with the limitations. They would have a few different dogs that all had their own specialties and hoped they kind of looked alike. We had to try our best not to pop too many surprises on the handlers because they really had to train these dogs to do those particular things for several weeks or months before we shot them. That was the most work I'd ever done on something in terms of having it all planned out, pre-visualized, and having the stunts and tricks prepared beforehand. So when they made it to set, everything would be ready to go. People say never work with dogs or children but those dogs were pretty good. I had more problems with the adult actors than the dogs."

From almost the very beginning, MGM was pushing Boaz to make a more kid-friendly movie, without all the violence and especially the killing that's a crucial part of the story. They wanted *Max* to be rated PG (which it was), something the grandparents could safely take their grandkids to. Even though the story was about a War Dog having served in Afghanistan, they wanted it to be more like *Benji* (1974), or something along those lines, something more family friendly. Boaz and Sheldon had always envisioned the movie as being a hard PG-13, and fortunately Boaz did not deviate from the initial concept, even though there was a lot of pressure on him to soften it up. Boaz was initially approached for the sequel, but he made his feelings quite clear about wanting to maintain the same gritty, realistic tone as the first. The studio had already come up with a concept and a title for the sequel, which was *Max 2: White House Hero* (2017), and Boaz flatly rejected it. When the studio would not budge, Boaz withdrew himself from consideration.

Boaz knew there would have to be some compromises but the whole time he rode the fine line between the two ratings. "I always felt *Max* should have been a PG-13 movie and the studio insisted that it be PG. Maybe that made sense from a financial standpoint but who knows. I really feel that I pushed the envelope of the PG rating and I feel certain scenes suffered from their decision. We had to edit the action or the dog fights in a certain way that would still preserve what we were going for or get the point across without going too far. Certain scenes had less impact than they could have had but at the same time, some people may have been shocked at the intensity of it being PG. So it was definitely an issue we faced when trying to finish the film."

When they did their preview of *Max*, they would have the highest audience approval rating MGM ever had up until that time and a real pleasant surprise to Boaz. "It scored so absurdly high and people enjoyed it so much. It was doing a certain thing by trying to be an edgy kid's film with emotion though it was hit pretty hard in the reviews. You would think most critics are open to things but I think the tone really threw them off. Some thought it was far too violent for a kid's movie and I think the film isn't really a gung-ho patriotic movie but it's respectful to the military and what people go through when they have family in the military. We really wanted it to show the devastation military families sometimes go through. It shows how emotionally taxing it is on this particular family with a loved one in the military. I think it was perceived by some critics as this red meat Americana movie." It wasn't received very well by the media and despite that, it did respectably well at the box office. As previously mentioned, its success quickly spawned a horrible sequel that went into production without any involvement from Boaz or Sheldon.

After the theatrical success of the film, there was a novelization commissioned by Harper Collins. Based on the screenplay by Boaz and Sheldon, it was written by a Young Adult author named Jennifer Li Shotz. The book sold quite well, and even ended up on the New York Times Bestseller list for Young Adult Fiction, apparently selling over 100,000 copies. The publisher contacted the two friends in regards to writing a series of books about *Max* which Sheldon knew just wouldn't work out. "We ended up having the same problems we had with MGM over the movie sequel. Both MGM and Harper Collins wanted the books to have a softer tone than the movie so they could be marketed as Young Adult fiction. This just didn't sit well with Boaz or me; we wanted the stories to have a harder edge, much like the movie. In the movie, three people die, and the two Rottweiler's who come after Max are shown being washed downriver, presumably to drown. I actually wrote a treatment for a subsequent novel, but the publisher and the studio both rejected it because it was too edgy for the market they were catering to." Ultimately, the publisher came up with their own title, *Hero*, which was a about a former search-and-rescue dog named Hero. They hired the same writer, Jennifer Li Shotz, to write these books. The series of *Hero* books did well enough that they spawned a sequel, titled *Scout*, about a puppy that grows up to be a dog that accompanies firefighters. According to the ads, these books are designed for age ranges from eight to twelve years. Boaz and Sheldon could have done quite well by sticking to the parameters set out by the studio and the publisher, though watered down Young Adult books were simply not within the purview of the guys who had written R rated movies like *Bloodsport* and *The Punisher*.

Max 2: White House Hero was made and it was everything the studio and the publisher kept asking for as far as being family friendly. In every other respect, it was just a disappointing movie. The studio hired Brian Levant to direct the film. He had directed a couple of other dog movies in the past, *Beethoven*(1992) and *Snow Dogs* (2002).Both were comedies, and Brian tried his best to make *Max 2* a comedy as well, rather than an action-adventure like the first one was. A movie about a War Dog that's returned home due to tragic circumstances simply won't translate into a comedic, kid-friendly sequel. Imagine trying to make a comedic, kid-safe, PG-rated sequel to *First Blood* and you'll understand just how daunting this task was. It's a shame because they killed what could have been a potentially lucrative franchise for them, for Boaz and Sheldon as well.

The influence of *Max* has never been more apparent than with the release of *Dog* (2022). The film stars Channing Tatum as a former Army Ranger who must make a trip down the Pacific coast in order to attend a funeral. Tatum's character must travel with a Belgian Malinois named Lulu. The film also happens to mark the directorial debut of Tatum who shared duties with his *Magic Mike* (2012) screenwriter Reid Carolin. The pair also served as Executive Producers of the HBO documentary *War Dog: A Soldier's Best Friend* (2017). This film examines the relationship between veterans and their dogs during combat as well as during their transition back into civilian life. *Max* would open the door in a sense for these other projects to walk through. All three films do their duty shedding light on such an important and touching subject.

Conclusion

With a career in Hollywood spanning nearly forty years, Sheldon Lettich has cemented himself in history. As a child in the 80s, I was fortunate enough to have lived through the era of the action star. I was there watching *Bloodsport* in a theater on opening weekend as I was for *Lionheart*, *Double Impact*, *Only the Strong*, and *Rambo III*. I had the posters for those films hanging in my room and I saw the name, Sheldon Lettich, on all of them. In 1988, when I was fourteen, I had no idea, nor would I have ever dreamed, I would be writing the biography of the man who helped propel Jean-Claude Van Damme into superstardom, who helped launch the career of Mark Dacascos, or wrote one of the most influential martial arts films since *Enter the Dragon*, *Bloodsport*.

I have no problem being labeled a fanboy, but my opinion of those films is echoed by millions of people around the world. In this book, you've learned about the international success of many of his projects, and you also heard from several of his colleagues. Every one of them had nothing but praise for the man. Some of them even acknowledged the fact he may even be instrumentally responsible for so many other classic films, just by how he networked and introduced people to one another. He introduced Tarantino to Bender, Raimi to Van Damme, and Yakin to Spiegel. These pairings have all gone on to their own successes and Lettich had a small part in it.

It really seems as if Sheldon unintentionally grew his family while making these films, many of his colleagues think of him as family or even like a brother. Luis Esteban is one of them. "Sheldon is one of those people, he hasn't gone through five different marriages, and he's been married to the same woman. He was always there for his three daughters. None of us are perfect but he always hung in there. He never went off and played the casting couch or let the fact that he was with these major action stars get to his head. He was friends with Sam Raimi, Lawrence Bender, and Quentin Tarantino and they were part of this vigilant little army of filmmakers. He's the furthest from a Harvey Weinstein that you can imagine. When you go into his office, it's filled with history books. He loves history. Sheldon never studied martial arts and never had an ego. He went and learned, applied his skills, and accomplished so much. The thing that always impressed me was how he always took care of his family. He was always there for them, even my daughter spent countless nights having sleepovers with his daughters and vice versa. We became like an extended family through our daughters. Even Jean-Claude's kids, Bianca and Kristopher, they all would hang out together and this extended family just grew. I got to know a lot of influential people in the business and Sheldon played things much differently. He wasn't doing the questionable things they were doing. Between the drugs, the women (or men), that just wasn't Sheldon. I've always thought of him as being a very honorable man."

He has always been very supportive to his friends, especially those trying to find their own path in Hollywood. Sheldon would actually visit the sets of some of the films they worked on. George Saunders has no problem attesting to this. "Sheldon was always very helpful to me when I was directing and would always offer up some very keen insights. I remember one scene in a film I acted in where I was tied up in the toilet with a beautiful porn star and the director on that project wasn't actually sure how to shoot it. Sheldon suggested he twist the camera 45 degrees into a "Dutch Angle" master shot, which turned out to be brilliant. So Sheldon was really innovative. He even helped me out when I was directing a promo with Eric Roberts and Mel Gibson's ex, Olga. I set-up and executed a few shots but completely forgot to do a close-up of our lead actress, who was quite beautiful. Sheldon was paying close enough attention to make sure I achieved that shot before moving on. From a business standpoint, Sheldon has been responsible for helping me get some really great jobs, especially some writing jobs at just the right time when I needed them financially. He's more than just a business associate, he's like my bigger, older, wiser brother and he makes a damn fine Manhattan martini, they're the best on the planet."

When talking with Boaz Yakin, I asked him what he felt was the most important thing for people to know about Sheldon and his answer was rather simple and sweet. "Our friendship has always been most important to me. Sheldon and I have known each other since 1985. He was one of the first people I met when I moved to Hollywood as a nineteen year old kid. I was living by myself and didn't have any friends out there and I was introduced to him, his wife Toni, who I believe was pregnant with their first daughter at the time. They took me into their home as part of their family and it was such a crucial friendship for me. Sheldon was a focal point of my emotional and social life in Los Angeles when I first moved out there. To this day, he really is a true, dear friend and you don't always keep friends that long on the better part of thirty five years. When I think about our connection, doing *Max* together, working on *Double Impact*, sure it was a major part of our lives but I've always thought of this as a friendship. We have some creative aspects to our friendship but overall, he and his family have been so much more to me than that. I will always be grateful to him for everything he has done."

Then there is someone like Mark Dacascos. Mark and Sheldon didn't remain particularly close after *Only the Strong*. Life and career get in the way and it's not easy for people to maintain a close friendship with everyone in their lives they've touched. They may not have been close but that doesn't mean they forget. Hearing Mark's words just helps to cement the type of person Sheldon is. "When I talk about Sheldon Lettich, I can't help but gush nothing but praise and gratitude to him. I feel so honored that he cast me in my first lead role and I was able to represent a beautiful art such as capoiera."

The impact Sheldon had on Mark is clearly felt in those words, but he doesn't stop there. "Any success I've had in acting is largely due to his taking a risk on me and I will never forget that. Sheldon really helped to push me to the next level and I'm forever grateful."

Sheldon's determination, dedication, and experience is certainly an admirable quality to his friends. Josh Becker was around long before Sheldon decided to get behind the moving camera; he was even around when Sheldon was still working behind the still camera. He also recognizes how important he was to helping make stars. "Sheldon made the decision to make films and he set out to make it happen, and he did! If he hadn't decided to get behind and support Van Damme, there wouldn't have been a Van Damme. He didn't discover him but he certainly made him a star. Sheldon knew the right way to craft a project completely suited for him. If he hadn't, Jean-Claude would of ended up in more movies like *Cyborg* in the sense that the director just didn't know how to use him, Sheldon always did. When he couldn't get Van Damme, he found someone else. He found Mark Dacascos and look where he is now."

As mentioned before, Sheldon and Brian Thompson both started in the business together. They even rose to prominence together in the action genre. Being there together and working on various projects over the years, it would be logical to inquire about growth. "I wish I could say there was a remarkable growth curve because Sheldon and I have been there together as newbies with lots of energetic ideas, then seeing him grow into this seasoned director who knew exactly what he wants and how to go about achieving it within the schedule. It's a maturity that comes along with experience. The first tool he really understood well was the camera since he worked as a photographer. Some directors just don't understand the camera or the mechanics of the frame or lighting but he started with that. I really feel that gave him a leg up in the business."

That business has been very kind to the filmmaker. Even though the shift away from the traditional action stars has made getting those types of films financed far more difficult. Sheldon hasn't directed a film since 2006 nor had a script produced since 2015. That doesn't mean for a second he's given up on film. He's continually going through the motions, hoping for something to stick. One such project he continues to pursue is *Metro Dog* which Luis Esteban has been trying to set up as a producer. "Sheldon and I really put a lot of work into developing *Metro Dog,* and it's one of those projects where if you don't have the money to do it right, it would most likely turn out very bad. Sheldon did *Max* with Boaz and that film turned out really great. That was sort of the hope for *Metro Dog* but it just hasn't come together yet. It's taken much longer than we wanted to get it going for any number of reasons. It's set in modern day Moscow and with the current political climate it's just been a long road. We'll keep trying though as long as Sheldon has the energy."

To crawl from the jungles of Vietnam to drinking Martinis in a high class Hollywood restaurant is not an easy feet. What other filmmakers have been to war before making it big in Hollywood? Becker has nothing but respect for Sheldon and his transition for the military to film. "There are only two Vietnam War vets who really made it as filmmakers in Hollywood, Sheldon and Oliver Stone. They had experiences as differently as humanly possible and nobody has written or shown the types of experiences Sheldon had in Vietnam. You watch any of those movies like *Platoon* (1986) or *Born on the 4th of July* (1989), and you get the sense it was just pure fucking misery. With Sheldon, he doesn't gripe about any truly miserable moments he may have had in Vietnam. At least, he doesn't harp on those bad experiences or dwell upon them. After the Marines were pulled out in 1969, he volunteered for the elite Force Recon unit. This guy was jumping out of helicopters over the everglades, and he did it over thirty times!" He certainly lived a full life even before making films. It's rare for someone to do so much in a single lifetime, but Sheldon accomplished it all.

The admiration from Josh doesn't end there. "When he made the decision to make films, he was all in and I knew it. I knew Sheldon long before he made that decision. He's a pretty decisive guy, once he made that decision, he just did it. He used his own money to do Firefight so he could show everyone he knew how to make a movie. Then he did that! With his background, he knew how to make an empty room look exciting."

He may have pulled all this off in his lifetime, but he never stopped reading or learning. According to Thompson, Sheldon continuously enjoys expanding his knowledge. "In his quiet, unassuming way, he knows so much about so many things, and he's such a voracious reader. He never flaunts his knowledge, even though he's an unassuming human encyclopedia. I don't think I've ever seen or heard him yell. Actors can sometimes be difficult and I've seen him get assertive with Jean-Claude, but it wasn't in a bossy forceful way, it was just him, taking control of a situation that needed to be controlled." Along with the knowledge, the love he's surrounded by helps to drive him. Being close to him for as long as he has, Thompson would know firsthand. "Sheldon gives the impression of someone who feels loved and he wears the effects of having four women in his life who adore him, his wife and three daughters, they just love him. He has a quiet heart that knows it's appreciated by them."

It's pretty obvious just how revered Sheldon is by those in his circle. When asked for a final comment to sum up Sheldon's life, Saunders offers his take. "Sheldon has had a life and a career that's well lived. He had a very inauspicious beginning who just sort of fell into filmmaking. People really like and trust him." This is Sheldon's life and his films are his legacy. Many of them are now considered timeless classics. Popular culture still references them, most recently the hit Netflix series *Cobra Kai* (2018-) references *Bloodsport* in numerous episodes. Even the film *Lady Bloodfight* (2016) which was directed by Chris Nahon and features rising action star Amy Johnston, is a gender reversed remake/reboot of the film and at one time was titled *Lady Bloodsport*. *Sense8* (2015-2018), another Netflix series, which was created by the Wachowskis, had one of the main characters obsessed with Van Damme and referenced *Lionheart* quite frequently during the first season.

We all know that those films were milestones for Jean-Claude and he deserves every bit of success he has worked so hard far. The man is a legend and a superstar. If it weren't for Sheldon, those films would not have happened. It's important to think about these things because making a film isn't a solo effort; it's the team as a whole. Sheldon has led his various teams to victory numerous times. Even though Hollywood and how it operates has changed so much, he is still filled with energy ready to share his next story with the world. This isn't the end of a career, it's a celebration of accomplishments, an inside look if you will at a life, a career, at a man who has brought so much to the world of film. All the kicks, all the explosions, and all the Van Damage he's helped to create will live on forever, being passed down from generation to generation. In doing so, these movies will continue to be inspiring to fans of the action genre for many years to come.

Acknowledgments

I would like to take some time to thank all the people who have contributed to, inspired, or supported me during this journey. I'll be forever grateful to Sheldon Lettich for trusting me to bring his story to the written page. There's no way for me to express how important those films were to me growing up and being entrusted by him to do this book has helped to give me the confidence to continue pursing things I'm passionate about. Sam Firstenberg, Josh Becker, Boaz Yakin, George Saunders, Luis Esteban, Brian Thompson, and Mark Dacascos, thank you so much for donating your time to me, for telling me stories from the set, and giving me a glimpse behind-the-scenes of these classic films. A tip of the hat to Ben Ohmart and Bear Manor Media for stepping up and publishing these tales of an era in Hollywood so many of us refuse to let go of. I also need to give a big shout-out to Alan Pirie for his excellent work on the cover. To david j. moore for taking me under his wing, for giving me a chance, opening up his home and most of all being a friend. To Melissa Hannon and Horror Geek Life for giving me an outlet for my writing, allowing me to explore the obscure and niche corners of cinema and music, and for suggesting the *Lionheart* retrospective which laid the groundwork for this book.

Most importantly, I would like to thank my family. Without their love, support, and understanding, I wouldn't still be pushing forward. My Mom and Dad never complained (at least not out loud) when I asked them to drive me to the video store or drop me off and pick me up from the movies. I don't think I even remember them ever telling me no. To my wife Geri, for always believing in me, putting up with my fandom, and not running away after I made you watch *Only the Strong* on one of our first dates. I know I'm a weird dad, opting to put my daughters in short films or forcing them to watch movies they may not have wanted to see but were important to me growing up. I've never been more proud of anyone in my life than those two girls. Kayla and Zoe couldn't be more different but I know in my heart they will continue to grow and evolve into amazing women who can conquer the world, they just have to believe in themselves the way their Mom and Dad do.

Printed in the USA
CPSIA information can be obtained
at www.ICGtesting.com
CBHW072250070424
6542CB00004B/8